KEY TO
FIRST YEAR LATIN

BY

ROBERT J. HENLE, S.J.

LOYOLA PRESS.
Chicago

LOYOLA PRESS.
3441 N. Ashland Avenue
Chicago, Illinois 60657
(800) 621-1008
www.loyolapress.com

ISBN-13: 978-0-8294-1205-5
ISBN-10: 0-8294-1205-0

Printed in the United States of America.
12 13 14 15 16 17 18 19 Bang 10 9 8 7 6 5 4 3 2

TABLE OF CONTENTS

INTRODUCTION

This key is intended as an aid to the busy teacher. It should serve to unlock readily and speedily whatever may be difficult or obscure, and to reassure those who wish to be certain that their own interpretations are the ones which the author himself would accept. A few points in connection with the key and its use merit a word of comment.

1. In the English translations of Latin exercises the literal meanings of Latin words and sentences are usually given, since the main purpose is to make the Latin text clear rather than to give an example of good style. Occasionally (especially when a literal translation results in pidgin English) a freer translation is added in parentheses. While it may often be necessary to demand a literal translation first in order to make the meaning and the sentence structure clear, the final translation accepted by the teacher should always be pure, idiomatic English.

2. In translating English exercises into Latin this key seldom gives more than one version. "You" could often be either singular or plural; "they put" could be present, imperfect, or perfect; "I see" can be translated by three or more verbs. It would have been impossible to give every variant translation, nor would any useful purpose have been served by so doing.

3. Certain extremely simple exercises involving nothing more than a knowledge of word meanings and syntactical forms are left unanswered. It was also considered unnecessary to diagram the sentences which the pupil is instructed to diagram, as all such sentences follow the simple models given in FIRST YEAR LATIN.

4. The English translations of passages from the New Testament are from the 1941 edition of the Confraternity of Christian Doctrine, published by St. Anthony Guild Press.

5. Numerical references such as "See No. . . . " are in all cases, without exception, to the author's LATIN GRAMMAR.

UNIT ONE

Exercise 1.—See No. 31.

Exercise 2.—See No. 31 for the cases and their translations.

Exercise 3.—1. The final *a* of the nominative is short; of the ablative, long. 2. By dropping the case ending of the genitive singular. 3. By the genitive singular.

Exercise 4.—All are feminine except *nauta, nautae,* which is masculine because it names a male person.

Exercise 5.—1. Mary prays. 2. The sailors pray. 3. The sailor prays. 4. The sailors do not pray. 5. They see. 6. The sailor sees. 7. Mary sees. 8. He (or she) sees. 9. The sailors do not see. 10. He (she) does not pray.

Exercise 6.—1. The sailors praise the land. 2. The sailors see the province. 3. Mary praises the forests. 4. The sailor sees the forests. 5. The sailor sees the gate. 6. They do not praise the province. 7. The sailors praise Mary. 8. They praise the victory. 9. The sailors praise fame. 10. He (she) praises Mary. 11. He (she) sees the province.

Exercise 7.—1. Marīam laudant. 2. Nautae prōvinciam vident. 3. Nautae glōriam laudant. 4. Portam videt. 5. Nauta prōvinciam nōn laudat. 6. Silvam laudant. 7. Nautās videt. 8. Victōriam laudat. 9. Portam vident. 10. Marīa nautās nōn laudat. 11. Nautae terram vident.

Exercise 8.—1. The glory (fame) of the province. 2. The sailor's victory (the victory of the sailor). 3. Mary's glory (fame). 4. The sailor's glory (fame). 5. The forest of the province. 6. The sailors' victory. 7. The gate of the province.

Exercise 9.—1. Victōria nautae. 2. Victōria Marīae. 3. Porta prōvinciae. 4. Glōria Marīae. 5. Victōria nautārum. 6. Silva prōvinciae.

Exercise 10.—See No. 34.

Exercise 11.—See No. 34.

Exercise 12.—1. The glory of God. 2. The friend of the slave. 3. The friend of God. 4. The victory of God. 5. The glory of Christ. 6. The glory of Mary. 7. The victory of the Christians. 8. The servant of God. 9. The friend of Christ. 10. The Son of God.

Exercise 13.—1. The Christians pray. 2. The friends of God praise the Christians. 3. The Christians praise the Son of God. 4. The Christians praise Mary. 5. The sailors do not see the slaves. 6. The slaves praise the Christians. 7. The Christians praise the servants of God. 8. They see the glory of God. 9. The Christians praise Christ. 10. Mary and Christ praise the friends of God. 11. God sees the land and the forests. He sees the sailors, the slaves, and the Christians. 12. The Christians praise the Son of Mary.

Exercise 14.—1. Chrīstiānī Fīlium Marīae laudant. 2. Marīa Deī Fīlium videt. 3. Chrīstiānī Chrīstī victōriam laudant. 4. Marīa Deum laudat. 5. Deus glōriam Chrīstī laudat. 6. Chrīstus amīcōs Marīae laudat. 7. Marīae servī Chrīstum laudant. 8. Deī amīcī Marīam laudant. 9. Nautae servōrum victōriam nōn laudant. 10. Marīa Deī glōriam et Chrīstī victōriam videt. 11. Deus terram videt; silvās videt.

Exercise 15.—See No. 37.

Exercise 16.—1. The kingdom of Christ. 2. The danger of the servants. 3. The power of God. 4. The rewards of a Christian. 5. The gate of heaven. 6. The reward of Mary. 7. The danger of the friend. 8. The victory of Christ.

Exercise 17.—1. The friends of God praise the kingdom of Christ. 2. Mary sees the reward and victory of Christ. 3. The sailors see the sky and the earth. 4. God sees the dangers of Christians. 5. God does not praise wars. 6. The servants of Christ praise the empire of Christ. 7. Mary sees the glory of the kingdom of Christ. 8. The Son of God praises the rewards of Mary. 9. The sailors do not praise the dangers of war.

Exercise 18.—1. (a) Nauta, m., No. 32. (b) Porta, f., No. 33. (c) Rēgnum, n., No. 38. (d) Chrīstus, m., No. 35. (e) Marīa, f., No. 33. (f) Praemium, n., No. 38. 2. See Nos. 9-10. 3. Adverbs usually come before the words they modify; verbs usually stand last in the sentence. 4. The nominative is short, the ablative long.

Exercise 19.—1. Christ gave glory to God. 2. They did not give swords to the slaves but they gave swords to the sailors. 3. The sailors gave victory to (their) friends. 4. God gave rewards to the friends of Mary. 5. God gave royal power to (His) Son. 6. The Christians gave glory to Mary and to the Son of Mary. 7. God gave the earth to Christ. 8. The sailors praise the glory of war but they do not praise the dangers of war. (No indirect object.) 9. He gave the province to (his) friend. 10. God gave glory and victory to the Christians. 11. He gave the sword to a friend.

Exercise 20.—1. Deus Chrīstō rēgnum dedit. 2. Gladium amīcō dedit sed nōn servō. 3. Chrīstiānī glōriam Deō dedērunt. 4. Servīs prōvinciam nōn dedērunt. 5. Deī Fīlius Caelum Chrīstiānīs dedit. 6. Nautae perīcula bellī nōn laudant sed victōriam et praemia bellī laudant. 7. Deus rēgnum et imperium Chrīstō dedit. 8. Nautae caelum vident.

Exercise 21.—1. Chrīstiānus ōrat. The Christian prays. 2. Chrīstiānī ōrant. The Christians pray. 3. Marīa Deum videt. Mary sees God. 4. Nautae terram vident. The sailors see the land. 5. Servus Chrīstī Caelum laudat. The servant of Christ praises heaven. 6. Amīcī Deī Chrīstum laudant. The friends of God praise Christ. 7. Chrīstus Deum videt. Christ sees God. 8. Deus terrās videt. God sees the earth. 9. Fīlius Deī Deum laudat. The Son of God praises God. 10. Marīa glōriam Deō dedit. Mary gave glory to God. 11. Servīs gladiōs nōn dedit. He did not give swords to the slaves. 12. Chrīstiānī rēgnum et imperium Chrīstī laudant. Christians praise the kingdom and power of Christ.

Exercise 22.—1. In the town. 2. In the forest. 3. With the Gaul. 4. With Mary. 5. On account of the glory of Rome. 6. After (the) victory. 7. In the forests of Gaul. 8. With the sailor. 9. On account of the dangers of the town. 10. On earth. 11. On account of (the) victory. 12. In the gates of Rome. 13. With God. 14. On account of the rewards of the Gauls. 15. In the sky. 16. After the victory of the Romans. 17. With (the) friends. 18. In the forest. 19. In the gates of the town. 20. With the Romans. 21. In Gaul. 22. On account of the glory of war. 23. In the provinces. 24. In the province. 25. With the servant. 26. After the war. 27. With the Roman. 28. In the kingdom. 29. In the towns. 30. With the sons. 31. On account of danger. 32. In the forests and towns. 33. After the danger. 34. With Christ. 35. In war. 36. With the Christians. 37. With the Gauls. 38. On account of war. 39. Behind the town. 40. In the gate.

Exercise 23.—1. Cum Marīā. 2. Post bellum. 3. Cum Deō. 4. Propter bellum. 5. In oppidō. 6. Post perīculum. 7. Propter praemium. 8. Cum Deī Fīliō. 9. Propter Chrīstiānōs. 10. In Caelō. 11. Propter rēgnum. 12. Cum amīcīs. 13. In Galliā. 14. Cum Rōmānīs. 15. Cum nautīs. 16. In silvīs. 17. In terrā. 18. In prōvinciīs. 19. Cum servō. 20. In perīculō. 21. Propter imperium. 22. Cum Gallō. 23. Post oppidum. 24. In terrā. 25. Propter Rōmae glōriam.

Exercise 24.—1. "You are sons of God." 2. Christ is the Son of Mary. 3. Christians are servants of God. 4. Heaven is the reward of Christians. 5. Mary is in heaven with God. 6. The war is in the province. (There is a war in the province.) 7. We are sons of God. 8. You are a friend of God. 9. The Gauls are in Gaul, but the Romans are not in Gaul. 10. The Gauls are in the towns and in the forests. 11. The Romans did not give swords to the Gauls. 12. The forests are in Gaul. (There are forests in Gaul.) 13. Rome is not in Gaul. 14. On account of war the Gauls are not friends of the Romans. 15. The swords are in the town.

(There are swords in the town.) 16. You are sailors. 17. The sailors are not in the forests. 18. I am with a friend in the province. 19. The forests are behind the town. 20. The sailors are Christians. 21. We are in the town. 22. The Roman gave a reward to the servant. 23. They are friends of God. 24. You are a Christian but you are a servant of the Roman. 25. You are not in heaven.

Exercise 25.—1. Chrīstus est Deī Fīlius. 2. Nautae caelum vident sed nōn terram. 3. Chrīstiānī servī Chrīstī sunt. 4. Sumus amīcī Deī. 5. Marīa cum Chrīstō in Caelō est. 6. Servī sunt in oppidīs et in silvīs. 7. Chrīstiānī Deum propter glōriam Chrīstī laudant. 8. Gallī sunt in Galliā. 9. Estis fīliī Deī. 10. Es servus Chrīstī. 11. In terrā sum. 12. Caelum est praemium servōrum Chrīstī. 13. Post bellum—praemia victōriae! 14. Rōmānī sunt in prōvinciīs. 15. Marīa est "Porta Caelī." 16. Servī sunt in oppidīs. 17. In Galliā nōn estis.

Exercise 26.—On the map you see Rome and the empire of the Romans. The Romans inhabit Rome. You see the provinces of the empire of the Romans (belonging to the Roman Empire). You see Gaul. The Romans conquered the Gauls in war. The swords are not in (There are no swords in) the towns of the Gauls, because after the war the Gauls gave the swords to the Romans. And so after the victories of the Romans there is a province in Gaul. (And so after these victories there is a Roman province in Gaul.) Gauls and Romans inhabit the province. There are dangers in the forests of Gaul, because the Gauls are not friends of the Romans. The Gauls are slaves of the Romans, because the Romans conquered the Gauls. And so the Gauls do not praise the power (empire) of the Romans, but the Romans praise the power (empire) on account of the glory of war.

Exercise 27.—You see Christians. You see Mary and Christ and God. The Christians are on earth, but Christ and Mary are in heaven with God. The dangers of the Christians are on earth, but the rewards are in heaven. Therefore Christians pray on earth. Mary prays with Christians because Christians are sons of Mary. Christians praise Mary because Christ is the Son of Mary. They praise Christ because He is the Son of God.

Exercise 28.—The gender of the nouns listed on pages 36, 44, and 51 and the numbers of the rules in the GRAMMAR are as follows: lēx, f., 50; rēx, m., 46; dux, m.,[1] 46; lūx, f., 50; homō, m., 46; imperātor,

---

[1] *Dux* and *hostis* are common nouns. In this book they are always masculine, as the leaders and enemies to whom reference is made are men, not women. They therefore follow No. 46 and are exceptions to No. 50.

m., 49; vēritās, f., 50; pars, f., 50; collis, m., exception to 50; hostis, m., 46; gēns, f., 50; caedēs, f., 50; flūmen, n., 51; iter, n., exception to 49; corpus, n., 52; vulnus, n., 52; agmen, n., 51; nōmen, n., 51.

Exercise 29.—Like lēx: frāter, frātris; pater, patris; māter, mātris; clāmor, clāmōris; prīnceps, prīncipis. Like pars: collis, collis; hostis, hostis; gēns, gentis; caedēs, caedis; mōns, montis.

Exercise 30.—1. Lēx, f., No. 50; rēx, m., No. 46; dux, m., No. 46; lūx, f., No. 50; homō, m., No. 46; imperātor, m., No. 46; vēritās, f., No. 50. 2. See No. 57. 3. (a) Lēgum; (b) ducum; (c) rēgum; (d) hominum; (e) imperātōrum. None have the characteristics noted in Nos. 60-61.

Exercise 31.—See Introduction, 3.

Exercise 32.—1. The light of truth. 2. King of kings. 3. King of men. 4. The law of God. 5. King of Christians. 6. On account of the law of God. 7. With the king. 8. On account of the truth.

Exercise 33.—1. Post rēgem. 2. Hominibus. 3. Lūx vēritātis. 4. Imperātōrī. 5. Propter lēgem Chrīstī. 6. Cum duce Gallōrum.

Exercise 34.—1. Christ is the King of Kings. 2. Men see the light. 3. Sailors are men. (*Hominēs* is a predicate noun.) 4. Christians praise the truth of Christ. 5. There is no light in the forests. 6. Romans do not praise the law and truth of Christ. 7. The commanders in chief of the Romans conquered the Gauls. 8. The leaders of the Gauls do not praise the law and power of the Romans. 9. Christ is King of men because He is God. 10. The leader of the Romans is in Gaul because the war is in Gaul (because there is a war in Gaul). (*Quod* is used here as a conjunction which joins a subordinate clause to a main clause.) 11. The Romans gave rewards to the commander in chief and the leaders because they conquered the Gauls. (*Ducibus* is the dative of indirect object.) 12. The Romans conquered the leaders and kings of the Gauls.

Exercise 35.—1. Imperātor ducēs Gallōrum nōn laudat. 2. Chrīstus lūx hominum est quod vēritātem hominibus dedit. 3. Gallī lēgēs Rōmānōrum nōn laudant. 4. Chrīstus est Rēx Rēgum. 5. Ducēs Rōmānōrum sunt in Galliā. Itaque rēgēs Gallōrum servī Rōmānōrum sunt. 6. Imperātor perīcula bellī videt.

Exercise 36.—1. The Gauls did not give rewards to Caesar, the commander in chief of the Romans. 2. The slave heard the voice of Caesar, the commander in chief. 3. God, the King of heaven and earth, gave salvation to men. 4. Caesar, the leader of the Romans, heard the voices of the Gauls in the forests. 5. For the sake of (on account of) the salvation of men Christ is man. 6. Christ, the Son of God, is the Son of Mary. 7. The Gauls, slaves of the Romans, do not praise the Romans. 8. Christians praise Christ, the Son of Mary.

Box, page 40.—Saint John, the servant of Christ, heard the voice of Christ: "I am the Way and the Truth and the Life."

Exercise 37.—The words to be completed are: 1. Rēx. 2. Filiō. 3. Imperātor. 4. Fīliī. 5. Imperātōrem. The translations: 1. Christ, the King of men, is in heaven. 2. The salvation of men is in Christ, the Son of God. 3. Caesar, the commander in chief of the Romans, is in Gaul. 4. The voice of Christ, the Son of God, is the voice of God. 5. The Romans praise Caesar, the commander in chief.

Exercise 38.—1. Chrīstus, Fīlius Deī, est homō propter salūtem hominum. 2. Vōcem Chrīstī, Fīliī Marīae, audīvit. 3. Chrīstus, Fīlius Deī, est Rēx Rēgum. 4. Deus Chrīstō, amīcō hominum, rēgnum dedit. 5. Chrīstiānī Chrīstum, Rēgem et amīcum hominum, laudant. 6. Caesar, imperātor Rōmānōrum, vōcēs Gallōrum audīvit. 7. Propter salūtem prōvinciae Caesar, imperātor, est in Galliā.

Exercise 39.—1. Porta. 2. Silva. 3. Gladius. 4. Rēx. 5. Homō. 6. Oppidum.

Exercise 40.—See Introduction, 3.

Box, page 43.—The voice of the people is the voice of God.

Exercise 41.—1. There are dangers in the forests of Gaul. 2. There is no peace in Gaul because Caesar is in Gaul with soldiers. 3. There are roads in the province. 4. The people praise the leader of the soldiers on account of (his) courage. 5. The Romans constructed roads in the province. 6. There is peace in heaven. 7. There are Christians in heaven. 8. In peace and in war Christians pray. 9. There are soldiers on the road. 10. Caesar gave the soldiers the rewards of courage because they conquered the Gauls. 11. The leaders of the Gauls fortified the towns.

Exercise 42.—1. Sunt viae in Galliā. 2. Est bellum in prōvinciā. 3. Sunt mīlitēs in silvā. 4. Rōmānī viās mūnīvērunt. 5. Nōn est pāx in Galliā quod Caesar et mīlitēs in Galliā sunt. 6. Propter virtūtem mīlitum pāx in prōvinciā est. 7. Propter perīculum populī oppida mūnīvērunt. 8. Chrīstus est Via et Vēritās. 9. Virtūtem populī laudant.

Exercise 43.—See Nos. 45-61.

Box, page 45.—The peace of Christ in the kingdom of Christ.

Exercise 44.—See Introduction, 3.

Exercise 45.—1. Propter salūtem gentium. 2. Pars dūcum et mīli-tum. 3. Cum imperātōre hostium. 4. Propter caedem hominum. 5. In colle. 6. Cum hostibus. 7. In viā. 8. Ducēs gentium.

Exercise 46.—1. The leaders of the Romans conquered the enemy on a hill. (The leaders conquered the enemies of the Romans on the hill.) 2. On account of the slaughter of the soldiers there is a war in Gaul. 3. There are dangers in Gaul because the Gauls are enemies of the Romans. 4. Christ is the King of nations and the salvation of men because He is God. 5. Part of the enemy is in the forests, but part is on the hill. 6. In Gaul there are hills and forests, towns and roads. 7. The Romans conquered the kings and tribes of Gaul. 8. On account of the welfare of the people and the peace of the provinces the Romans constructed roads. 9. Men praise courage and truth. 10. After the slaughter of the enemy Caesar praises the soldiers for (on account of) their courage.

Exercise 47.—1. Pars hostium in oppidīs est, sed pars in colle est. 2. Propter caedem ducum gentis, Gallī Caesarem nōn laudant. 3. Chrīstus est Rēx gentium et populōrum. 4. Sunt collēs post oppidum. 5. Post victōriam est caedēs partis. ducum gentis. 6. Pars hostium in collibus et in silvīs est.

Exercise 48.—1. The final *a* of the nominative is short, of the ablative, long. 2. See Nos. 32-33, 35, 38, 46-52. 3. Christ, the Son of God, gave glory and a reward to the friends of God. Rules for cases: Fīlius, No. 473; praemium, No. 745; amīcīs, No. 737.

Exercise 49.—1. See Nos. 46-52. 2. See Nos. 59-63.

Exercise 50.—1. Acc. sing. 2. Gen. pl. 3. Gen. pl. 4. Gen. pl. 5. Gen. pl. 6. Gen. pl. 7. Gen. pl. 8. Gen. pl. 9. Gen. pl.

Exercise 51.—See Introduction, 3.

Exercise 52.—1. You Are Brothers. Christ is the King of men but He is (also) the brother of men, and God is the King of men but He is (also) the Father of men. And so men are brothers. And so war is the slaughter of brothers. And therefore God and Christ do not praise war. 2. The Slaughter of the Gauls. The Romans killed a part of the chiefs of the Gauls. And so God heard the shouting of mothers and of fathers and of brothers in the forests and mountains of Gaul. 3. In Gaul. There are forests and mountains and hills in Gaul. There are towns in the hills, but part of the tribes of the Gauls inhabit the mountains and forests. 4. Christ, the Leader of Men. Christ is the leader of men because He gave truth and law and light to men. Christ is the way and the truth. 5. "Our Tainted Nature's Solitary Boast." Mary is the Mother of Christ. But Christ is God because He is the Son of God the Father. And so Mary is the Mother of God. Christians praise Mary, the Mother of God. Mary is mother of men because Christ on the cross gave Mary to men. And so Christians are sons and servants of Mary. Mary is the gate of heaven.

Box, page 50.—I am a soldier of Christ.

Exercise 53.—1. Clāmōrem prīncipum audīvit. 2. Prīncipēs gentis occīdērunt. 3. Sunt perīcula in montibus. 4. Imperātor mātrēs et patrēs mīlitum laudat. 5. Frātrēs in Galliā cum Caesare sunt. 6. Propter bellum collēs mūnīvērunt. 7. Rōmānī viās in montibus mūnīvērunt.

Exercise 54.—See Introduction, 3.

Exercise 55.—1. In flūmine. 2. Propter vulnera. 3. In itinere. 4. In agmine. 5. In nōmine Marīae. 6. In corpore. 7. Cum agmine. 8. In itinere. 9. Post iter. 10. Nōmen flūminis. 11. Propter lēgem. 12. Cum imperātōribus. 13. Salūs gentium. 14. In monte.

Exercise 56.—1. On account of wounds the soldier is not in the column. 2. The general sees the soldiers' wounds. 3. There are bodies in the river. 4. There are rivers and forests in Gaul. 5. The Romans are on the march. 6. There are enemies in the forests and in the mountains. And so we are in danger. 7. Caesar sees the enemy's column. 8. Christians praise the name of Mary. 9. The enemy's column is on the river. 10. The Romans killed Christians because Christians praise the name of Christ.

Exercise 57.—1. Sunt corpora et gladiī in flūmine. 2. Agmen in montibus est. 3. Chrīstiānī in nōmine Chrīstī, Fīliī Deī, ōrant. 4. Sunt frātrēs et patrēs in agmine. 5. Sunt perīcula in itinere quod hostēs in collibus sunt. 6. Post iter collem mūnīvērunt. 7. Iter in montibus est. 8. Nautae terram et caelum vident. 9. Rēx propter salūtem rēgnī ōrat.

Exercise 58.—See Introduction, 3. The genders and the GRAMMAR numbers giving the rules for the genders are: nōmen, n., 51; rēx, m., 46; vēritās, f., 50; māter, f., 47; mōns, m., exception to 50; agmen, n., 51; dux, c., but in FIRST YEAR LATIN always m. because the leaders are men rather than women; mīles, m., 46; caedēs, f., 50; pater, m., 46; flūmen, n., 51; clāmor, m., 49; lūx, f., 50; homō, m., 46; virtūs, f., 50; iter, n., exception to 49; prīnceps, m., 46; pars, f., 50; hostis, c., but in FIRST YEAR LATIN always m. because the enemies are men; salūs, f., 50; collis, m., exception to 50; vōx, f., 50; frāter, m., 46; corpus, n., 52; imperātor, m., 46, 49; pāx, f., 50; vulnus, n., 52; gēns, f., 50.

Exercise 59.—1. "You are the light of the world." 2. Christ was in the world on account of (for) the salvation of men. 3. Christ gave light and a law, salvation and truth to men. 4. Caesar, commander in chief of the Romans, was with the soldiers in Gaul. 5. Christ is the salvation of the world. 6. The slaves praise the king's name. 7. The army of the enemy was in the mountains. 8. On account of the slaughter of the leading men there was no peace. 9. On account of wounds the soldiers were not on the march. 10. God, the Father of men, praises courage but He does not praise wars and slaughter. 11. The leader heard the cries of the slaves and the shouting of the soldiers. 12. After the war there were bodies on the hills and in the rivers, and the commander in chief heard the shouting of mothers. 13. Christians are Christ's brothers and Christ's soldiers. 14. The Romans killed a part of the leading men of the Gauls. 15. The tribes and peoples of Gaul do not praise the power of the Romans.

Exercise 60.—1. In nōmine rēgis. 2. Propter salūtem hominum. 3. In itinere. 4. In montibus et in collibus. 5. Cum prīncipibus gentium. 6. Lūcem mundī vident. 7. Post caedem ducum. 8. Erant corpora in viā. 9. Propter virtūtem mīlitis. 10. Virtūtēs Chrīstiānōrum laudat. 11. In pāce et in bellō. 12. Vōcem imperātōris audīvit. 13. Partem hostium occīdērunt. 14. Lēgēs gentis laudant. 15. Caesar praemia mīlitibus dedit. 16. Propter vulnera prīncipum. 17. Imperātor clāmōrem pātrum audīvit. 18. Agmen in flūmine erat. 19. Mātrēs agmen vident. 20. Propter salūtem gentis. 21. Vōcēs frātrum audīvit. 22. Deus vēritātem hominibus dedit. 23. Propter salūtem agminis. 24. In itinere. 25. Erat iter in montibus. 26. Caesar gladiōs prīncipī nōn dedit. 27. Gallī praemium imperātōrī dedērunt.

Exercise 61.—1. Chrīstus est Fīlius Deī. 2. Marīa Māter Deī et hominum est. 3. Mīles in colle est. 4. Mīles agmen hostium videt. 5. Servī viam mūnīvērunt. 6. Rōmānī Chrīstiānōs occīdērunt.

Exercise 62.—See No. 65.

Exercise 63.—See Introduction, 3.

Exercise 64.—1. Propter metum perīculī. 2. In senātū. 3. Cum exercitū Caesaris. 4. Post adventum Chrīstī. 5. Cum equitātū Gallōrum. 6. Impetus hostium. 7. Cum spīritū Deī. 8. In portū.

Exercise 65.—1. Now there are harbors in Gaul. (Abl.; no idea of motion.) 2. After the coming of the Romans there was war in Gaul. 3. Caesar came into the province with the cavalry. (Acc.; motion toward.) 4. Caesar, however, was not with the army. 5. On account of fear of the Romans the Gauls came into the forests. 6. The sailors see the harbor. 7. The Senate praises Caesar because the Romans conquered the enemy. 8. They made an attack against the enemy. 9. After the arrival of the cavalry the soldiers made an attack against the Gauls. 10. The Gauls were on the hill. Caesar's soldiers, however, made an attack against the Gauls. They killed the leaders and chiefs of the Gauls and conquered the Gauls. After the war, on account of fear of Caesar, the enemy did not make an attack against the Romans. 11. The Gauls killed the senate.

Exercise 66.—See Introduction, 3.

Exercise 67.—The Slaughter of the Christians. After the coming of Christ the light of truth was in the world, but the Romans were not friends of Christ and of truth. The Christians, however, were friends of Christ. There were many Christians in the empire of the Romans. They were in the harbors and in the towns of the provinces and in the forests and in the mountains. They were in the army and in the cavalry and in the Senate. They were slaves and soldiers; they were mothers and fathers, Gauls and Romans. On account of fear of Christ the King, however, and on account of the name of the Christians' God, the Romans killed the Christians. After the slaughter of the Christians the Romans were not friends and servants of God. The Christians, however, because the Romans killed the Christians on account of the law of Christ, are now in heaven with Mary and Christ and see the glory of God the Father.

1. The light of truth. 2. No. 3. Yes. 4. In the harbors, towns, forests, and mountains; in the army, cavalry, and Senate. 5. Slaves and soldiers, mothers and fathers, Gauls and Romans. 6. They killed them.

Exercise 68.—The Conquest of Gaul. Gallī nōn erant amīcī Caesaris et senātūs. Itaque Caesar in Galliam cum equitātū et mīlitibus vēnit. Gallī autem, propter metum Caesaris, in silvās et in montēs vēnērunt. Exercitus Caesaris in silvīs hostium erat, et perīcula erant. Rōmānī autem in hostēs impetum fēcērunt. Ducēs et prīncipēs Gallōrum occīdērunt. Equitātum et exercitum Gallōrum vīcērunt, et portūs et oppida et collēs Galliae mūnīvērunt. Itaque senātus propter glōriam bellī et virtūtem mīlitum Caesarem nunc laudat. Propter metum mīlitum Gallī nunc amīcī et servī senātūs sunt.

Exercise 69.—God Is Everywhere. "God is a spirit." He is in heaven and on earth. He sees the world. He sees men. He sees the soldiers and the sailors and the servants. He sees the mothers and the fathers, the brothers and the sons. He praises men on account of virtue (courage), but He does not praise (them) on account of slaughter.

Exercise 70.—See No. 69.

Exercise 71.—See Introduction, 3.

Exercise 72.—1. The soldiers were in battle line. 2. The Romans killed the Christians on account of the (their) faith. 3. The soldiers placed hope of victory in courage. 4. The Romans made an attack against the enemy's battle line. 5. The Gauls see the battle line of the Romans on the hill. 6. In Christ is the hope of the world. 7. God praises Christians on account of faith and virtue. 8. The soldiers see the affair.

Exercise 73.—1. Caesar in aciē erat. 2. Fidem mīlitis laudant. 3. Senātus rem nōn laudat. 4. Gallī in aciem Rōmānōrum impetum fēcērunt. 5. Spem in Deō posuērunt.

Exercise 74.—1. *Hostium*, declined like *pars*, No. 60; *virtūtum*, regular; *hominum*, regular; *gentium*, like *pars*, No. 61. 2. *Homō*, m., No. 46; *rēs*, f., No. 70; *nauta*, m., No. 32; *māter*, f., No. 47; *vēritās*, f., No. 50; *pāx*, f., No. 50; *gēns*, f., No. 50; *servus*, m., No. 35; *equitātus*, m., No. 66; *praemium*, n., No. 38; *Rōmānus*, m., No. 35.

Exercise 75.—1. Chrīstiānī propter cōpiam grātiae Chrīstī Deō grātiās agunt. 2. Propter metum Caesaris gentēs in castra impetum nōn fēcērunt. 3. Erat cōpia gladiōrum in castrīs. 4. Imperātor propter victōriam in grātiā cum rēge erat. 5. In castra impetum fēcērunt. 6. Cōpiae hostium in prōvinciā nōn erant. 7. Spem in grātiā Chrīstī posuērunt. 8. Propter caedem prīncipum bellum erat in Galliā. Caesar in Galliam cum cōpiīs et equitātū et impedīmentīs vēnit. Cōpiae hostium in colle erant. Rōmānī autem post collem castra posuērunt. Gallī propter metum Caesaris in castra impetum nōn fēcērunt. Rōmānī autem in Gallōs impetum fēcērunt. Gallī in equitātū spem posuērunt, sed Rōmānī equitātum Gallōrum occīdērunt et collem cēpērunt. Ducēs et castra et impedīmenta Gallōrum cēpērunt. Post bellum erat pāx in Galliā et Rōmānī in prōvinciam vēnērunt.

Exercise 76.—The Camp of the Romans. You see the army of the Romans in camp. You see soldiers and leaders and the commander in chief. You see the soldiers' swords. You do not see the baggage, but the baggage is in the camp. There is an abundance of all things in the camp. The soldiers pitched camp on a hill but not in the forest. The battle line came into the camp with the baggage train. The enemy, however, made an attack against the camp, but the troops of the Romans conquered the enemy. Now the commander in chief praises the soldiers and the leaders on account of (their) courage and the leaders give thanks to the soldiers on account of the victory. On account of the victory the commander in chief came into favor with the Senate.

Exercise 77.—"Woe to the Conquered!" The Gauls were enemies of the Romans. Therefore the Romans came into Gaul with troops and pitched camp. In the camp there were soldiers and cavalry and slaves and the soldiers' baggage. There was an abundance of swords in the camp. There were battle lines on the hills, in the mountains, and in the forest. The Gauls made an attack against the Romans; the Romans, however, made an attack against the Gauls. The Romans placed hope of victory in courage; the Gauls placed hope of safety in courage. The Romans, however, conquered the Gauls. They killed part (some) of the leading men (chiefs) and the leaders of the Gauls; they captured the harbors and towns of the Gauls. And so the Gauls gave an abundance of swords and slaves to the Romans. After the war there was peace in Gaul, but there were camps of the Romans in Gaul and the Gauls were slaves of the Romans. The commander in chief of the Romans was Caesar. The Senate praises Caesar and the army on account of the victory and the courage of the soldiers, and the Romans give thanks to Caesar.

Exercise 78.—Brothers in Christ. On account of the grace of God we are Christians. And therefore we are brothers on account of the law of Christ: "You are brothers."

Exercise 79.—Castra. Mōns (silva). Mīles. Via. Senātus. Portus: Agmen. Impedīmenta. Aciēs. Equitātus. Lēx. Imperātor (dux). Collis. Flūmen.

Exercise 80.—Who Is Christ? Christ, the Son of God, is the son of Mary. Therefore He is man and God. Christ is King of men because He is God. In Christ is man's salvation because, on account of the salvation of men, He came into the world. He is the "Light of the World" because He gave men truth. And so Christians give thanks to God and to Christ, and praise Christ, King and Commander.

Exercise 81.—The genders and the GRAMMAR numbers giving the rules for the genders are: 1, n., 52; 2, m., 35; 3, f., 70; 4, f., 50; 5, f., 33; 6, n., 51; 7, m., 46; 8, f., 33; 9, n., 38; 10, f., 33; 11, n., 52; 12, n., 38; 13, c., but here m. by 46; 14, n., 51; 15, m., 35; 16, f., 47; 17, n., 51; 18, n., 38; 19, m., 35; 20, m., 46; 21, n., exception to 49; 22, c., but here m. by 46; 23, f., 33; 24, f., 50; 25, m., 46; 26, m., 35; 27, f., 33; 28, m., exception to 50; 29, m., 35; 30, m., exception to 50; 31, f., 33; 32, m., 46; 33, m., 35; 34, c., but here m. by 46; 35, m., 35; 36, n., 38; 37, f., 50; 38, f., 50; 39, m., 32; 40, f., 33; 41, m., 46; 42, m., 35; 43, f., 50; 44, m., 66.

Exercise 82.—The genders and the GRAMMAR numbers giving the rules for the genders are: 1, f., 50; 2, m., 46; 3, f., 70; 4, m., 35; 5, m., 35; 6, m., 66; 7, m., 66; 8, f., 33; 9, m., 66; 10, f., 50; 11, f., 70; 12, m., 66; 13, f., 50; 14, f., 50; 15, f., 70; 16, m., 49.

Exercise 83.—1. God, the father of men, is in heaven. 2. God gave a law to men. (*Hominibus,* dat., indirect object.) 3. On account of (For the sake of) men's salvation Christ was man on earth. 4. Christ is the light of the world. (*Lūx,* predicate noun.) 5. Christ, the Son of God, is King of tribes and peoples. (*Fīlius,* appositive.) 6. After the coming of Christ there was truth in the world. (*Adventum,* acc. after *post.*) 7. The spirit of God was in Christ. 8. The kingdom of Christ is the kingdom of heaven. 9. Christians pray in the name of Christ. 10. Mary, with Christ in the kingdom of heaven, now sees the glory of God. (*Rēgnō,* abl. after *in,* no motion expressed.) 11. Mary, the Mother of God, is the gate of heaven. 12. Heaven is the reward of virtue. 13. God praises the faith of Christians. (*Fidem,* direct object.) 14. You are brothers. 15. A friend is the servant of a (his) friend. 16. Soldiers praise peace. 17. Rome is not in Gaul, but there is a province of the Romans in Gaul. 18. The Gauls inhabit Gaul. 19. The sailors see the harbors. 20. The Romans constructed roads in the provinces. 21. Christians do not praise the slaughter of the enemy's leading men. 22. Caesar did not give the command of Gaul to the Gauls. 23. The commander in chief heard the shouting and cries of the enemy. 24. On account of wounds the soldiers did not make the march. 25. On account of (Through) fear the leader praises the king. 26. On account of war there were soldiers and a supply of swords in the town. (*Erant* agrees with *mīlitēs et cōpia;* see No. 471.) 27. The enemy was in the mountains and on the hills. 28. The bodies of the soldiers were in the forest. 29. They killed a part of the cavalry in the river. 30. The Senate and the leading men give thanks to the army on account of the victory. (*Exercituī,* indirect object.) 31. The Romans placed hope in courage. 32. Caesar came into camp with troops and baggage. 33. On account of the influence of Caesar the leading men of the Gauls gave slaves to the Romans. 34. The enemy was behind the Romans' battle line. The cavalry, however, came into the battle line. And so the Romans conquered and killed the enemy. (*Aciem,* acc. after *in,* expressing motion toward.) 35. Caesar came into the forests of Gaul. The leading men of the Gauls, however, saw the affair. They therefore made an attack against Caesar's battle line. 36. Soldiers in battle line pray because they are in danger.

UNIT TWO

Exercise 84.—1. In the deep river. 2. With a great army. 3. After the great war. 4. With holy Mary. 5. On a long road. 6. With good men. 7. With large forces. 8. With many soldiers. 9. In great danger. 10. In high mountains. 11. With a good man. 12. After a long march. 13. On account of many wounds. 14. With a bad servant.

14 FIRST YEAR LATIN

Exercise 85.—1. Cum multīs mīlitibus. 2. In altīs montibus. 3. Propter lēgem sānctam Deī. 4. Cum homine bonō. 5. Magna corpora. 6. Cum prīmīs Chrīstiānīs. 7. Lēgēs malae. 8. Alta flūmina. 9. Longa via. 10. Propter magnum metum Rōmānōrum. 11. Magnus clāmor. 12. Sāncta Marīa.

Exercise 86.—1. Many Christians were in the first battle line. (Abl. after *in*, no motion expressed.) 2. Holy Mary prays. 3. A long column came into the high mountains. (Acc. after *in*, expressing motion toward.) 4. The bad sailor does not pray. 5. A good leader praises the great courage of the soldiers. (*Bonus*, adj. of quality follows noun; *magnam*, adj. of quantity precedes noun.) 6. In a long column there are many soldiers and much baggage.

Exercise 87.—1. Ducēs bonī pācem laudant. 2. Rēgēs malī multōs Chrīstiānōs occīdērunt. 3. Longum agmen in silvīs erat, sed prīma aciēs in altīs montibus erat. 4. Propter magnam glōriam Rōmae multī hominēs lēgēs Rōmānōrum laudant. 5. Sunt magnī montēs et alta flūmina in Americā. 6. Chrīstiānī servī sānctae Marīae sumus.

Exercise 88.—1. Angusta. 2. Bonus. 3. Tūtī. 4. Rōmāna. 5. Chrīstiānī. 6. Malae. 7. Reliqua. 8. Sānctī. 9. Altum. 10. Prīmī. 11. Sānctus. 12. Multae. 13. Tūtī. 14. Magnī. 15. Malus. 16. Longa. 17. Sānctus. 18. Tūtī.

Box, page 77.—The welfare of the people is the highest law. Let the welfare of the people be the highest law.

Box, page 78.—Glory be to the Father, and to the Son, and to the Holy Spirit.

Exercise 89.—1. The Roman legions were in front of (before) the camp. 2. Holy Mary prays for bad men and for good men. 3. Many Gauls were before the gates of the camp. 4. The leading men were in front of a high wall. 5. The Roman soldiers pitched camp in front of (before) the wall of the large town. 6. Christians pray for (their) friends. 7. On behalf of the good king the soldiers made an attack against the enemy. 8. There was a great scarcity of grain in Gaul. 9. The rest of the Christian soldiers were in the first battle line before the forest. 10. Slaves praise a good master.

Exercise 90.—There was a great scarcity of grain in the Roman camp because the Gauls did not give a supply of grain to the Romans and there were no crops in Gaul. The Gauls were not friends of the Romans. Caesar, therefore, came into Gaul with troops and baggage. Caesar's column was long. The road was in (ran through) narrow and high mountains. The Gauls therefore made an attack against the long column, but the Roman legions conquered the Gauls. And so the remaining Gauls came into a safe city. The Romans, however, pitched camp before the high wall. Caesar's first battle line was in front of the camp. The Gauls, however, on account of (their) great fear of Caesar, did not make an attack against the Roman camp. And so the Romans made an attack against the Gauls and conquered the Gauls. They killed many Gauls and a great part of Gaul's leading men. After Caesar's victory there was peace in Gaul. And so the Gauls gave the Romans a large supply of grain, and there was no scarcity of grain in the Roman camp.

Box, page 79.—Holy, holy, holy, Lord God of hosts (armies).

Exercise 91.—1. Prō magnīs castrīs altum flūmen est. 2. Mūrī oppidī sunt altī. 3. Caesar erat magnus imperātor. 4. Erat magna inopia frūmentī. 5. Erant multae legiōnēs cum Caesare in Galliā. 6. Sāncta Marīa prō hominibus ōrat. 7. Chrīstus Dominus prō mundō ōrat. 8. Servī Rōmānī dominōs nōn laudant. 9. Sunt magna frūmenta in Galliā.

Exercise 92.—1. The column was long. (Longum, predicate adjective; nom. sing., n., with agmen.) 2. The remaining Gauls were not safe. (Reliquī, nom. pl., m., with Gallī; adj. of quantity precedes noun.) 3. On behalf of the good commander in chief the Christian soldiers made an attack against the enemy. (Chrīstiānī, nom. pl., m., with mīlitēs; adj. of quality follows noun. Bonō, abl. sing., m., with imperātōre; adj. of quality follows noun.) 4. The road was narrow. (Forms of sum may stand anywhere.) 5. The long column came into the high mountains. (Longum, nom. sing., n., with agmen; adj. of quantity precedes noun.) 6. The first legion was in battle line. (Prīma, nom. sing., f., with legiō; adj. of quantity precedes noun.) 7. There was a great scarcity of grain in the remaining tribes. (Magna, nom. sing., f., with inopia; adj. of quantity precedes noun. Reliquīs, abl. pl., f., with gentibus; adj. of quantity precedes noun.) 8. Bad men do not pray for the rest of the men. (Malī, nom. pl., m., with hominēs; adj. of quality follows noun.) 9. There are many rivers in Gaul. (Multa, nom. pl., n., with flūmina; adj. of quantity precedes noun.) 10. The master, a good and holy man, gave grain to the servants. (Bonus, nom. sing., m., with homō; adj. of quality follows noun.) 11. The Roman legions were in battle line before the high wall. (Altō, abl. sing., m., with mūrō; adj. of quantity generally, but not invariably, precedes noun.)

Box, page 80.—In the name of the Lord.

Exercise 93.—1. Malās. 2. Bonīs. 3. Magnum. 4. Magnā. 5. Rōmānō. 6. Bonīs. 7. Multīs. 8. Chrīstiānam. 9. Magnam. 10. Rōmāna. 11. Longā. 12. Magnum.

Box, page 81.—The earth is the Lord's! Great is the glory of the Lord!

Exercise 94.—1. With Caesar, the Roman general. 2. On account of the welfare of the Roman people. 3. In the high mountains. 4. After a great slaughter. 5. On account of many wounds. 6. On account of the welfare of the remaining tribes. 7. For the holy name. 8. In the deep river.

Exercise 95.—1. See No. 78. 2. See No. 78. 3. (1) Homine fortī, hominēs fortēs, hominum fortium. (2) Omnī Chrīstiānō, omnēs Chrīstiānī, omnium Chrīstiānōrum. (3) Duce nōbilī, ducēs nōbilēs, ducum nōbilium. (4) Brevī itinere, brevia itinera, brevium itinerum. (5) Viā difficilī, viae difficilēs, viārum difficilium. (6) Bellō gravī, bella gravia, bellōrum gravium. 4. (1) Salūtem commūnem, salūte commūnī. (2) Omnem Galliam, omnī Galliā. (3) Rem gravem, rē gravī. (4) Metum gravem, metū gravī. (5) Oppidum nōbile, oppidō nōbilī. (6) Omnem spem, omnī spē. (7) Vulnus grave, vulnere gravī. (8) Viam facilem, viā facilī. (9) Nōmen nōbile, nōmine nōbilī. 5. (a) Difficilī. On a different route. (b) Omnibus. With all the troops. (c) Nōbilī. For a noble king. (d) Fortī. For a brave friend. (e) Nōbilī. For a noble (renowned) leader. (f) Grave. After a severe war. (g) Gravem. On account of severe fear. (h) Omnī. With all the cavalry. (i) Fortibus. With the brave soldiers. (j) Gravia. On account of serious wounds. (k) Commūnem. On account of the common welfare. (l) Nōbile. Behind the renowned town.

Exercise 96.—1. Fortis, nōbilis. Christ the Lord, King of men, was strong and noble. 2. Brevis. The hope of the Gauls was short. 3. Nōbilis. The renowned leader was in the first battle line. 4. Fortēs. Before the camp there were brave soldiers. 5. Omnem. They placed all hope of safety in courage. 6. Omnem. Christians place all hope of salvation in the name of Christ. 7. Gravem. On account of a serious affair Caesar came into Gaul. 8. Commūnem. On account of the common welfare all the Gauls made an attack against the province. 9. Difficilis. On account of the mountains and forests the route was difficult. 10. Facilis. On account of the courage of the Gauls the thing was not easy.

Exercise 97.—1. Perīculum erat grave. 2. Estis fortēs. 3. Propter salūtem commūnem hominum Chrīstus in mundum vēnit. 4. Via erat difficilis. 5. Omnēs hominēs magnam virtūtem laudant. 6. Erant mīlitēs fortēs et ducēs nōbilēs in exercitū Rōmānō. 7. Iter nōn erat facile. 8. Montēs magnī et altī sunt. 9. Omnis imperātor virtūtem et fidem laudat. 10. Caesar imperātor magnus et nōbilis erat. 11. Victōria nōn erat facilis. 12. Iter erat breve. 13. Gladiī Rōmānī erant gravēs. 14. Rēs erat gravis. 15. Chrīstus dominus nōbilis et dux fortis est. Itaque omnēs hominēs bonī et sānctī Chrīstum Dominum laudant. 16. Lēgēs Rōmānae erant gravēs. 17. Flūmina longa et alta Americae sunt nōbilia.

Exercise 98.—1. The Gauls were eager for fame. 2. The son is like the father. 3. The Gauls were next to (were the tribe living nearest to) the province. 4. Mary is full of grace. 5. Gaul was full of Romans. 6. The town was full of soldiers and of swords. 7. The province is full of all good things. 8. Heaven is full of the glory of God. 9. We are eager for all good things. 10. They were next to Gaul (lived nearer to Gaul than any others). 11. Holy men are like Christ.

Exercise 99.—1. Gladiōrum (gladiīs). 2. Victōriae. 3. Galliae. 4. Rōmānōrum (Rōmānīs). 5. Fīnitimārum. 6. Mīlitis (mīlitī). 7. Bellī.

Box, page 88.—All for Jesus.

Exercise 100.—The name of Jesus is the (a) holy name. It is a name noble and full of hope. All Christians pray in the name of Jesus; all praise Jesus; all give thanks to Jesus; all in heaven with Mary see Jesus. In Jesus' name the first Christians conquered the Romans. On account of Jesus God the Father gave the first Christians the reward of victory. And so Jesus Christ is both Lord and King of all men.

Exercise 101.—1. Christians praise both Jesus Christ and Mary. 2. Rome is a city both great and renowned. 3. Caesar was eager for both fame and power. 4. At dawn the brave cavalry made an attack against the rest of the enemy. 5. On account of serious dangers and the soldiers' many wounds the Romans made a short march into the province.

Exercise 102.—What do you see in the picture? In the picture you see a Roman column. It is a long column, but you see a part of the column. You see the standards of the legion and the swords of the soldiers. Part of the column is on the bridge. The cavalry, however, is not on the bridge. You see the commander in chief. He comes first. There is a baggage train in the column. In the baggage train is a supply of grain and of all things. You see the city and the high wall.

Exercise 103.—Sunt multī pontēs in flūminibus longīs et altīs in Americā. 2. Mīlitēs Rōmānī propter nōmen Jēsū multōs Chrīstiānōs occīdērunt. 3. In Americā oppida magna et nōbilia sunt. 4. Chrīstiānī omnem spem et fidem in Dominō Jēsū Chrīstō posuērunt. 5. Et nautae et mīlitēs Deum laudant. 6. Urbs Rōma magna et nōbilis est. 7. Prīmā lūce imperātor signum dedit. Itaque equitēs in hostēs impetum fēcērunt et magnam partem prīncipum gentis occīdērunt. 8. Vidētis signa legiōnum. 9. Vulnera mīlitum fortium sunt multa et gravia. 10. Hostēs equitem Rōmānum occīdērunt. 11. Pontēs mūnīvērunt. 12. Quid Chrīs-tiānī laudant?

Box, page 90.—The Sign of the Cross. In the name of the Father and of the Son and of the Holy Spirit. Amen.

Reading No. 3.—What is victory? It is the reward of courage. What is war? It is the slaughter of brothers. What is a soldier? He is the bulwark of empire.

UNIT THREE

Exercise 104.—Laudāre, pācāre, oppugnāre, occupāre, parāre.

Exercise 105.—See No. 152.

Exercise 106.—1. See No. 152. 2. They all have -*āre* in the present infinitive. 3. See No. 162.

Exercise 107.—1. 3rd pl., they pray, are praying, do pray. 2. 3rd pl., they fight, are fighting, do fight. 3. 2nd sing., you seize, are seizing, do seize. 4. 2nd pl., you pray, are praying, do pray. 5. 3rd sing., he prays, is praying, does pray. 6. 1st pl., we prepare, are preparing, do prepare. 7. 3rd sing., he seizes, is seizing, does seize. 8. 1st pl., we seize, are seizing, do seize. 9. 2nd sing., you pray, are praying, do pray. 10. 1st sing., I prepare, am preparing, do prepare.

Exercise 108.—1. Parant. 2. Oppugnat. 3. Laudās or laudātis. 4. Ōrant. 5. Parāmus. 6. Laudō.

Exercise 109.—1. Ōrat. 2. Parās or parātis. 3. Quid laudat? 4. Ōrā-mus. 5. Oppida occupant. 6. Oppidum oppugnant. 7. Virtūtem laudant. 8. Gladiōs parat. 9. Ōrat. 10. Quid laudant?

Exercise 110.—1. Laudant. The Romans praise Caesar. 2. Laudat. Caesar does not praise the first legion. 3. Parant. The enemy is prepar-ing war. 4. Occupat. The renowned leader seizes the city and the harbor. 5. Oppugnant. The soldiers attack the camp.

Exercise 111.—All good men pray, but bad men do not pray. Chris-tians pray in the name of Christ. A good king prays for (his) kingdom and soldiers. A good leader prays for (his) soldiers. On account of the dangers of war both soldiers and sailors pray. Both fathers and mothers pray for (their) sons. Sons pray for (their) fathers and mothers. Friends pray for (their) friends. Christ prays for all men.

When we pray, we praise God. All Christians praise God, the Father of all men, because He prepares many good things for men. After vic-tory and safety soldiers praise God; fathers and mothers praise God on account of peace and the safety of (their) sons.

Exercise 112.—Bad kings and leaders prepare (for) war. A bad king, eager for glory and power, gets swords and legions ready. He prepares camps full of swords and grain. He attacks and seizes neighboring cities and towns. The bad king's soldiers seize both forests and hills. They are eager for victory but not for peace. God, however, does not prepare rewards for bad soldiers and kings!

Exercise 113.—You are good men. Therefore you praise peace and virtue and pray for all men. You do not prepare (for) war, for you are not eager for fame and victory. You do not attack neighboring cities; you do not seize the towns of neighboring tribes; you prepare swords and legions, not on account of war, but on account of peace (not because you want war, but because you want peace).

Exercise 114.—1. We Christians pray for all men. (*Chrīstiānī* agrees with *we*, understood from *ōrāmus.*) 2. You praise brave soldiers. 3. You are not attacking the city. 4. You are preparing a supply of swords. 5. We Christians praise the Holy Spirit. (*Chrīstiānī* agrees with *we*, understood from *laudāmus.*) 6. You all praise a brave and holy man. (*Omnēs* agrees with *you*, understood from *laudātis.*)

Exercise 115.—1. Imperātōrēs Rōmānī virtūtem et fidem mīlitum fortium laudant. Mīlitēs Rōmānī fortēs cōpiam gladiōrum parant. Urbēs et oppida oppugnant. Collēs et montēs et pontēs occupant. Mūrus imperiī sunt. Omnis spēs victōriae et salūtis in virtūte legiōnum fortium est. 2. Omnēs Chrīstiānī estis. Itaque omnēs Jēsum Chrīstum, Fīlium Deī, et Marīam, Mātrem Chrīstī, laudātis. Prō omnibus hominibus, mīlitibus et nautīs, prīncipibus et servīs ōrātis. In nōmine Jēsū Chrīstī ōrātis, et Patrem et Fīlium et Spīritum Sānctum laudātis. 3. Caesarem laudāmus quod imperātor magnus et fortis est. 4. Dux castra oppugnat. 5. Bellum parant. 6. Pācem laudāmus, sed bellum nōn laudāmus. 7. Ducēs frūmentum et gladiōs parant.

Exercise 116.—1 and 2. (a) *Collium*, like pars; see No. 60. (b) *Frātrum*, exception; see No. 62. (c) *Prīncipum*, like *lēx*. (d) *Gravium*, regular, adj. of 3rd decl. 3. The soldiers are before the gates. (*Portīs*, abl. pl. of *porta, ae,* f.; after *prō.*)

Exercise 117.—See Nos. 152, 153, 162, 163.

Exercise 118.—See Introduction, 3.

Exercise 119.—See Introduction, 3.

Exercise 120.—1. Pugnābant. The brave cavalry was fighting with a great number of the enemy (against a large force of the enemy). 2. Laudābant. Christians were praising Christ, the King of all nations. 3. Portābant. The centurions were not carrying the grain. 4. Superābat. A high mountain surpasses (rises above) the hills. 5. Laudābat. The

Roman people were praising the victories of the remaining legions.
6. Ōrābant. Good Christians were praying for (their) brothers (brethren). 7. Superābat. The Roman cavalry were surpassing the Gauls in courage. 8. Pugnābat. A great number of centurions were fighting in the first battle line.

Exercise 121.—1. Servī in oppida frūmentum portābant. 2. Legiōnēs Rōmānae cum gentibus Galliae pugnābant. 3. Equitātus magnum Gallōrum numerum superābat. 4. Centuriō in prīmā aciē pugnābat. 5. Caesar hostēs superābat.

Exercise 122.—See Introduction, 3.

Exercise 123.—1. (a) m., No. 46; (b) f., No. 50; (c) m., exception to No. 50. 2. (a) Legiōnēs; (b) virtūtēs; (c) corpora; (d) gravēs, gravēs, gravia. 3. The centurions did not give swords to the slaves. (Servīs, dat. pl. of servus, ī, m., indirect object.)

Exercise 124.—See Nos. 162-164.

Exercise 125.—See Introduction, 3.

Exercise 126.—1. God will give truth to all nations. 2. Meanwhile the commander in chief will call the centurions into winter quarters. 3. God will call holy men into heaven after death. 4. On account of the fear of death (Because of their fear of death) the chiefs of the remaining tribes will give grain to the Romans. 5. The slaves will carry the grain into winter quarters. 6. The centurion will call the leading men into winter quarters.

Exercise 127.—1. In Caelō Deum laudābimus. 2. Rēgēs malī bellum parābunt. 3. Rōmam laudābis. 4. Dominum Deum exercituum laudābō. 5. Omnibus hominibus bonīs Deus magna praemia dabit. 6. Caesar mīlitēs in hīberna vocābit. 7. Post mortem Caesaris Gallī servī Rōmānōrum erant. 8. Interim centuriō in aciem legiōnēs vocābit.

Exercise 128.—1. Caesar was commander in chief of the Romans. (Imperātor is nominative, a predicate noun.) 2. (a) f., No. 50; (b) m., No. 46; (c) f., No. 50. 3. (a) Morte; (b) centuriōne; (c) gravī; (d) senātū; (e) rēgnō; (f) vōce; (g) fidē.

Exercise 129.—1. Who will praise Caesar after the slaughter of the leading men of Gaul? 2. Why do you call the Senate? 3. Where are the enemy's winter quarters? 4. Who does not praise God? 5. Where are the Roman troops? 6. Why did they pitch camp in an unfavorable place? 7. Why does he seize foreign cities? 8. Why were the foreign tribes preparing for war? 9. Why was he seizing every place?

Exercise 130.—1. Cūr mīlitēs locō aliēnō pugnābant? 2. Quis magnum imperātōrem Caesarem superābit? 3. Quid parābant? 4. Quis portūs

et urbēs aliēnās occupat? 5. Ubi prīmā lūce pugnābunt? 6. Homō
cupidus glōriae virtūtem aliēnam nōn laudat.

Exercise 131.—1. Why do we praise God? We praise God because
God is good and is the Lord of heaven and earth. 2. Why were the
Romans fighting with the Gauls? The Romans were fighting with the
Gauls on account of the slaughter of the centurions. 3. Why were the
Romans praising Caesar? Rōmānī Caesarem laudābant quod erat dux
fortis. The Romans were praising Caesar because he was a brave leader.
4. Why do Christians praise the Holy Spirit? Chrīstiānī Sānctum
Spīritum laudant quod Deus est. Christians praise the Holy Spirit because He is God. 5. Why do Christians praise Mary? Chrīstiānī Marīam
laudant quod māter Chrīstī est. Christians praise Mary because she is
the Mother of Christ. 6. Why do we pray in the name of Jesus Christ?
In nōmine Jēsū Chrīstī ōrāmus quod salūs mundī est. We pray in the
name of Jesus Christ because He is the salvation of the world. 7. Who
was carrying the large supply of grain? The slave was carrying the
large supply of grain. 8. What does a good leader prepare? A good
leader prepares swords and a supply of grain. 9. Who will fight for a
good leader? Mīlitēs fortēs prō duce bonō pugnābunt. Brave soldiers
will fight for a good leader. 10. Who was calling the slave? The master
was calling the slave. 11. Who was commander in chief of the Romans
in Gaul? Caesar imperātor Rōmānōrum in Galliā erat. Caesar was
commander in chief of the Romans in Gaul. 12. Who will give great
rewards to good men? Deus magna praemia hominibus bonīs dabit. God
will give great rewards to good men. 13. In war what do good leaders
seize? In bellō ducēs bonī montēs et collēs, portūs et pontēs occupant.
In war good leaders seize mountains and hills, harbors and bridges.
14. Who is Christ? Chrīstus Fīlius Deī et frāter omnium hominum est.
Christ is the Son of God and every man's brother. 15. Who prays for
all men? Chrīstus prō omnibus hominibus ōrat. Christ prays for all men.
16. Where does Mary now pray? Mary now prays in heaven. 17. Where
is God? God is in heaven and on earth and in every place. 18. Where
was Caesar fighting? Caesar in Galliā pugnābat. Caesar was fighting in
Gaul. 19. Where is the Romans' baggage train? Impedīmenta Rōmānōrum in ponte sunt. The Romans' baggage train is on the bridge.
20. Where will God give a reward to holy men after death? Deus
praemium hominibus sānctīs in Caelō post mortem dabit. God will give
a reward to holy men in heaven after death.

Exercise 132.—1. Were the Romans always fighting? 2. Were they
preparing (laying in a supply of) grain after the long march? 3. You

22 FIRST YEAR LATIN

will praise the mountains and forests and rivers of Gaul. 4. Were the Romans fighting with the Gauls on the march? 5. After the war were there many bodies in the rivers and in the forests? 6. Are the baggage train and the legions in the column? 7. Were you praising the name of Mary? 8. On account of wounds (Because of their wounds) they did not make a long march. 9. Does the Roman army surpass the Gauls? 10. Were holy men always praying? 11. I will always praise the law and the truth of Christ. 12. Is the commander in chief giving the signal? 13. After the speech of the chief are the Romans giving the Gauls a supply of grain? 14. Will the centurion call the cavalry at dawn? 15. Do Christians pray in the name of Christ? 16. Did the Gauls always make an attack against the columns of the Romans? 17. Was there a large bridge on (over) the deep river? 18. Were the Gauls attacking the winter quarters? 19. We were praising the victory and glory of Christ. 20. Was the commander in chief praising the centurion on account of (his) great courage and many wounds? 21. Do kings give great rewards to (their) friends? 22. Will he seize the hills? 23. Meanwhile, on account of Caesar's favor, the Gauls are carrying grain into the winter quarters. 24. Was the sailor praying on account of fear of (because he was afraid of receiving) wounds? 25. Was the leader preparing (laying in a supply of) grain and swords? 26. We will praise Christ, the King of glory. 27. Who was seizing the places? 28. Was the cavalry fighting in the forest? 29. Were the slaves carrying a great number of swords? 30. On account of the fear of wounds and of death, sailors and soldiers always pray in war. 31. God heard the prayers of many Christians. 32. Was the cavalry fighting in an unfavorable and narrow place?

Page 118.—The Christian Prayer, the Doxology. Glory be to the Father and to the Son and to the Holy Spirit. As it was in the beginning, is now, and ever shall be, world without end. Amen.

Exercise 133.—1. Laudāsne semper nōmina Jēsū et Marīae? 2. Laudābimusne Deum in Caelō? 3. Chrīstiānī semper ōrant, sīcut Chrīstus amīcōs suōs monuit. 4. Propter ōrātiōnēs Chrīstiānōrum Deus multīs hominibus grātiam dabit. 5. Propter ōrātiōnem imperātōris prīncipēs gentium bellum parābunt. 6. In prīncipiō bellī Rōmānī hostēs superābant. 7. Suntne multa flūmina longa et nōbilia in Americā? 8. Eratne iter longum et difficile? 9. Propter multa et gravia vulnera mīlitum exercitus iter breve in hīberna fēcit. 10. Eratne iter plēnum perīculōrum? 11. Erantne agmina Caesaris tūta in Galliā? 12. Vocābitne post mortem in Caelum Deus omnēs hominēs bonōs (sānctōs)? 13. Eratne locus aliēnus? 14. Quid servī Rōmānī ōrābant? 15. Eratne in imperiō Rōmānō magnus servōrum numerus? 16. Superābantne Rōmānī omnēs gentēs Galliae? 17. Servī corpus prīncipis portābant. 18. Occupābuntne nautae et mīlitēs Americānī portūs et urbēs aliēnās? 19. Agmen Rōmānum castra oppugnābat. 20. Interim ubi reliquī Gallī pugnābant?

Exercise 134.—1. Because their present active infinitives end in *-ēre.* 2. See No. 152. 3. See Nos. 165, 168, 171.

Exercise 135.—See Introduction, 3.

Exercise 136.—See Introduction, 3.

Exercise 137.—See Introduction, 3.

Exercise 138.—1. You fear. 2. He will advise the leader. 3. He was terrifying the enemy. 4. They were advising the brother. 5. They have command. 6. They terrify the people. 7. He was having a part. 8. You will fear the cavalry.

Exercise 139.—1. Terret. The shouting of the enemy does not terrify the Roman soldiers because the Romans are brave. 2. Timēbunt. Many men are brave in peace; in war, however, they will fear the enemy. 3. Monēbunt. On account of fear the slaves will warn the master. 4. Terret. Fear of God terrifies bad men. 5. Monēbant. On account of the favor of Caesar (To gain favor with Caesar) the Gauls were warning the Romans. 6. Timent. All men fear wounds and death. 7. Habēbant. The legions had a large supply of arms.

Exercise 140.—1. All men fear difficult things. 2. On account of a serious affair the centurions will warn the general. 3. The shouting of the enemy in difficult and narrow places terrifies the legions. 4. A bad king has unfavorable affairs (suffers reverses). 5. The Roman people were not afraid of (were not fearing) serious dangers or difficult things. 6. Many tribes do not have arms.

Exercise 141.—1. (a) Legiōnēs; (b) flūmina; (c) corpora; (d) centuriōnēs; (e) facilēs, facilēs, facilia. 2. Cupidī victōriae et glōriae sunt. 3. He was carrying grain into camp. (*Castra,* acc. pl. after *in,* expressing motion toward.)

Exercise 142.—Portus Margarītārius. Hostēs semper bellum parābant, quod cupidī imperiī et glōriae et victōriae erant. Copiās Americānās autem timēbant; nautās et mīlitēs Americānōs timēbant. Prīncipēs hostium populum monēbant et terrēbant: "Americānī cupidī imperiī sunt. Magnam armōrum copiam et magnum nautārum et mīlitum numerum habent. Portūs et oppida oppugnābunt. Itaque copiam armōrum et omnium rērum parābimus. Cum legiōnibus hostium pugnābimus et superābimus." Itaque bellum parābant.

In Americā autem erat pāx. Populus Americānus cupidus bellī nōn

24 FIRST YEAR LATIN

erat; imperātōrēs cupidī glōriae bellī nōn erant. Nōn multī prīncipēs senātum et populum monēbant.

Ante diem septimum Īdūs Decembrēs, 1941, hostēs impetum in Portum Margarītārium fēcērunt. Multōs nautās et mīlitēs occīdērunt. Bellum erat!

Nunc autem hostēs superāmus; gentēs Japōniae terrēmus. Nautae et mīlitēs fortēs prō Americā pugnant. In locīs aliēnīs et plēnīs magnōrum perīculōrum pugnant; sed cupidī victōriae, praemiī virtūtis, nunc sunt. Superābunt hostēs!

Exercise 143.—1. Oppugnant. 2. Portant (habent). 3. Terret. 4. Superant. 5. Monet (vocat). 6. Pugnant.

Exercise 144.—See Introduction. 3.

Exercise 145.—Marcus, a Roman centurion, gives his mother greeting. I am now with the army in Gaul. There is a large army in Gaul because the Gauls are fighting with the Romans. Caesar, a brave man, is commander in chief of all the legions. I praise Caesar because he is a good leader—he sees everything and prepares everything.

I am not now in danger. We are in camp. The enemy does not attack the Roman camp because they are not brave. Galba is in camp with me. He is a good man and a friend to me.

We were often fighting with the Gauls and overcoming (them). And so now many Gauls are slaves and they are with us in the camp. They give grain to us. They carry the baggage into camp and prepare many things for us.

After the first victory Caesar was praising me in camp on account of (my) courage and reliability. At dawn the enemy made an attack against us. Both Galba and I were fighting in the first battle line and many Gauls were fighting with us, but they were not terrifying us or overcoming us. Caesar was watching us. And so Caesar was praising us on account of (our) courage. I now have great fame and after the war Caesar will give me a great reward. Do you not praise your son? Farewell.

Exercise 146.—1. Mē monet. 2. Nōs senātum et prīncipēs monēbimus. 3. Ego collem occupō, sed Caesar pontem occupat. 4. Nōs videt. 5. Ego Spīritum Sānctum laudō. 6. Prō mē pugnant. 7. Mēcum pugnat. 8. Gallī nōbīs praemia dabant. 9. Dabitne mihi praemium? 10. Nōbīscum pugnābant. 11. Chrīstiānī prō mē ōrant. 12. Sāncta Marīa prō nōbīs ōrat. 13. Nōs Patrem et Fīlium et Spīritum Sānctum in Caelō vidēbimus. 14. Multī et fortēs mīlitēs mēcum pugnant. 15. Datne Deus nōbīs grātiam?

Exercise 147.—1. Ego tibi praemium dabō. 2. Dominus prō vōbīs pugnat. 3. Deus vōbīs praemium Caelum dabit. 4. Ego tē monēbam. 5. Dominus tē vocat. 6. Dominus est tēcum. 7. Vōs victōriam Chrīstī laudābitis. 8. Tū ducem monēbis. 9. Movetne tē metus mortis? 10. Prō vōbīs ōrābimus.

Exercise 148.—An Examination of Professed Christians by a Roman Judge.

PROCONSUL. Are you a Christian?

CHRISTIAN. Yes, I am a Christian.

PROCONSUL. And you, are you a Christian?

SECOND CHRISTIAN. Yes, I also am a Christian. We are all Christians.

PROCONSUL. What? You are all Christians?

FIRST CHRISTIAN. We are.

PROCONSUL. Why do you not praise the gods of the Romans?

FIRST CHRISTIAN. We do not praise the gods of the Romans because they are not true (gods).

PROCONSUL. I warn you! If you will praise the gods of the Romans, I will give you rewards, but . . .

SECOND CHRISTIAN. Fear of death and of wounds does not move us. We praise the Lord of heaven and earth, "the King of Kings and ruler of all nations." Christ prayed for us. The grace of Christ is in us. And so what will terrify us? We do not fear you.

PROCONSUL. Christ! Who is Christ? The Romans killed Christ because He was an evil man.

FIRST CHRISTIAN. Christ is the Son of God and nevertheless the brother of all men.

PROCONSUL. Why do you not praise the Roman emperor?

FIRST CHRISTIAN. We always praise the Roman emperor, but we do not praise the slaughter of holy men, nor shall we praise (it). Nevertheless we always pray for and always shall pray for the emperor. We Christians—as Christ advised us—pray for all men, for kings, chiefs. soldiers, slaves.

PROCONSUL. Nevertheless I am warning you! After death what will you have?

FIRST CHRISTIAN. You will not move us. We hold (fast to) the faith and the truth of Christ and always will hold fast (to them). Christ is the salvation of men. In Christ is the hope of all nations. After death He will give us a great reward; with Christ in heaven we shall see the Father and the Son and the Holy Spirit forever.

OTHER CHRISTIANS. So be it!

PROCONSUL. Where is the Christians' God? I have not seen (was not seeing) the God of the Christians and I do not see Him (now).

SECOND CHRISTIAN. He is in every place but we do not see God now. God is not a body. Nevertheless after death you will see (Him), and He will not give you a reward.

PROCONSUL. By Hercules! Are you warning me? Fear of the Christians' God does not terrify me, nor will it. I, however, have command. The swords of the Roman soldiers will terrify you!

CHRISTIANS. The sword does not terrify us, nor the power of the world. The power of God, however, terrifies and moves us. In God is salvation.

PROCONSUL. Are you all Christians?

CHRISTIANS. We are all Christians.

PROCONSUL. And so it is decreed that all these Christians be punished by the sword.

CHRISTIANS. Thanks be to God! We shall pray for you. Christ calls us into heaven!

Exercise 149.—See Nos. 9, 10. 2. (a) Laudābat; in polysyllabic words, if the second last syllable is long, it is accented. (b) Impedīmenta; same as (a). 3. Sunt perīcula in silvīs.

Box, page 132.—Peace be with you!

Exercise 150.—See Introduction, 3.

Exercise 151.—1. You were praising Caesar. And so he will give you a reward. (*Is* refers to *Caesarem*, and agrees in number and gender: sing., masc.) 2. Caesar does not see the enemy's column. Will you warn him? (*Eum* refers to *Caesar;* sing., masc.) 3. Mary was holy. And so God gave her a reward. (*Eī* refers to *Maria;* sing., fem.) 4. The enemy made an attack against the winter quarters. The brave soldiers, however, were withstanding their attack. (*Eōrum* refers to *mīlitēs;* pl., masc.) 5. Mary is the mother of God. Therefore we Christians praise her. (*Eam* refers to *Maria;* sing., fem.) 6. A friend is in danger. And so we will pray for him. (*Eō* refers to *amīcus;* sing., masc.) 7. The enemy is seizing the town. Will they hold it? (*Id* refers to *oppidum;* sing., neut.) 8. The enemy is preparing for war, but we shall withstand their attack. (*Eōrum* refers to *hostēs;* pl., masc.) 9. Caesar is calling the leaders of the Gauls into winter quarters, but they are not friends of the Senate and the Roman people. (*Eī* refers to *ducēs;* pl., masc.) 10. Mothers are good. Their virtue is great. We always praise them, and God will give them great rewards. (*Eārum, eās,* and *eīs* refer to *mātrēs;* pl., fem.) 11. Caesar is a Roman commander, but the Senate does not praise his courage. (*Ējus* refers to *Caesar;* sing., masc.) 12. Caesar will seize the town of the Gauls, but you will not warn them. (*Eōs* refers to *Gallōrum;* pl., masc.) 13. There are many holy men. God will give them rewards. (*Eīs* refers to *hominēs;* pl., masc.) 14. Christ is Mary's son and is now in heaven with her. (*Eā* refers to *Marīae;* sing., fem.) 15. Soldiers are always in danger. Therefore we pray for them. (*Eīs* refers to *milites;* pl., masc.) 16. Caesar is in camp. A slave is giving a sword to him. (*Eī* refers to *Caesar;* sing., masc.) 17. All the Gauls are in (under) arms. They have placed hope of victory in courage. Their cavalry is brave. There is a supply of grain in their towns. They hold both bridges and hills. Caesar heard those things; nevertheless he does not fear them (the Gauls). (*Eōrum* [both times] refers to *Gallī;* pl., masc. *Ea* has no expressed antecedent.)

Exercise 152.—1. Senātus Caesarem laudat quod is prō populō Rōmānō in fīnibus Gallōrum pugnat. 2. Viae bonae sunt. Eās Rōmānī mūnīvērunt. 3. Caesar cum Gallīs in fīnibus eōrum pugnābat. Oppida et urbēs eōrum occupābat. Gallī impetūs ējus nōn sustinēbant. 4. Nōs Chrīstum et Marīam mātrem ējus laudāmus. Ea sāncta erat. Deus eī magnum praemium dedit. Omnēs hominēs sānctī eam et ējus Fīlium in Caelō vidēbunt. Eī cum eā ōrābunt omnēs prō nōbīs. 5. Gallī nōn amīcī Rōmānōrum erant. Gallī eīs frūmentum nōn dabant, et eōs nōn laudābant. Gallī cum eīs pugnābant. 6. Chrīstus lūx mundī et salūs omnium hominum est. Eum in terrā nunc laudāmus, et cum eō Deum in Caelō in saecula saeculōrum laudābimus. 7. Legiōnēs Rōmānās propter victōriās eārum laudāmus. Eae prō senātū et populō Rōmānō pugnābant. Gallī cum eīs pugnābant, sed eae Gallōs superābant. Caesar imperātor eārum erat et propter virtūtem et fidem eārum eās laudābat. Itaque senātus eīs magna praemia dabat. 8. Hostēs frūmentum et arma in oppidum portant. Tenēbuntne eī id? 9. Gallī castra parant. In eīs prō salūte commūnī Galliae pugnābunt. Ea tamen nōn tenēbunt. Caesar eōs superābit et ea occupābit. 10. Hīberna Rōmānōrum in fīnibus hostium erant. Hostēs ea oppugnābant et occupābant. 11. Gallī impetum in agmina Rōmāna saepe fēcērunt, sed Rōmānī impetūs eōrum sustinēbant.

Box, page 135.—I sustain (support, uphold) wings (their wings).

Exercise 153.—1. Prō nōbīs saepe ōrāmus. 2. Prō sē ōrat. 3. Prō tē ōrās. 4. Prō sē ōrant. 5. Eum laudant. 6. Legiō prō sē ōrat. 7. Prō mē ōrō. 8. Eōs videt. 9. Prō vōbīs ōrātis. 10. Eum nōn laudat. 11. Prō sē ōrat. 12. In nōbīs grātiam Deī habēmus.

Exercise 154.—1. Hominēs sānctī sē nōn laudant. 2. Mātrēs nōn sē sed fīliōs laudant. 3. Hominēs saepe sē nōn vident sīcut eōs vidēmus.

4. Chrīstiānī prō sē et prō omnibus hominibus saepe ōrant. Deus enim eīs et omnibus hominibus propter ōrātiōnēs eōrum grātiam dat. 5. Caesar sē nōn laudābat.[1] 6. Legiō etiam sē laudābat. 7. Marīa nōn prō sē sed prō nōbīs nunc ōrat, in Caelō enim et māter etiam omnium hominum est. 8. Post victōriās Rōmānōrum Gallī sē saepe occīdēbant.

Exercise 155.—Roman Virtue and Christian Virtue. Marcus Tullius Cicero, a great and good orator, often praised truth and virtue. Concerning virtue he said, "Virtue is praised for itself." (*Sē* refers to *virtūs;* reflexive.) In speeches he often praised good men, but the evil he did not praise. He sustained many dangers; death and swords he did not fear; he was always praising the name of the Roman people.

Cicero nevertheless was not a Christian. (Christ came into the world after his death.) (*Ējus* refers to *Cicerō;* modifies *mortem.*) And so Cicero, eager for fame, often praised himself. (*Sē* refers to *Cicerō;* reflexive.) All the Romans praised themselves often. (*Sē* refers to *Rōmānī;* reflexive.) The Senate praised itself. (*Sē* refers to *senātus;* reflexive.) The Roman emperors and leaders also praised themselves. (*Sē* refers to *imperātōrēs* and *ducēs;* reflexive.) Holy men, however, praise not themselves but God, just as Mary, the mother of all Christians, did not praise herself. (The first *sē* refers to *hominēs*, the second to *Marīa;* both are reflexive.) After the Annunciation she prayed: My soul doth magnify the Lord . . . for He has done great things unto me . . . and holy is His name. (*Ea* refers to *Marīa* in the preceding sentence; personal pronoun used as subject.)

Cicero and all the Romans placed hope in themselves. (*Sē* refers to *Cicerō* and *Rōmānī;* reflexive.) Christians, however, place hope not in themselves but in the grace of Christ. (*Sē* refers to *Chrīstiānī;* reflexive.)

Cicero sustained many serious dangers because he was both good and desirous of fame. Christians, however, withstand dangers because they have Christ with them. (*Sē* refers to *Chrīstiānī;* reflexive, used for *cum sē.*) For Christians carry Jesus Christ in themselves. (*Sē* refers to *Chrīstiānī;* reflexive.) And so the name of Christians was also "Christophers" (Christ-bearers).

Exercise 156.—1. 3rd. 2. 1st. 3. 2nd. 4. 3rd. 5. 3rd. 6. 1st. 7. 2nd. 8. 3rd. 9. 1st. 10. 2nd. 11. 3rd. 12. 2nd.

Exercise 157.—1. Because all the infinitives end in *-ere.* 2. See No. 166. 3. (a) Gerit, gerunt. (b) Defendit, defendunt. (c) Īnstruit, īnstruunt.

[1] In impressions antedating 1947, *prō sē nōn ōrābat.*

Exercise 158.—See Introduction, 3.

Exercise 159.—1. A Roman soldier sees the enemy. The enemy, however, does not see him. 2. The soldier sends a slave into the camp. 3. The slave warns Caesar in the camp. "The enemy is on the river. There is danger for us!" 4. Caesar calls the leaders and the centurions. 5. The centurions call the soldiers. They draw them up before the camp. 6. Caesar leads the soldiers. "We will terrify the enemy! Bravely we will fight!" 7. Meanwhile the enemy sees the Roman soldier. He, however, defends himself bravely. 8. The enemy sees the legion and Caesar. Fear of Caesar terrifies them. "It is Caesar! He will overcome us! There is danger!" The leading men of the enemy draw up (their) forces. They defend themselves. 9. The Romans carry on the affair bravely and conquer the enemy. The enemy give themselves up to Caesar. 10. Caesar leads soldiers and enemies into camp; he draws up all the soldiers and praises (them).

Exercise 160.—1. Legiōnēs Rōmānae fortiter sē defendunt quod sunt cupidae glōriae bellī. 2. Caesar in fīnēs hostium exercitum dūcit; hostēs eum vident et timent. 3. Rōmānī semper bellum fortiter gerunt cum hostibus. 4. Centuriō prō mūrō legiōnem īnstruit. 5. Mittitne centuriōnēs gentibus fīnitimīs? 6. Caesar gladium gerit. 7. Rōmānī cum populīs et gentibus fīnitimīs bellum saepe gerunt. 8. Dūcitne servus agmen in locum angustum et difficilem? 9. Imperātor senātum fortiter monet. 10. Rēx exercitum īnstruit; nōs autem eum et exercitum ējus superābimus.

Exercise 161.—See No. 169.

Exercise 162.—See Introduction, 3.

Exercise 163.—1. Gerēbant, vincēbant. The Gauls were waging war with the Romans but they were not overcoming them. 2. Petēbant. After Caesar's victory the Gauls were seeking peace. 3. Vincit. Christ conquers the world. 4. Pellēbam. I was driving the enemy onto the bridge. 5. Īnstruēbant. The enemy was drawing up soldiers before the camp. 6. Mittēbatne. Was Caesar sending a dispatch? 7. Petēbat. The king was seeking peace. 8. Pellunt. The brave soldiers are routing the enemy.

Exercise 164.—1. On account of fear of the Romans the Gauls were waging war with them. The Romans, however, were always conquering (them). 2. We were begging for grain. You were not sending grain. 3. The Roman legions always conquer the enemy. 4. Caesar routs the Gauls.

Exercise 165.—1. Imperātor litterās mittēbat et cōpiam frūmentī et gladiōrum petēbat. 2. Nōs hostēs saepe pellēbāmus. Eōs saepe vincē-bāmus. Tamen fortiter bellum gerēbant et sē dēfendēbant. 3. Prīmam aciem in altum flūmen pellēbant. 4. Imperātor litterās mittit. Servus in prōvinciam eās portābit.

Exercise 166.—See Introduction, 3.

Exercise 167.—1. You will send the legions into camp. 2. We will send a dispatch concerning many things. 3. The Romans are always con-tending with the Gauls. 4. Where will the Romans pitch camp? 5. I shall not send grain. 6. Will you send slaves? 7. They will pitch camp there. 8. At dawn the remaining Gauls will hasten into the mountains. 9. He will place hope of safety in courage. 10. I shall drive them into the river. 11. The Senate will act concerning a serious affair.

Exercise 168.—1. Ibi castra pōnēmus. 2. Cum gente dē pāce agent. 3. Cum omnibus cōpiīs in oppidum contendet. 4. Cum Gallīs contendent. 5. Fidem in virtūte reliquārum legiōnum pōnent.

Exercise 169.—See Introduction, 3.

Exercise 170.—See Introduction, 3.

Exercise 171.—1. Fear terrifies you. 2. The Senate will assemble. 3. They were withstanding the attack. 4. They see the harbor. 5. They will fear the cavalry. 6. They are pitching camp. 7. They will contend for victory. 8. They are fortifying the town. 9. He will call the cen-turion. 10. He defends himself. 11. He will send the army into Gaul. 12. They were coming through the forest. 13. They were treating of the affair. 14. He hears a cry. 15. The Spirit of God leads him. 16. He was waging war. 17. Caesar's coming will terrify you. 18. He praises God. 19. He will seize the hill. 20. He is drawing up the troops. 21. You will overcome them. 22. He was attacking the city. 23. You are praying. 24. They were preparing arms. 25. I did not have slaves. 26. I will warn you. 27. They will hold the bridge. 28. They will carry the standard. 29. They are fighting bravely. 30. He will give swords. 31. I will conquer the enemy. 32. You are moving the camp. 33. I will beg for (request) peace. 34. You are repulsing the cavalry. 35. They were listening to (hearing) the speech.

Exercise 172.—1. Leaders often fortify towns and bridges. 2. Part of the enemy is coming through the forest; (another) part of them, however, is coming through the province. 3. Do you hear the cries of the slaves? 4. On account of the common welfare the Romans were building long roads through the provinces. 5. We heard the shouting of the horsemen. 6. The general will come into the Senate. The Senate will hear his speech. 7. The leaders and chiefs of the Gauls will assemble in the town. 8. At dawn the Senate will assemble in a safe place. It will act concerning a serious matter. 9. Meanwhile Caesar was coming through the province with all the troops. 10. The horsemen were warning Caesar about his danger. And so he is fortifying the camp.

Exercise 173.—1. In castra conveniunt. 2. Rōmānī longās viās mūniēbant. 3. Pontēs mūniēbant. 4. Prīmā lūce convenient. 5. Veniuntne Rōmānī in fīnēs hostium? 6. Audiuntne vōcēs et clāmōrem equitum? 7. Venietne agmen per prōvinciam? 8. Ducēs gentis in montēs conveniēbant. 9. Dēfendentne lēgem Rōmānam? 10. Lūx et vēritās Chrīstī mē dūcunt. 11. Ōrātiōnem prīncipis audiēbant. 12. Post adventum Caesaris Gallī oppida mūniēbant. 13. Propter virtūtem et fidem eōrum imperātor centuriōnēs laudābat. 14. Hostēs sē fortiter dēfendēbant. 15. Erant servī in collibus. 16. Pars prīncipum nunc convenit. 17. Post caedem prīncipum Gallī equitēs timēbunt. 18. Propter victōriam in grātiam cum rēge veniēbant. 19. Cum imperātōre dē pāce agēbant. 20. Exercitus per silvās veniēbat. 21. Ibi castra ponent, sed Caesar ea oppugnābit. 22. In nōmine Jēsū Chrīstī ōrābimus. Itaque Deus nōbīs grātiam dabit. 23. Vulnera sāncta Chrīstī laudāmus. 24. Per Chrīstum pācem et salūtem petēmus. 25. In Galliam veniētis et flūmina alta et magnōs montēs et oppida et magnās urbēs vidēbitis. Ducēs fortēs et nōbilēs vidēbitis. Est cōpia frūmentī in urbibus. Galliam et Gallōs laudābitis.

Exercise 174.—The Senate (About the Senate). In the Roman Senate there are many noble and brave men. The Roman state (the Roman Senate and the people) has an empire of many tribes and provinces. The Senate assembles often. Kings of foreign tribes often come into the Senate. Often they are seeking peace; often they are requesting a supply of arms and rations. The leading men of Rome often come into the Senate. They often treat of serious matters and of the welfare of the Roman people. They act regarding laws, wars, and the provinces. All foreign tribes fear the Senate.

Exercise 175.—1. Rōma urbs magna et nōbilis erat. 2. Hostēs undique erant. 3. Multa flūmina Galliae erant alta et longa. 4. Eritisne fortēs? 5. Undique sunt montēs. 6. Castra Rōmāna erant plēna gladiōrum et tēlōrum. 7. In Caelō cum Deō erimus. 8. Cupidī grātiae Deī erāmus. 9. Chrīstiānī et fīiii Deī estis. 10. Mīles Chrīstī sum. 11. Via angusta et difficilis est. 12. Montēs Galliae sunt altī. 13. Itinera Caesaris longa et difficilia saepe erant. 14. Propter grātiam Deī tūtī eritis. 15. Chrīstus dux bonus et nōbilis est. 16. Rōmānī cupidī glōriae erant. 17. Estisne similēs Chrīstō? 18. In Caelō multī hominēs sānctī erunt. 19. Gallī fīnitimī prōvinciae sunt. 20. Glōria Rōmae semper erit magna. 21. Nōs Chrīstiānī et servī Deī sumus. 22. Multī rēgēs erant malī. 23. Reliquī mīlitēs erant tūtī. 24. Erāsne in prīmā acie? 25. Cum Caesare nōn eram. 26. Nōn omnēs Chrīstiānī sunt similēs Chrīstō. 27. Sunt in prōvinciā multae et magnae urbēs.

Exercise 176.—1. We are in Caesar's camp on account of fear of the enemy. 2. From all sides there was the shouting of the enemy. 3. There was serious danger in the province. 4. The Gauls are always eager for power. 5. All men are desirous of fame. 6. Were there darts in the camp? 7. On all sides there were mountains and forests. 8. In heaven we shall be with Christ. 9. Were the mountains high and difficult? 10. Caesar was eager for power. 11. Is Christ the son of both Mary and God? 12. Is Mary full of grace? 13. You, however, are all brothers. 14. Was Christ in the world on our account? 15. We were not in the forest. 16. Caesar was in the first battle line. 17. I will be brave. 18. I was with the army in Gaul. 19. Are you a horseman? Are you a soldier? 20. All holy men are like Christ.

Exercise 177.—1. The winter quarters were not far from a town of the Gauls. 2. Caesar was a long way from camp. 3. The winter quarters are not far away from Caesar. 4. The legions will be away. 5. Caesar was away. 6. Rome is at a great distance from us. 7. God is not far from us. 8. War and the danger of death are far away from heaven.

Exercise 178.—1. Ā castrīs absum. 2. Ab oppidō nōn longē aberat. 3. Ā flūmine longē aberant. 4. Flūmen ā silvīs nōn longē abest. 5. Gallia ā vōbīs longē abest.

Exercise 179.—See Introduction, 3.

Exercise 180.—See Introduction, 3.

Exercise 181.—A Dream of Judgment.

The Voice of the Angel. Who are you?

Second Voice. I am a king. On earth I held the kingdom and command of the Romans.

Voice of the Angel. Do you seek a reward and glory now?

Second Voice. Yes, I do. I had great fame on earth and always shall. All men praised me. I was a great emperor. I waged many wars strongly. A good leader, I prepared everything; I prepared rations and arms; I fortified camps and towns; I equipped and stationed soldiers. The soldiers always placed hope in me. I often fought with the soldiers in the first battle line. I led them through mountains and forests. In Gaul and in all the provinces I contended with the enemy. Fear of the enemy neither moved nor terrified me. I have seized the territory of many tribes. I have attacked both many towns and great cities. I have strongly (vigorously) defended the Roman provinces and their cities. I have terrified the enemies of the Roman name and bravely withstood their attacks. I have sent cavalry and soldiers against them—the enemy always gave way. I routed the enemy and surpassed them in war and conquered.

THE VOICE OF THE ANGEL. The man praises himself strongly (very much indeed).

SECOND VOICE. On account of me, the tribes (living) near the provinces feared the Roman legions; they often sent (their) chiefs into the camp of the Romans concerning peace. The chiefs and kings treated with me about peace. They gave themselves up to me. I called the chiefs of the Gauls into the camp. They came together into the camp. I demanded grain. They carried a large supply into the camp. All men feared me. All tribes heard the name of the Roman king.

VOICE OF THE ANGEL. Why have you waged war with many tribes? Why did you rout and terrify and conquer them?

VOX REGIS. For the glory and the welfare of the Roman state!

THIRD VOICE. No! Not on account of that, but because he was eager for glory and power! He did not seek peace, but swords and wars and slaughter. He filled rivers and forests and towns with bodies; he gave soldiers and sailors to slaughter because he sought glory for himself. I will give him (his) reward.

VOX REGIS. Who are you?

THIRD VOICE. Ah! You did not see me but I was not far away from you. I saw everything. I did not warn you, however. I was always with you on earth—and now you will remain with me forever!

VOICF OF THE ANGEL. Who are you?

THE NEW VOICE. I am a Christian.

VOICE OF THE ANGEL. What do you seek? Do you seek glory with Christ?

CHRISTIANUS. I seek God and Christ.

THE GUARDIAN ANGEL. He will neither defend nor praise himself. But I was always with him. He was a slave of the Roman emperor. However, he bravely held the law of Christ; he prayed in the name of Christ. The emperor, however, held him in chains because he was a Christian. But fear of death and of wounds neither moved nor terrified him. He placed hope in the grace of Christ and always held the faith. And so the Romans killed him.

A NEW VOICE. Enter into the joy of your Lord.

VOICES ON ALL SIDES. Glory be to the Father and to the Son and to the Holy Spirit, as it was in the beginning, is now, and ever shall be, world without end. Amen.

Exercise 182.—1. Caesar mīlitēs in ponte et prō castrīs collocāvit. 2. Chrīstus in terrā nōn mānsit. 3. Mūrōs hominibus complēvērunt. 4. Caesar cōpiam frūmentī parāvit. 5. Rōmānī hostibus nōn saepe **cessērunt.** 6. **Ubi fuistī?** 7. Senātus Caesarem saepe laudāvit propter ējus victōriās. 8. Caesar perīculum et mortem nōn timuit. 9. In Galliā multī Rōmānī fuērunt. 10. Vīcēruntne Rōmānī Gallōs? 11. Ēgēruntne cum prīncipe dē pāce? 12. Prīmā lūce prīncipēs Gallōrum convēnērunt. 13. Equitēs nōn cessērunt, sed impetum fortiter sustinuērunt. 14. Quis Gallōs vīcit et urbēs et oppida eōrum occupāvit? 15. Gallī Caesarem nōn laudāvērunt, sed eum timuērunt. 16. Rōmamne vīdistī?

Exercise 183.—1. The leading men had incited the tribes next (living nearest) to the province because they were eager for victory. (*Prōvinciae* is dative with *fīnitimās; victōriae* is genitive with *cupidī.*) 2. Meanwhile the cavalry had confused the remaining Gauls. (*Reliquōs* is accusative, agreeing with *Gallōs*, direct object.) 3. Good Christians had kept the faith and truth of Christ. 4. The general had set fire to the cities and towns. 5. Many Gauls had aided the Roman legions. 6. The leader of the enemy had filled the hills with men. (*Hominibus*, ablative without a preposition, used with *complēverat.*) 7. The cavalry had confused the enemy's column. 8. Courage had kept (preserved, saved) Rome. 9. At dawn Caesar had seized both the hills and the bridges. 10. The Senate had given the province to Caesar. (*Caesarī* is dative, indirect object.)

Exercise 184.—1. Rēx servōs incitāverat. 2. Deus eōs adjūverat. 3. Fidem servāverant. 4. Equitēs hostēs perturbāverant. 5. Servī oppidum incenderant. 6. In senātum prīncipēs Galliae vocāverant. 7. In silvīs equitēs collocāverat. Hostēs in eōs impetum fēcērunt.

Exercise 185.—1. Senātus Caesarem laudāvit. 2. Gallī Caesarem semper timuerant. 3. Equitēs hostēs terruērunt. 4. Mīlitēs frūmenta incenderant. 5. Servī hostēs adjūverant. 6. Fidem servāvērunt. 7. Nōn cessērunt. 8. Urbem tenuērunt. 9. Castra mōvērunt. 10. Pontem occupāvit. 11. Multa tēla parāverant. 12. Servī arma habuerant. 13. Agmen Rōmānum vīdērunt. 14. Impetum nōn sustinuērunt. 15. Sē dēfendit. 16. Arma in Galliam mīsērunt. 17. Servī in castra frūmentum portāverant. 18. Rōmānī Gallōs superāverant. 19. Prō rēge ōrāverant. 20. Prīncipēs vocāvit.

UNIT FOUR

Exercise 186.—1. Cum puerīs bonīs. 2. Prō virīs nōbilibus. 3. In agrōs bonōs. 4. Ager plēnus puerōrum (puerīs). 5. In agrīs. 6. Cum virō fortī. 7. In magnō agrō. 8. Puer similis virō fortī. 9. Propter glōriam virōrum fortium. 10. Per agrōs Gallōrum. 11. Mors virī fortis. 12. Propter caedem mātrum et puerōrum. 13. Fortūna bona virī fortis et nōbilis.

Exercise 187.—1. Roman men were brave and fought bravely with the enemy. Thus they guarded (preserved) Rome. For fortune aids brave men. 2. Many enemies came across the mountains into Italy. Nevertheless the Romans conquered them. 3. A good boy is a mother's glory. For all fathers and mothers always praise good boys but do not praise bad boys. 4. At that time, after the arrival of the Roman army, there was a great scarcity of grain in Gaul. For the Romans had set fire to the crops in the fields. 5. In Italy there were good fields, noble men, and good boys. 6. The Roman general came into the fields of the enemy with all (his) troops. He burned the crops; he attacked towns and cities; he led the men and boys into camp.

Review Questions.—Sentence 2. *Eōs* agrees in number and gender with *hostēs,* but not in case. Sentence 5. The literal translation would be: "Good fields, . . . were in Italy." English idiom prefers, "There were . . ." See page 42.

Exercise 188.—1. Omnēs hominēs fortūnam bonam laudant. 2. Hannibal, vir fortis et nōbilis, trāns montēs vēnit et magnam partem Italiae occupat. 3. Puerī bonī saepe ōrant. 4. Puerī arma parant. 5. Trāns flūmen in agrōs vēnērunt et frūmenta incendunt. 6. In agrīs hostium cōpiās collocat. 7. Prō nōbīs virī fortēs pugnant. 8. In agrīs Italiae virōs collocat. 9. Ita nōs mīlitēs fortēs glōriam nōminis Rōmānī servāmus. 10. Puerī in agrīs virōs adjuvant. 11. Quis puerum vocat? 12. Portatne puer litterās in Italiam? 13. Quid puerō dās? 14. Superāvēruntne Gallōs? 15. Quid puer portat? 16. Quis gentēs Galliae incitat? 17. Virōs malōs nōn adjuvāmus. 18. Prō portā castrōrum mīlitēs collocat. 19. Urbēs Italiae oppugnant.

Reading No. 4.—Italy and Gaul. Italy is a land both great and good. Do you see Italy on the map? Is Italy large? Is it long? Rome was in Italy, a great and renowned city. Do you see Rome on the map? Rome is on the Tiber River. Do you see the river on the map? In Italy there were many large cities, long rivers, and high mountains. There were also fields full of crops. In the fields of Italy the Romans had waged many wars with neighboring tribes and had finally conquered all Italy. Thus the Romans held command (were masters) of Italy. In all parts of Italy all the men and boys were praising and defending the Roman name.

The Alps are great and high mountains. Do you see the mountains on the map? Across the Alps at that time were both the Roman Province and Gaul. Many generals came across the mountains into Italy. Hannibal, a brave and renowned man, came into Italy through difficult mountains with all (his) troops and thus waged war with the Romans in the fields of Italy. Then Caesar led the Roman legions across the mountains into the fields (territory) of the Gauls. Napoleon too, a brave general, hastened across the mountains with large forces into Italy, and seized all of Italy.

Rome, as you see on the map, is far distant from Gaul. In Gaul also there were cities and towns and good fields. There were rivers and mountains. You see them on the map. You see also the territory of the Roman Province. Caesar held command of it and waged wars with the Gauls. After Caesar's victories the Romans held command of all Gaul.

Box, page 167.—Rome—the mother of Italy (Rome is the mother of Italy).

Exercise 189.—See Nos. 75 and 76 for adjectives; Nos. 34, 37, 57, and 69 for nouns.

Exercise 190.—1. Cum cōpiīs integrīs. 2. Prō hominibus līberīs. 3. In Gallōs miserōs. 4. Cum legiōnibus integrīs. 5. In cīvitāte līberā. 6. Cum servīs miserīs. 7. Post victōriam hominum līberōrum. 8. Propter fortūnam miseram. 9. Propter glōriam cīvitātis līberae.

Box, page 169.—The Lord will be with you at all times and in every place.

Exercise 191.—1. Noble and free men have guarded (preserved) the American state. 2. The Romans, brave men and free, conquered the wretched Gauls in many battles. For fortune also aided the Romans. 3. The leaders (officers) stationed fresh legions in the first battle line. 4. The Romans stormed the towns of the Gauls; they seized their fields, burned the (their) crops, killed chiefs, leaders, mothers, fathers, men, and boys. Thus they conquered them. 5. Hannibal, a brave and renowned man, hastened across the mountains into the fields of Italy with all (his) forces. The Romans bravely contended (fought) with him. They defended the cities and towns of Italy. After many battles and great slaughter the Romans overcame him. Thus they guarded (preserved) the glory of the Roman name.

Review Questions.—Sentence 2. *Virī* is in apposition with *Rōmānī*. Sentence 4. *Eōrum* and *eōs* agree with their antecedent, *Gallōrum,* in number and gender.

Box, page 170.—Mountaineers are always free.

Exercise 192.—1. In proelium cōpiās integrās dūcēbat. 2. Prīnceps Gallōs miserōs dēfendēbat. 3. Rōmānī cīvitātēs līberās vincēbant. 4. Rōmānī multīs proeliīs Gallōs vīcērunt. 5. Post proelium frūmenta et oppida incendēbant. 6. Mīlitēs, virī līberī et fortēs, hostēs pellēbant. 7. Dē servō miserō cum dominō agēbat. 8. Post proelium castra pōnēbant. 9. Legiōnēs integrae nōn cēdēbant. 10. Cum cōpiīs integrīs in Galliam contendēbat. 11. Servī arma nōn portābant. 12. Gallī miserī pācem petēbant. 13. Mittēbatne litterās in Italiam? 14. Post proelium cōpiās integrās īnstruēbat. 15. Americānī cīvitātem līberam dēfendēbāmus. 16. Puerōs et virōs in agrōs mittēbant. 17. Americānī semper erimus līberī.

Exercise 193.—1. Servī nōn sunt līberī. 2. Cīvitās Americāna est lībera. 3. Nōn omnēs servī Rōmānī miserī erant. 4. Ego vir līber sum. 5. Ego puer miser nōn sum. 6. Washingtonius erat vir fortis et nōbilis.

Reading No. 5.—Eternal Rome. The Romans always placed hope of safety and victory in courage. In wars they prepared everything; they fortified towns and camps; they had soldiers and cavalry; they got ready a supply of grain. (Their) Leaders and generals were often great and noble. But (it was) not because of all these things that the Romans conquered. For many tribes had all these things and yet did not conquer (their) enemies. Nevertheless the Romans conquered many great (powerful) enemies. Enemies had often attacked (their) camps, conquered the legions, seized fields and cities. The Roman state nevertheless did not seek (beg for) peace. Their leading men (leaders) did not treat of (discuss) peace in the Senate. They were eager for victory and power and glory. And so the Romans always conquered the enemy. Victory was the Romans' on account of Roman courage (Victory came to the Romans because of Roman courage). And so the glory of the Roman name was great, and both the Romans and the foreign tribes praised eternal Rome.

Box, page 172.—Rome—mother of kings and leaders.

Exercise 194.—See Nos. 72 and 76.

Exercise 195.—See Nos. 72, 76; 34, 37, and 57.

Moments at Mass No. 1.—The Lord be with you! And with thy spirit.

Exercise 196.—1. Propter fortūnam vestram (tuam). 2. In agrīs nostrīs. 3. Cum virīs nostrīs fortibus. 4. Post mortem meam. 5. In cīvitāte vestrā (tuā). 6. Propter glōriam patrum nostrōrum.

Exercise 197.—1. Our fathers, men both free and brave, contended with the enemy in many battles. Thus they both defended and guarded our state. And so now we have a state both renowned and free. 2. We will treat with you concerning the welfare of your soldiers. 3. I do not praise you because of the slaughter of the wretched slaves, nor do I praise your courage. 4. I will send my fresh legions into the first battle line. 5. We will storm your towns and your cities. We will burn the (your) crops. We will terrify your boys and your mothers. Thus we will conquer your soldiers. 6. War is difficult and full of dangers. The enemy comes across the mountains. They come into your fields. You will fight bravely with them and you will not treat with them about (will not sue for) peace. Fortune also will aid you.

Box, page 176.—"The Mother of God is my Mother!"

Exercise 198.—1. Mīlitēs nostrī fortēs impetūs vestrōs nōn timent. 2. Imperātōrem vestrum monēbō. 3. Cīvitās nostra semper lībera erit. 4. Equitēs nostrī mīlitēs vestrōs terrēbunt. 5. Agrōs vestrōs et urbēs vestrās vidēbimus. 6. Mīlitēs nostrī, virī fortēs et līberī, collem tenēbant. 7. Prīmā lūce castra nostra movēbimus. 8. Equitēs nostrōs nōn sustinēbunt. 9. In urbe meā manēbō. 10. Mīlitibus vestrīs mūrum complēbātis. 11. Servus tuus mē monet. 12. Audīsne equitēs nostrōs? 13. Tenētisne castra vestra? 14. Sustinēbuntne virī nostrī impetum eōrum? 15. Mīlitēs vestrōs nōn timeō, virī enim nostrī fortēs eōs sustinēbunt.

Reading No. 6.—The Second Punic War. Hannibal, a brave and noble man, was at that time the commander in chief of the Carthaginians. He had always been the enemy of the Roman people. He was eager for victory and power. And so he was bravely waging war with the Romans.

He was in Spain with a large army. He had with him a great number of soldiers and cavalry and elephants. With all (his) forces he hastened through Gaul (for as yet there was no Roman province in Gaul). He led the soldiers through great forests. He led the army across deep rivers. The Alps were high and great mountains. The way (pass) through them was difficult and narrow. Many tribes of the Gauls were waging war with him. He finally repulsed the Gauls in many battles and came through the mountains into Italy with soldiers, baggage train, and elephants.

"It is (There is) Italy! In Italy there are good fields and an abundance of all things. There are also towns and many great cities. The

Romans hold them now, but we will overcome the Romans. We will hold (have possession of) the cities and the fields, and seize even Rome (as well). The Romans are brave, but we too are brave. They shall not overcome us. And so we will place all hope of victory in courage! Fortune also will aid us; for fortune always aids the brave. After the victory I will give you great rewards and we shall have the great glory of war (the glory we gain through the war will be great)!"

Questions on Reading No. 6.—1. Hannibal erat imperātor Carthāginiēnsium. 2. Erat vir fortis et nōbilis. 3. In Hispāniā erat. 4. Sēcum magnum exercitum habēbat. 5. In Italiam per montēs vēnit.

UNIT FIVE

Exercise 199.—1. Passive. 2. Passive. 3. Active. 4. Passive. 5. Active. 6. Active, passive. 7. Passive. 8. Passive. 9. Passive. 10. Passive. 11. Active.

Exercise 200.—See Introduction, 3.

Exercise 201.—(1) Administrātur, it is being managed; administrantur, they are being managed; administrābātur, it was being managed; administrābantur, they were being managed; administrābitur, it will be managed; administrābuntur, they will be managed. (2) Appellātur, he is being addressed; appellantur, they are being addressed; appellābātur, he was being addressed; appellābantur, they were being addressed; appellābitur, he will be addressed; appellābuntur, they will be addressed. (3) Cōnfirmātur, he is being encouraged; cōnfirmantur, they are being encouraged; cōnfirmābātur, he was being encouraged; cōnfirmābantur, they were being encouraged; cōnfirmābitur, he will be encouraged; cōnfirmābuntur, they will be encouraged.

Exercise 202.—1. It is being managed. 2. He is being called upon. 3. They are being attacked. 4. He is being encouraged. 5. He (It) is being placed. 6. You will be praised. 7. They were being encouraged. 8. They were being managed. 9. They are being helped. 10. We were being called upon. 11. We are being praised. 12. He (It) is being given.

Exercise 203.—1. Cōnfirmor; I encourage, I am being encouraged. 2. Appellābar; I was calling upon, I was being called upon. 3. Cōnfirmābantur; they were encouraging, they were being encouraged. 4. Dabātur; he was giving, he was being given. 5. Administrāris; you are managing, you are being managed. 6. Cōnfirmātur; he is encouraging, he is being encouraged. 7. Administrābātur; he was managing, he was being managed. 8. Adjuvābitur; he will aid, he will be aided. 9. Appellāmur; we are calling upon, we are being called upon. 10. Adjuvāminī; you are aiding, you are being aided. 11. Cōnfirmābuntur; they will encourage, they will be encouraged. 12. Collocantur; they are placing, they are being placed. 13. Cōnfirmantur; they are encouraging, they are being encouraged. 14. Datur; he is giving, he is being given. 15. Collocābāris; you were placing, you were being placed.

Exercise 204.—1. Mary was being called upon. 2. The province will be managed. 3. The friends are being encouraged. 4. Gaul is being managed. 5. The Romans were being strengthened. 6. The world is being managed. 7. The wars are being managed. 8. God is called the King of men. 9. The commander in chief will be called upon. 10. Peace will be strengthened. 11. The chiefs are being called upon. 12. The courage of the legions was being strengthened. 13. The Holy Spirit is being called upon. 14. The affair was being managed. 15. Hope of victory is being strengthened. 16. The centurions will be called upon. 17. Brave men will be encouraged. 18. Rome will not be attacked. 19. Land and sky are being praised. 20. The leader's dispatch is being given to the enemy. 21. The sailors were not being aided. 22. The winter quarters were being attacked. 23. The standard is being given to the legions. 24. Glory will be given to God. 25. A great number of slaves was being given to him. 26. Salvation and truth are being given to us through Christ. 27. Rewards will be given to the soldiers. 28. The victory of the sailors will be praised. 29. Many men will be stationed on the hill. 30. Neighboring tribes are being helped. 31. A part of the soldiers is being stationed in the territory of the enemy. 32. Bad boys are not praised. 33. Arms were being given to Caesar. 34. The town will be attacked. 35. The Roman people were (was) being helped. 36. Soldiers are being stationed on the wall. 37. Good fortune was being praised. 38. On account of the favor of Caesar grain is being given to the Romans. 39. The name of God will always be praised. 40. On account of fear of wounds and death (the) soldiers are calling upon God. 41. Soldiers are being stationed on the bridge. 42. Jesus Christ our Lord will be praised.

Exercise 205.—1. Often on account of the fear of wounds and death peace is praised. 2. There were brave and free men in Caesar's army. They were praised; for they bravely attacked cities and towns. 3. Will peace be strengthened (established) after battles, and wars, and slaughter? 4. God is always called upon in danger. 5. Everything was being managed bravely, because Caesar, a brave and renowned man, was commander in chief of the Romans. 6. Either Lincoln or Washington was the chief (greatest) of all American leaders. They are therefore praised and always will be praised. 7. Why are bad boys not praised? 8. Glory is given to God through Jesus Christ. 9. Soldiers were being stationed both in the forest and in the fields; the enemy made an attack against (upon) them. 10. A bad king will not be aided. 11. Soldiers are being praised on account of (because of their) courage. Centurions also are being praised on account of (for their) courage and reliability. The leaders and generals are managing the affair bravely. And so they also are being praised. 12. Good Christians keep the law of Christ both in peace and in war. And so a great reward will be given to them in heaven. 13. You are Americans. You are both free and brave. And so you will always be praised. 14. The leaders were not being praised, for they were far away from the battles and the camps.

Exercise 206.—1. Centuriōnēs appellantur. 2. Deus appellābitur. 3. Rēs administrātur. 4. Pāx cōnfirmābātur. 5. Mīlitēs in agrīs collocan tur. 6. Urbēs oppugnantur. 7. Mīles adjuvātur. 8. Frūmentum mīlitibus dabitur. 9. Amīcī nostrī cōnfirmābuntur. 10. Mīlitēs nostrī adjuvābantur. 11. Exercitus cōnfirmātur. 12. Fidēs nostra cōnfirmābitur. 13. Bellum administrātur. 14. Vōs laudābiminī. 15. Nōs cōnfirmāmur. 16. Eī adjuvābantur.

Exercise 207.—1. Ā rēge. 2. Ab hostibus. 3. Ab equitibus. 4. Ā Marīā. 5. Ab omnibus servīs. 6. Ab hostium duce.

Exercise 208.—1. Peace is often not preserved (The cause of peace is often not advanced) by soldiers, for they are eager for the glory of war. *(Ā mīlitibus.)* 2. Command will be managed (exercised) by Caesar, a brave and good man. *(Ā Caesare.)* 3. A supply of grain was not preserved (kept) by the slaves. *(Ā servīs.)* 4. After the battle we were encouraged by the general. *(Ab imperātōre.)* 5. Are holy persons praised by good men? *(Ā virīs.)* 6. Rome is far away from America. (This is the "booby-trap.") 7. The forest will be seized by the cavalry. *(Ab equitibus.)* 8. Is the Roman Senate praised by many men? *(Ā virīs.)* 9. Everything was being attended to by a good leader. *(Ā duce.)* 10. The centurions were being called upon by the commander in chief. *(Ab imperātōre.)* 11. The commander in chief will be called by the Senate. *(Ā senātū.)*

Exercise 209.—1. Cīvitās nostra lībera ā virīs līberīs et fortibus cōnservābitur. 2. Omnēs mīlitēs ab imperātōre in proelium vocābuntur; nam numerus hostium magnus est, et victōriae cupidī sunt. 3. Fidēs ā multīs Chrīstiānīs nōbilibus servābātur. 4. Multī agrī aliēnī ā mīlitibus Rōmānīs occupābantur. 5. Ducēs Gallōrum ā Caesare saepe vocābantur.

6. Servī ā dominō vocābantur. 7. Cīvitās Americāna ab omnibus hominibus līberīs laudātur.

Exercise 210.—Is the world being managed by God? The world is both preserved and managed by God. For in the beginning God made heaven and earth and all things on account of (for) us men and He is the Father of men. We men are preserved by God and everything is given to us by God. Truth and salvation are given to us by God; grain and an abundance of all things are both prepared and preserved for us by God. And so in danger of death God is called upon by sailors; in the dangers of war He is called upon by soldiers; always and in all places (everywhere) He is called upon by mothers and fathers, by men and boys, by Christians and by all men. For God is good, and men are always both aided and strengthened by Him. And so God is always praised by good and holy men, for He is the Father of all men.

Exercise 211.—At that time command of (supreme authority over) the Roman people was seized by Caesar. He was a brave man, for (both) enemies were overcome by him, and friends encouraged. After his death peace was strengthened by the Roman emperors through arms and legions (by means of armed forces). Not all men, however, were free, for many men were wretched slaves. The Pāx Rōmāna was established by the emperors, but the liberty of all men was not preserved by the Romans.

Exercise 212.—The American state is being preserved by brave soldiers and always will be preserved. The American soldiers will not be overcome by the enemy, also brave (even by a brave enemy). American men on account of courage and reliability will always be praised by us and by all men.

Reading No. 7.—Hannibal had led his army across great and high mountains. The enemy of the Roman people was in Italy. And so the Romans were in great danger. The Roman army was in Spain. Scipio had been with the Roman legions in Gaul. He, however, sent the army into Spain and hastened into Italy.

The Gauls were holding the parts of Italy next to (nearest) the Alps. They were enemies of the Roman people and had often waged war with the Romans. And so Hannibal led (his) army into their territory and was being helped by them. There Scipio, leader of the Romans, fought with Hannibal, but Hannibal conquered him. The Romans nevertheless did not sue for peace.

Therefore the cavalry of both the Romans and the enemy were fighting bravely. Meanwhile the Roman general sent his troops into battle. The elephants and horsemen of the enemy terrified the Roman cavalry and overcame it. Then the Roman legions made an attack against (upon) the soldiers of the enemy. The Roman soldiers were brave and were fighting bravely. Nevertheless they were being overcome by the enemy. Then a part of the enemy's soldiers made an attack against the Romans from the rear. And thus the enemy made an attack against the Romans from all sides. Nevertheless part of the Romans came (got) through the enemy and came safe (safely) into a Roman town. The Gauls and the Carthaginians killed all the remaining Romans. Not many (Few) Romans came safe (safely) into camp. The victory was Hannibal's. Fortune had aided not the Romans but the enemy.

1. Hannibal trāns Alpēs cum exercitū vēnerat. 2. Exercitūs Rōmānī in Hispāniā et in Rōmā erant. 3. Scīpiō imperātor Rōmānōrum erat. 4. Equitēs Rōmānī hostēs nōn superāvērunt. 5. Hostēs, nōn Rōmānī, vīcērunt.

Exercise 213.—"Bellum ā duce fortī administrātur. Ante bellum omnēs rēs ab eō parābantur; frūmentum et arma in oppida prōvinciae ā servīs portābantur; collēs et pontēs ā legiōnibus occupābantur; virtūs mīlitum ā centuriōnibus cōnfirmābātur. Nunc, in perīculīs bellī, imperātor legiōnum Rōmānārum et ā mīlitibus Rōmānīs et ab hostibus laudātur. Hostēs enim terruit, et metus eōrum est glōria imperātōris Rōmānī. Cūr ā senātū Rōmānō nōn laudātur? Cūr ab omnibus vōbīs nōn adjuvātur? Hominēs bonī eum nunc laudant et semper laudābunt."

Exercise 214.—See Introduction, 3.

Exercise 215.—1. They are being restrained. 2. It was being held. 3. You will be terrified. 4. It is being held. 5. They are being terrified. 6. It is seen. 7. It will be occupied. 8. They were being terrified. 9. You were being restrained. 10. They will be held.

Exercise 216.—1. The enemy is often terrified by the Roman cavalry. 2. The enemy's attack will be withstood by the brave soldiers. 3. Many boys were seen in the fields. 4. Noble and great men will neither be terrified nor overcome. 5. The hill is being filled with fresh soldiers. 6. The rest of the enemy was being held in on all sides by the Romans. 7. Afterwards the standard will be moved by the centurion. 8. On account of (Because of his) grave (serious, severe) fear the enemy was terrified. 9. Good men will not be terrified on account of (because of, by) fear of death. 10. High mountains are seen on all sides by the Helvetians. 11. The enemy is being held in on all sides. 12. The place was filled with the shouting of wretched soldiers. 13. Afterwards command was held by Caesar. 14. Royal power is often held by a king eager for glory. 15. The bridge is being held by brave soldiers. 16. The Gauls (living) nearest to the province are being terrified. 17. They were neither moved nor terrified on account of (by) the fear of death. 18. The attack is being withstood. 19. The Roman legions are not being terrified. 20. The Romans are not being terrified by the Gauls, brave men. 21. All the soldiers will be held (kept) in the camp. 22. Afterwards the camp will be moved across the river. 23. The boy was terrified because he was far away from (his) father and mother. 24. Free men were not being restrained. 25. The town full of rations will be occupied.

Exercise 217.—1. Mīlitēs ab imperātōre continēbantur. 2. Imperium ā Caesare obtinētur. 3. Hostēs ab equitibus terrentur. 4. Agmen Rōmānum ā Gallīs vidēbitur. 5. Oppidum aut ā nōbīs obtinēbitur aut ab hostibus occupābitur. 6. Pōns ab equitibus obtinētur. 7. Posteā rēgnum ab eō obtinēbitur. 8. Neque ā mīlitibus neque ab equitibus terrēbimur. 9. Ab equitibus continēbantur.

Exercise 218.—1. Christians praise God both by voice (word) and by virtue (virtuous deed). *(All italicized words in this exercise are ablatives of means.)* 2. The Romans did not conquer the Christians by means of swords. 3. The Roman state was preserved by arms and by courage. 4 The Romans always defended the winter quarters with darts and swords. 5. The courage of the brave cavalry was being strengthened by rewards. 6. Meanwhile the centurions will be advised by Caesar's dispatch. 7. The Helvetians are held in on all sides by high mountains and a deep river.

Exercise 219.—1. Tēlīs castra dēfendērunt. 2. Virtūs mīlitum ōrātiōne centuriōnis cōnfirmābitur.[1] 3. Gladiīs oppugnāvērunt. 4. Cīvitās Rōmāna virtūte Senātūs Populīque Rōmānī cōnservābātur. 5. Rōmānī urbēs mūrīs mūnīvērunt.

Reading No. 8.—Hannibal's victory was great. The Roman Senate and People, however, were not suing for peace. They prepared fresh troops. Arms and darts were being prepared.

Hannibal stationed a great number of soldiers on a hill; the cavalry, however, he placed on the right and on the left part (sides). And so the Roman general, eager for battle and victory, led the Roman army into narrow places (a narrow place). Suddenly the Romans saw the enemy. They were being held in on all sides by the enemy. There was no hope of safety (escape). The Romans were being (both) terrified by darts and confused by the cavalry. Then the enemy made an attack on the

---

[1] In impressions antedating 1947, *cōnfirmābātur*.

Romans from all sides. The slaughter of the Romans was great. The place was filled with the shouting of the wretched Romans. A part of the Romans, however, came (got) through the enemy. The cavalry of the enemy, however, killed them afterwards (later).

The enemy's victory was great. The danger of the Romans was serious. Nevertheless even then the Romans did not treat with the enemy about peace. They were placing hope of salvation in courage (depended on their courage for final victory).

Exercise 220.—See Nos. 247, 250, and 253.

Exercise 221.—1. He was being handed over. 2. He was being sent away. 3. They are being killed. 4. They will be guided. 5. They are being placed. 6. You are being sent away. 7. They were being killed. 8. It is being burned. 9. They are being routed. 10. He is being led. 11. He was being conquered. 12. They were being handed over.

Exercise 222.—1. Trādar; I will hand over, I will be handed over. 2. Dīmittēbātur; he was sending away, he was being sent away. 3. Occīduntur; they are killing, they are being killed. 4. Dēfendiminī; you are defending, you are being defended. 5. Dīmittitur; he is sending away, he is being sent away. 6. Trādētur; he will hand over, he will be handed over. 7. Occīdēmur; we will kill, we will be killed. 8. Pōnēbāris; you were placing, you were being placed. 9. Trāditur; he is handing over, he is being handed over. 10. Dīmittor; I am sending away, I am being sent away. 11. Occīdēris; you will kill, you will be killed. 12. Dūcentur; they will lead, they will be led. 13. Incenditur; he burns, it is being burned. 14. Pellēbantur; they were routing, they were being routed. 15. Sustinēminī; you will withstand, you will be withstood.

Exercise 223.—1. The chiefs of the enemy are being handed over to the Senate. 2. The Gaul is being killed. 3. The evil man will be killed by the Senate. 4. Italy is being defended by the Romans. 5. The Gauls will be both repulsed and killed. 6. The army is being led into the territory of the enemy. 7. Thanks are given to God. 8. The cavalry was being sent away against the neighboring tribes. 9. You are being sent into Gaul. 10. Rome will be defended. 11. Slaves are often killed. 12. Almost all the neighboring tribes are being conquered. 13. The column is being led by Caesar. 14. The enemy nevertheless will be conquered. 15. The city will not be handed over to the enemy. 16. The cavalry is being sent away against the remaining tribes. 17. The camp was being defended with darts. 18. The Romans will neither be routed nor killed. 19. Kings eager for glory often wage war with neighboring tribes. 20. The crops are often burned in the fields.

Exercise 224.—1. Equitēs hostium tēlīs occīdēbantur. 2. Senātus dīmittitur. 3. Omnēs ferē gladiī et tēla ā ducibus Gallōrum trādentur. 4. Omnēs ferē gentēs Galliae ā Rōmānīs vincēbantur. 5. Urbēs nostrae et oppida nostra ā mīlitibus fortibus dēfenduntur. 6. Agmen in Galliam ab imperātōre dūcētur. 7. Equitēs hostium ab equitibus nostrīs pellentur. 8. Gallī sine spē pugnābant. 9. Grātiae senātuī aguntur.

Exercise 225.—1. Often in war the forests are burned by the enemy. (*Hostibus*, ablative of agent.) 2. Rome was preserved by the courage of the legions. (*Virtūte*, ablative of means.) 3. The centurions are sent away against almost all the neighboring tribes by Caesar. (*Caesare*, ablative of agent.) 4. The Roman forces are not being repulsed by the Gauls. (*Gallīs*, ablative of agent.) 5. The courage of soldiers is always strengthened by the hope of victory. (*Spē*, ablative of means.) 6. Often after a battle the chiefs of the enemy were killed by the Romans. (*Rōmānīs*, ablative of agent.) 7. The chiefs will not be dismissed by Caesar. (*Caesare*, ablative of agent.) 8. He is being killed by darts. (*Tēlīs*, ablative of means.) 9. The Roman soldier sees an enemy. He kills him with darts. (*Tēlīs*, ablative of means.) 10. Soldiers will be led (in) from all sides; camp will be pitched on a hill; arms and grain will be carried into the camp. (*Colle*, ablative after *in*, expressing place where; *castra*, accusative after *in*, expressing motion.—These are the "booby-traps.")

Exercise 226.—1. Omnēs rēs ab imperātōre administrābantur. (*By the general*, ablative of agent.) 2. Castra mūrō mūnīvērunt. (*With a wall*, ablative of means.) 3. Prīncipēs gladiō occīdit. (*With a sword*, ablative of means.) 4. Pāx virtūte legiōnum cōnfirmābātur. (*By the courage*, ablative of means.) 5. Ab equitibus Rōmānīs dēfendēbantur. (*By Roman cavalry*, ablative of agent.) 6. Urbs ā Gallīs trādēbātur. (*By the Gauls*, ablative of agent.) 7. Virtūte mīlitum Rōmānōrum hostēs vīcit. (*By the courage*, ablative of means.) 8. Prīncipēs ab imperātōre Rōmānō dīmittuntur. (*By the Roman general*, ablative of agent.)

Reading No. 9.—Hannibal had a great number of soldiers but not so many horsemen. Scipio did not have so many soldiers; (he had), however, many horsemen. Hannibal had elephants also. The Romans did not have elephants.

Exercise 227.—1. It is heard. 2. They are being fortified. 3. It was being heard. 4. They will be fortified. 5. I am being heard. 6. They were being fortified. 7. He will be heard. 8. It was being fortified. 9. They are being heard.

Exercise 228.—1. The camps were always fortified by the Romans.

(*Rōmānīs,* ablative of agent; *mūniēbantur,* imperfect passive.) 2. What is heard by you (What do you hear)? 3. I came with Caesar through the mountains into Gaul. (*Caesare,* ablative with *cum; montēs,* accusative after *per; Galliam,* accusative after *in,* expressing motion toward.) 4. The city is being fortified by a king eager for victory. (*Victōriae,* genitive with *cupidō.*) 5. We give thanks to Christ, the Son of God. (*Fīliō,* dative, in apposition to *Chrīstō,* indirect object; *Deī,* possessive genitive.) 6. Meanwhile both the hills and the bridges were being fortified by the legions. 7. There was fear in the camp because the shouting of the enemy was heard. (*Fuit,* agrees with its subject *metus; castrīs,* ablative after *in,* expressing place; *quod,* the conjunction *because.*) 8. Rewards will not be given to bad boys. (*Puerīs,* dative, indirect object.) 9. Where is Rome? (*Ubi,* the interrogative adverb *where.*) 10. The son is often like the father. (*Patris,* genitive with *similis.*) 11. The tribes next to (living near) the enemy's territory often seek a supply of arms. (*Fīnibus,* dative with *finitimae; hostium,* possessive genitive.) 12. Was Lincoln like Washington? (*Washingtoniō,* dative with *similis.*) 13. Fresh legions are being sent against the enemy. (*Hostēs,* accusative after *in,* expressing motion toward.) 14. The shouting of the remaining sailors was heard. (*Reliquōrum,* adjective modifying *nautārum.*) 15. Mary is full of grace. (*Grātiā,* ablative with *plēna.*) 16. The forest is full of dangers. (*Perīculōrum,* genitive with *plēnae.*) 17. On account of fear of the enemy the legions were being drawn up before the gates. (*Metum,* accusative after *propter; portīs,* ablative after *prō.*) 18. The city is being fortified by a wall. (*Mūrō,* ablative of means.) 19. Who will fight for the king? (*Rēge,* ablative after *prō.*) 20. The baggage train was large (There was a large baggage train). 21. After the war there was peace. (*Bellum,* accusative after *post.*) 22. Caesar was general of the Romans. (*Imperātor,* predicate nominative.) 23. The places were narrow and difficult. (*Loca,* nominative plural of *locus, ī;* subject nominative.) 24. Rome is far (a great distance) from Gaul. (*Galliā,* ablative of place from which with *ā* and *abest; longē,* adverb.) 25. The town was being filled with soldiers. 26. The soldier was not like the leader. (*Ducī,* dative with *similis.*) 27. The Romans always defended Rome by courage and arms. (*Virtūte,* ablative of means.) 28. Why did they not (make a) march through the mountains? (*Cūr,* interrogative adverb.) 29. The soldiers sent (hurled) darts against the enemy from all sides. 30. The leader seized the royal power.

Picture captions, page 204.—He is coming with Romans. He is being killed with a sword.

Exercise 229.—1. Gladiīs oppugnāvērunt. 2. Caesar cum Gallīs oppugnābat. 3. Equitēs in castrīs cum mīlitibus erant. 4. Castra mūrō mūniēbantur. 5. Marīa in Caelō cum Deō est. 6. Clāmōre equitēs terruērunt.

Reading No. 10.—Hannibal and Scipio both drew up (their) soldiers. The courage and hope of the soldiers were being strengthened (buoyed up) by the speeches of the generals. "We will place hope in courage! We will fight bravely! We shall either conquer or be conquered!"

Hannibal gave the signal. The elephants were sent against the Roman battle line.

The elephants therefore neither terrified the Romans nor confused the battle line.

Meanwhile the Roman cavalry made an attack against the enemy's cavalry. The enemy, however, did not withstand the attack. And so the cavalry of the enemy yielded.

Then the first battle line of the enemy was sent by Hannibal against the Romans. The affair (this phase) was carried on with the sword (Fighting at this point was with the sword). Both the Romans and the enemy were fighting bravely. The cries and shouting of the men were heard on all sides. Many were killed by darts and swords, both of the enemy and of the Romans. The Roman soldiers, however, were withstanding (continued to withstand) the attack. And so both Scipio and Hannibal sent fresh soldiers into the battle.

The Romans, however, were not being overcome by the fresh soldiers. The enemy therefore was in great danger.

Then the Roman cavalry made an attack against the enemy from the rear. And so the enemy was being held in (surrounded) on all sides by the Romans. The slaughter of the wretched enemy was great. For the Romans either killed or captured almost all the enemy.

After the battle the enemy sought peace. So, after many victories of the enemy (won by the enemy) and a great slaughter of (great losses among) the Romans, the Romans conquered the enemy by courage and arms.

Exercise 230.—See Nos. 255-266.

Exercise 231.—See Introduction, 3.

Exercise 232.—See Nos. 346-348.

Exercise 233.—1. Laudātī. You have been praised. 2. Trāditum.

The town has been handed over. 3. Retentī. The chiefs were kept. 4. Comparāta. A supply of grain has been prepared. 5. Explōrāta. All the places have been reconnoitered. 6. Pressī. The enemy was (hard) pressed. 7. Laudātus. You have been praised. 8. Laudātī. We have been praised. 9. Audītae. Cries were heard. 10. Retentī. The sailors were held back. 11. Superātus. The army has been overcome. 12. Mōta. The camp has been moved.

Exercise 234.—1. Estis. 2. Sunt. 3. Es. 4. Est. 5. Sunt. 6. Erāmus. 7. Est. 8. Sunt.

Exercise 235.—1. You had been praised. 2. You were warned. 3. The cavalry was overcome. 4. The bridge was burned. 5. The grain was carried. 6. The camp was defended. 7. Almost all places had been seized. 8. They were repulsed. 9. We were led. 10. They (These things) were carried on. 11. The town had been attacked. 12. Arms were handed over to them. 13. You were heard. 14. We had been greatly terrified. 15. The soldiers were drawn up. 16. A dispatch was sent. 17. The mountain had been filled with men. 18. Darts were prepared. 19. We were conquered. 20. You had been called. 21. Peace was sought. 22. Grain was given to them. 23. It was done. 24. The affair was managed. 25. The camp had been moved. 26. The centurions had been called. 27. The Gauls were (hard) pressed. 28. A supply of darts had been prepared. 29. The leaders were kept. 30. They were killed. 31. The mountains had been reconnoitered. 32. The chiefs had been sent away. 33. The attack had been withstood. 34. Hope was placed in courage. 35. The town was fortified. 36. The legions were stationed there. 37. All things had been made ready. 38. Peace was strengthened (confirmed). 39. We were terrified. 40. The crops were burned in the fields. 41. I was aided. 42. You were repulsed. 43. You were seen. 44. He was routed. 45. I had been violently disturbed. 46. Command was held. 47. The law was not preserved. 48. The neighboring tribes had been aroused. 49. The first legion was (hard) pressed. 50. The standard had been guarded. 51. We were held in from (on) all sides. 52. They were (hard) pressed.

Exercise 236.—1. (Ego) ā Caesare laudātus sum. 2. (Tū) ā servō monitus es. 3. Nōs ab hostibus victī sumus. 4. Magnus numerus servōrum ā Rōmānīs habitus est. 5. Frūmentum in hīberna portātum erat. 6. Oppidum fortiter dēfēnsum erat. 7. Collēs ab equitibus occupātī sunt. 8. Rōmānī ab imperātōre fortī ductī sunt. 9. Bellum cum Gallīs gessum erat. 10. Urbs oppugnāta erat. 11. Hostibus ā duce trāditī sumus. 12. Ōrātiō ā prīncipibus audīta est. 13. Vōs tēlīs territī erātis. 14. Legiōnēs ā Caesare īnstrūctae sunt. 15. Litterae ā prīncipe missae sunt.

16. Mūrus virīs complētus est. 17. Arma comparāta erant. 18. Nōn victī sumus. 19. Deus appellātus erat. 20. Pāx petīta est. 21. Gladiī mīlitibus datī sunt. 22. Hostēs in silvās pulsī sunt. 23. Bellum ab imperātōre fortī administrātum est. 24. Castra in locum tūtum mōta erant. 25. Centuriōnēs ab imperātōre vocātī erant. 26. Hostēs tēlīs pulsī sunt. 27. Omnēs rēs parātae erant (Omnia parāta erant). 28. Rēx retentus erat. 29. Ducēs gladiīs occīsī erant. 30. Omnia lōca explōrāta erant. 31. Servī dīmissī sunt. 32. Impetum ab aciē sustentum est. 33. Ibi castra posita erant. 34. Castra mūrō mūnīta sunt. 35. Eques in ponte collocātus erat. 36. Pāx cōnfirmāta erat. 37. Frūmentum ā Rōmānīs incēnsum erat. 38. Et ā servīs et ab hominibus līberīs adjūtī sunt. 39. Mīlitēs convēnerant. 40. Ab equite vīsus erat. 41. Equitēs pulsī sunt. 42. Prīma aciēs perturbāta est. 43. Rēgnum ā virō bonō obtentum est. 44. Cīvitās ā virīs fortibus cōnservāta erat. 45. Legiō in castra missa est. 46. Fidēs ā multīs Chrīstiānīs servāta est. 47. Mīlitēs ā ducibus contentī sunt.

Exercise 237.—All Wars Are Alike. 1. On account of war swords and darts had been got ready by the Romans; today also many great (supplies of) arms are being made ready by the Americans. 2. In the camps of the Romans there was often a great scarcity of everything; in American camps too there is often a scarcity of things. 3. In the wars of the Romans all places were often reconnoitered by the cavalry; in modern wars, however, all places are reconnoitered by airmen. 4. At that time the enemy was often (hard) pressed by the cavalry; today the enemy is (hard) pressed by tanks. 5. The Gallic war was managed (waged) by Caesar. Who manages (wages) the common general war today? 6. Caesar, general of the Romans, was praised on account (because) of (his) victory. Will the American leaders be praised on account (because) of (their) victory?

Reading No. 11.—"Are you . . . are you Roman soldiers?"

CENTURIO. We are Roman cavalry. But you . . .

PROFESSOR. Where are you?

C. We are in Gaul. We are in the fields of the enemy. Now, as you see, we are in a great forest.

P. Who is your general?

C. Caesar is our general, a man both renowned and brave. The war is being strongly (well) managed by him.

P. War? Is war being waged?

C. Just so. The Roman legions are now fighting with the Gauls. Is the shouting of both the enemy and the Romans heard by you?

P. Did the Gauls prepare war? Were they eager for war?

C. Yes. They were eager for victory and the glory of war. And so before the war arms and darts were got ready by the Gauls. Their courage was strengthened by the leaders and chiefs. Towns and cities were fortified by them. Grain was carried into the towns by the Gauls and their slaves. Thus all things had been made ready.

P. But what are the Gauls doing now?

C. They are defending the towns and fields with darts and arms. The hills and bridges are being seized by them, for they are waging war with us.

P. And Caesar? What did he do before the war?

C. Camp was pitched by him on a hill. Grain was carried into the camp by slaves. Arms and darts were also got ready by him. The cavalry was (constantly) sent away by Caesar into the territory of the enemy. All places were reconnoitered by them. We fortified our camp with a wall. Caesar strengthened the courage and hope of the soldiers . by a speech and with rewards.

P. Will the Gauls be conquered by you?

C. Yes. The Gauls fight bravely, but they will not conquer us. We will conquer them with arms and by courage. For the Romans neither are conquered nor treat with the enemy about peace. Behold! The Gauls are already (now) being both terrified and killed by the Roman soldiers. A slaughter! Cities, towns, hills, forests, harbors, fields will be seized by the Roman army. Command of all Gaul will be held by (in the hands of) Caesar! We will carry on the affair with swords! Many Gauls will be killed by us. The crops will be burned by the Roman cavalry; bridges and towns will be burned by the legions. After the war grain and slaves and arms will be handed over to us by the Gauls. Thus peace will be strengthened (established) in Gaul. The victory will be ours! Ah, victory!

P. But what are you doing now?

C. We are being sent into battle by Caesar. Behold, we are behind the enemy's battle line! We have come by a long route through the forest and . . . There is the signal! The signal is being given by Caesar! (Forward) Against the enemy!

UNIT SIX

Exercise 238.—See Introduction, 3.
Exercise 239.—See Introduction, 3.

Exercise 240.—See Introduction, 3.

Exercise 241.—See Introduction, 3.

Box, page 227.—I will praise my God in my life (as long as I live).

Exercise 242.—1. He is fortifying the camp with a wall (rampart) in order that he may defend it. (*Castra . . . mūnit,* main clause; *ut . . . dēfendat,* subordinate clause.) 2. Do we give rewards to friends in order that we may strengthen friendship? (*Damusne . . . amīcīs,* main; *ut . . . cōnfirmēmus,* subordinate.) 3. I am fighting bravely in order that I may preserve (save) my life. (*Fortiter pugnō,* main; *ut . . . cōnservem,* subordinate.) 4. They are fortifying the winter quarters with a ditch in order that they may withstand the enemy's attack. (*Hiberna . . . mūniunt,* main; *ut . . . sustineant,* subordinate.) 5. The cavalry is coming swiftly in order that it may burn the crops. (*Equitēs . . . veniunt,* main; *ut . . . incendant,* subordinate.)

Exercise 243.—3, 4, 6, 7, 8.

Exercise 244.—1. The soldiers eager for glory are fighting in order that they may conquer the enemy, that they may conquer the enemy, in order to conquer the enemy, to conquer the enemy. 2. Will free men always fight in order that they may preserve our state, etc., as above. 3. Arms are being prepared by us in order that we may save our lives, etc., as above. 4. They are fortifying the camp by means of a wall and a ditch in order that they may withstand the enemy's attack, etc., as above. 5. We will strengthen (encourage) friendship with all nations in order that we may keep peace with them, etc., as above.

Exercise 245.—1. Pugnant ut vītās virōrum bonōrum dēfendant. 2. Collem vallō mūnit ut eum teneat. 3. Frūmentum mittunt ut pācem cōnfirment. 4. Rōmānōs adjuvant ut amīcitiam cum eīs cōnfirment.

Box, page 229.—True happiness has been placed (lies) in virtue.

Exercise 246.—1. Grain is being carried into the camp by (the) slaves in order that there may be no scarcity of grain. (*Frūmentum . . . portātur,* main clause; *nē . . . sit,* subordinate clause. Present tense in subordinate clause after a primary tense in main clause. *Note.* The same explanation applies to all sentences in this exercise. For the diagram see page 227 in the text.) 2. Is he holding the soldiers in camp in order to wait for fresh troops? (*Continetne . . . castrīs,* main; *ut . . . exspectet,* subordinate.) 3. He is coming into the fields of the enemy in order to terrify them. (*In . . . venit,* main; *ut . . . terreat,* subordinate.) 4. The Gauls are fighting long and bitterly lest the Romans burn the crops. (*Gallī . . . pugnant,* main; *nē . . . incendant,* subordinate.) 5. He is strengthening the courage of the soldiers by a speech in order that they may be eager for victory. (*Virtūtem* . . . *cōnfirmat*, main; *ut* . . . *sint*, subordinate.) 6. He is giving rewards to the chiefs in order to strengthen friendship with their tribes. (*Praemia* . . . *dat*, main; *ut* . . . *cōnfirmet*, subordinate.) 7. The Gauls are fighting in order that they may not be slaves. (*Gallī pugnant*, main; *nē* . . . *sint*, subordinate.) 8. The centurion is helping his brother lest the enemy kill him. (*Centuriō* . . . *adjuvat*, main; *nē* . . . *occīdant*, subordinate.) 9. He is fortifying the camp by means of a rampart and a ditch, in order that the enemy may not take it by storm. (*Castra* . . . *mūnit*, main; *nē* . . . *expugnent*, subordinate.)

Exercise 247.—1. Pugnant ut vincant. 2. Oppidum oppugnant ut id expugnent. 3. Veniunt ut ōrātiōnem audiant. 4. Pontem occupant ut eum incendant. 5. Venient ut Rōmam videant. 6. Ōrant ut bonī sint. 7. Oppidum mūnient nē hostēs id expugnent. 8. Prīncipem monent ut vītam ējus cōnservent. 9. Pugnat ut rēx sit. 10. Cēdunt nē caedēs sit. 11. Mīlitēs collocant ut pontem dēfendant. 12. Arma trādunt ut pācem cōnfirment. 13. Arma parant ut bellum gerant. 14. Veniet ut imperātōrem occīdat. 15. Venit ut pācem petat. 16. Manēbit ut legiōnēs novās exspectet.

Exercise 248.—1. Deus nōs adjuvat nē hostēs nōs superent. 2. Marīa prō nōbīs ōrat ut grātiam Deī habeāmus. 3. Ego fortiter et diū pugnābō ut vītam tuam cōnservem. 4. Castra fossā mūnit ut ea dēfendat. 5. Caesarem exspectāmus nē hostēs nōs vincant. 6. Dūcitne legiōnēs novās in Galliam ut urbēs expugnet? 7. Frūmenta incendit ut in Galliā inopia frūmentī sit. 8. Amīcitiam cum omnibus gentibus cōnfirmat nē bellum sit. 9. Veniunt ut oppidum expugnent. 10. Hostēs eōs premunt. Itaque cēdent nē hostēs sē occīdant. 11. Conveniunt ut rēgem audiant.

Exercise 249.—See Introduction, 3. Suggested sentences are: 1. Imperātor eī praemia dat ut fortiter contendat. 2. Pugnābō ut hostēs vincam. 3. Virtūtem mīlitum cōnfirmat nē hostēs timeant. 4. Gallī castra Rōmānōrum expugnant. 5. Mīles ācriter pugnat ut imperātor sē laudet. 6. Caesar, imperātor fortis, hostēs populī Rōmānī vincet. 7. Exercitus Rōmānus fortiter pugnat. 8. Senātus Caesarem in Galliam mittit ut hostēs pellat. 9. Caesar in castrīs cōpiās novās exspectābit. 10. Frūmenta incendunt nē Caesar in agrōs suōs veniat. 11. Centuriō cum equitibus veniet. 12. Caesar armīs et virtūte Gallōs vincit. 13. Fortiter pugnat ut frātrem adjuvet. 14. Rōmānī venient ut urbem dēfendant. 15. Gallī pontem dēfendunt nē Caesar cōpiās in castra dūcat. 16. Virtūtem mīlitum ōrātiōne cōnfirmat. 17. Dux mīlitēs convocābit ut eōs appellēs. 18. Bellum fortiter geris. 19. Hīberna vallō mūniunt nē hostēs ea occupent. 20. Caesar legiōnēs integrās mittit nē Gallī equitēs occīdant. 21. Sānctī Chrīstiānōs adjuvant.

Box, page 232.—Life without literature is death.

Exercise 250.—1. Many men come to Italy to see Rome. (*Multī*, nominative modifying *hominēs*, the subject; *Italiam*, accusative after *in*, expressing motion toward.) 2. Men assemble swiftly both to see and to hear new things. (*Novās*, acc. modifying *rēs*, the object.) 3. Soldiers fight long and bravely in order to get the glory of victory. 4. The soldiers are striving bitterly with the enemy in order both to repulse them and to kill them. (*Hostibus*, ablative after *cum*.) 5. A bad master is praised by (his) wretched slaves in order that he may save their life. (*Miserīs*, abl. modifying *servīs; eōrum*, personal pronoun, modifying *vītam*.) 6. Caesar, a good and brave man, often fights in the battle line with the soldiers in order to strengthen (their) courage. (*Vir*, nom., in apposition to *Caesar; aciē*, abl. after *in*, expressing place; *virtūtem*, acc. object of the subordinate clause.) 7. The camp is being fortified by the Romans by means of a rampart and a ditch lest the enemy take it by storm. (*Ea*, acc. referring to *castra*.) 8. Leaders often both thank the soldiers and give rewards in order that they may fight bravely. (*Mīlitibus*, dat., indirect object.) 9. Are commanders often desirous of glory and victory? (*Glōriae*, genitive with *cupidī*.)

Reading No. 12.—

GUARD. Who are you?

VOICE OUTSIDE THE GATE. I am a Roman centurion. I come to treat with the chiefs about a serious matter.

GUARD. We will call them.

CHIEFS. Why do you come? What do you seek?

CENTURION. We come to ask for a supply of grain. There is a scarcity of grain in our camp. Caesar therefore sends us to get grain.

CHIEFS. But we do not have an abundant supply of grain, nor are there crops in the fields.

CENTURION. Nevertheless you shall give (it) to us. Are you friends of the Roman people? You shall give us the grain . . . in order that you may always be friends of the Roman people.

CHIEFS. We are also men. Boys and mothers and . . .

CENTURION. The tribe next (living nearest) to you did not give us grain. Already (their) towns and cities are being stormed and burned, the men and boys killed, the mothers led into camp to be slaves. You are nevertheless friends of the Roman people!

CHIEFS. We have always been friends of Caesar and of the Roman people. We have also (even) sent (him) horsemen. We have not waged war with him. We have always kept peace with Caesar and the Roman people.

CENTURION. And so why are you waiting? We seek grain!

CHIEFS. But we have no supply!

VOICES FROM THE CROWD. We will not give (it)! We will fight!

THE CHIEF. Caesar will (surely) come!

Exercise 251.—See Introduction, 3.

Exercise 252.—See Introduction, 3.

Exercise 253.—See Introduction, 3.

Exercise 254.—See Introduction, 3.

Exercise 255.—1. 3rd sing., present indicative. 2. 3rd sing., present subjunctive. 3. 3rd sing., imperfect subjunctive. 4. 3rd sing., future indicative. 5. 1st pl., present subjunctive. 6. 3rd pl., present subjunctive. 7. 3rd sing., imperfect subjunctive. 8. 3rd pl., imperfect subjunctive. 9. 1st sing., future indicative or present subjunctive. 10. 3rd sing., present indicative. 11. 3rd sing., imperfect subjunctive. 12. 3rd pl., imperfect subjunctive. 13. 2nd pl., present subjunctive. 14. 3rd sing., present subjunctive. 15. 3rd sing., present subjunctive.

Exercise 256.—1. Caesar often waited for new and fresh legions in order easily to conquer the enemy. (*Vinceret*, 3rd sing., imp. subj. of *vincō, vincere, vīcī, victus*, 3, tr.; used in a purpose clause after a secondary tense.) 2. The Gauls fortified the town by means of a high wall and a wide ditch lest the Romans should take it by storm. (*Id*, acc. sing., neuter pronoun, referring to *oppidum*, object of *expugnārent; expugnārent*, 3rd pl., imp. subj. of *expugnō*, 1, tr.; used in a negative purpose clause after secondary tense.) 3. The lieutenant called upon the centurions and the military tribunes to fight long and bravely. (*Pugnārent*, 3rd pl., imp. subj. of *pugnō*, 1, tr.; used in a purpose clause after a secondary tense.) 4. Did Hannibal lead all the troops (the entire army) across wide rivers and through high mountains to wage war with the Romans in Italy? (*Gereret*, 3rd sing., imp. subj. of *gerō, gerere, gessī, gestus*, 3, tr.; used in a purpose clause after a secondary tense.) 5. Jesus Christ, the Son of God, came into the world to give us life and salvation. (*Daret*, 3rd sing., imp. subj. of *dō, dare, dedī, datus*, 1, tr.; used in a purpose clause after a secondary tense.) 6. The Gauls often sent envoys into Caesar's camp to ask for peace and friendship. (*Peterent*, 3rd pl., imp. subj. of *petō, petere, petīvī, petītus*, 3, tr.; in a purpose clause after a secondary tense.) 7. A council is often called by emperors in order that they may treat of a serious matter in the council. (*Agant*, 3rd pl., pres. subj. of *agō*, *agere*, *ēgī*, *āctus*, 3, tr.; in a purpose clause after a primary tense.) 8. The leader gave the envoys rewards in order that they might praise the plan.

Exercise 257.—1. Pugnāvērunt ut vincerent. 2. Oppugnāvērunt oppidum ut id expugnārent. 3. Pontem occupāvērunt ut eum incenderent. 4. Vēnērunt ut cōnsilium audīrent. 5. Vēnērunt ut Rōmam vidērent. 6. Ōrāvērunt ut bonī essent. 7. Oppidum mūniunt nē hostēs id expugnent. 8. Prīncipem monuērunt ut vītam ējus cōnservārent. 9. Bellum gessit ut rēgnum occupāret. 10. Cēdunt nē caedēs sit. 11. Equitēs collocāvērunt ut collem dēfenderent. 12. Arma trādūxērunt ut pācem cōnservārent. 13. Arma parāvērunt ut bellum gererent. 14. Prīncipēs dīmissī sunt nē gentēs bellum gererent. 15. Vēnit ut rēgem occīderet. 16. Mīlitēs īnstrūctī sunt ut urbem dēfenderent. 17. Caesarem exspectāvit ut hostēs vinceret. 18. Vēnit ut pācem peteret. 19. Convēnērunt ut ōrātiōnem audīrent. 20. Mānsit ut prīncipem exspectāret.

Exercise 258.—1. Rōmānī castra fossā lātā mūnīvērunt nē hostēs ea facile expugnārent. 2. Caesar in conciliō virtūtem lēgātōrum et tribūnōrum mīlitum saepe cōnfirmāvit ut fortiter pugnārent. 3. Ācriter pugnāvērunt nē hostēs oppidum oppugnārent. 4. Occīdēbanturne saepe prīncipēs et ducēs hostium ā Caesare post bellum? 5. Lēgātus in castrīs mīlitēs retinuit nē hostēs cōnsilia vidērent. 6. Caesar in ponte mīlitēs collocāvit nē hostēs trāns flūmen lātum venīrent.

Reading No. 13.—The Death of (Two) Brave Brothers. In this battle many horsemen were killed, in (among) them a brave and renowned man, Piso Aquitanus. He was a friend of the Roman people. His brother had been wounded in battle and was being (hard) pressed by the enemy. There was no hope of safety (escape). Piso saw this: he saw his brother; and he saw the enemy. Nevertheless he hastened toward the enemy in order to aid his brother. But he was surrounded by the enemy and killed. Then Piso's brother was greatly moved by his (brother's) death and hastened toward the enemy. He fought bitterly, but he was also killed by the enemy. Thus (these) brave and good brothers were (both) killed. Do we praise them?

Answers, page 240.—1. Pīsō Aquītānus fuit vir fortis et nōbilis. 2. Frāter Pīsōnis ab hostibus premēbātur. 3. Et Pīsō et frāter ējus in hostēs contendērunt. 4. Pīsō in hostēs sē mīsit ut frātrem adjuvāret. 5. Pīsō Aquītānus occīsus est. 6. Frāter ējus etiam occīsus est.

Exercise 259.—1. Primary tenses: present, future, and future perfect; secondary: imperfect, perfect, and pluperfect. 2. The ablative without a preposition is used to express the non-living agent, the means, or the instrument.

Box, page 242.—I do all things and endure all things on account of Thee (for Thy sake).

Exercise 260.—1. Is God praised by all the saints? (*Ab sānctīs*, ablative of agent.) 2. The Gauls often exchanged hostages in order to strengthen peace. (*Sē*, reflexive pronoun, with *inter* and *dedērunt*, idiomatic use, to mean *exchange*.) 3. The brave do not yield on account of (through) fear. (*Fortēs*, adjective in masculine plural used as noun. See No. 845.) 4. Caesar, a brave man, did all things strongly (boldly). (*Omnia*, adjective in neuter accusative plural used as a noun.) 5. Caesar waged many wars in order to be commander and chief. 6. Does God help the brave? (*Fortēs*, adjective in masculine plural used as noun.) 7. Our men always fight bravely and eagerly to preserve our free state. (*Nostrī*, adjective in masculine plural used as noun.) 8. Fortune aids the brave. 9. Our men yielded lest there be a great slaughter. 10. I do all things by virtue (virtuously) in order to be a good servant of Christ. (*Virtūte*, ablative of means.) 11. The lieutenant hastened into the fields immediately in order not to be far from the battle. (*Nē*, conjunction in negative purpose clause.) 12. The saints sustain heavy toil on account of (endure heavy burdens for) Christ. 13. At once the enemy sent the cavalry into the battle line in order to confuse the ranks of our soldiers. 14. The chiefs were exchanging hostages in order that there might be peace in Gaul. 15. The chiefs of Gaul were always contending among themselves about (over) the command of all Gaul. 16. There was a route both difficult and narrow between the mountains and the river. 17. The leaders are treating among themselves in council of a serious matter.

Box, page 243.—Toil conquers all things.

Exercise 261.—1. Interim equitēs ab imperātōre in fīnēs hostium missī sunt ut cōnsilia eōrum explōrārent. 2. Rōmānī castra vallō saepe mūnīvērunt nē Gallī ea expugnārent. 3. Gallī pācem obsidibus cōnfirmāvērunt. 4. Equitēs in hostēs statim missī sunt ut ōrdinēs eōrum perturbārent. 5. Obsidēs inter sē saepe dedērunt ut pācem et amīcitiam cōnservārent. 6. Concilium in oppidum statim convēnit ut prīncipēs inter sē dē pāce et bellō agerent.

Exercise 262.—1. The ablative without a preposition is used to express the non-living agent, the means, or the instrument. 2. *Ā* or *ab* with the ablative is used to express the living agent. 3. Primary tenses: present, future, and future perfect.

Reading No. 14.—Hostages. The Gauls often exchanged hostages in order to strengthen friendship and peace. Therefore friendship was encouraged through the hostages and thus peace was strengthened in Gaul. The Gauls often gave hostages to the Romans also in order to strengthen faith (encourage trust). The Romans, however, gave no hostages to the Gauls, for, desirous of command over all of Gaul, they had conquered the tribes of Gaul by means of arms and courage. And so the Gauls feared the Romans and often waged war with them in order not to give them hostages.

The hostages, however, (As for the hostages, they) were boys and men, mothers and fathers. Often, also (too), they were sons of the chiefs and kings of the Gauls. But hostages were not free, for the Romans held them in camps, in winter quarters, and in towns in order that on account (for the sake) of their safety the Gauls would preserve peace. And so the hostages were often wretched. For if after peace (had been signed) the Gauls (again) waged war with the Romans, the Romans killed all their hostages in order that afterwards the Gauls would keep faith on account of fear. Thus the Gauls were often terrified by the slaughter of the hostages and did not wage war with the Romans in order to spare the lives of the hostages.

Answers, page 245.—1. Gallī inter sē obsidēs dedērunt ut pācem cōnfirmārent. 2. Gallī Rōmānīs obsidēs dabant ut fidem cōnfirmārent. 3. Obsidēs nōn erant līberī. 4. Obsidēs in castrīs et hībernīs et oppidīs ā Rōmānīs tenēbantur. 5. Obsidēs saepe erant miserī, nam nōn erant līberī; et sī Gallī bellum cum Rōmānīs gessērunt, Rōmānī eōs occīdēbant.

Box, page 245.—The courage of the soldiers lies in the leader's plan (Vain is the valor of the soldier if the leader is without a plan).

Exercise 263.—1. Quī. 2. Quōrum. 3. Cūjus. 4. Cui. 5. Quibus. 6. Quem. 7. Quōs. 8. Quibus. 9. Quō. 10. Quod. 11. Quō. 12. Cūjus. 13. Quae.

Exercise 264.—1. The Romans killed Christ, who was the Son of God. (*Quī*, masc. nom. sing.; agrees with *Chrīstum* in gender and number, but is the subject of the relative clause.) 2. Mary, whom we praise, is the mother of God. (*Quam*, fem. acc. sing.; agrees with *Marīa* in gender and number, but is the object of the relative clause.) 3. The tribes which were next to (nearest) the province sent envoys to seek help. (*Quae*, fem. nom. sing., agreeing with *gentēs;* subject of the relative clause.) 4. The legion which had been across the river was immediately sent into the forest to repulse the enemy. (*Quae*, fem. nom.

sing., agreeing with *legiō;* subject of the relative clause.) 5. We shall always remember the wars which our fathers waged. (*Quae,* neut. acc. pl., agreeing with *bella;* object of the relative clause.) 6. A town in which there was grain (The town in which the grain was) was being attacked by the Romans. (*Quō,* neut. abl. sing., agreeing with *oppidum;* abl. after *in.*) 7. The commanders whose memory we praise were brave. (*Quōrum,* masc. gen. pl., agreeing with *imperātōrēs;* possessive genitive with *memoriam.*) 8. In order to terrify the Gauls the lieutenant killed the hostages that he was holding in camp. (*Quōs,* masc. acc. pl., agreeing with *obsidēs;* object of the relative clause.) 9. I who am a Roman will not yield to you. (*Quī,* masc. nom. sing., agreeing with *ego;* subject of the relative clause.) 10. Caesar immediately sent reinforcements into the forest lest the enemy overcome our men. 11. The lieutenant killed a slave to whom the enemy had given a sword. (*Cui,* masc. dat. sing., agreeing with *servum;* indirect object of after *dederant.*) 12. The winter quarters in which the Romans are, are narrow. (*Quibus,* neut. abl. pl., agreeing with *hīberna;* abl. after *in.*) 13. Will you give grain to us who are Gauls? (*Quī,* masc. nom. sing., agreeing with *nōbīs;* subject of the relative clause.) 14. All men will remember the king for whom I have fought. (*Quō,* masc. abl. sing., agreeing with *rēgem;* abl. after *prō.*) 15. The Romans often killed those with whom they had fought. (*Quibuscum,* masc. abl. pl., agreeing with *eōs;* abl. after *cum.*) 16. Caesar, with whom I was, gave me rewards. (*Quōcum,* masc. abl. sing., agreeing with *Caesar;* abl. after *cum.*) 17. Those who keep the law of Christ are holy. (*Quī,* masc. nom. pl., agreeing with subject understood of *servant;* subject of the relative clause.) 18. The tribes into whose territory Caesar came fought bravely with him. (*Quārum,* fem. gen. pl., agreeing with *gentēs;* possessive gen. with *fīnēs.*) 19. The legions which I had seen across the wide river at dawn were led by Caesar into camp. (*Quās,* fem. acc. pl., agreeing with *legiōnēs;* object of the relative clause.) 20. Caesar held the power for which he was eager. (*Cūjus,* neut. gen. sing., agreeing with and modifying *imperium;* gen. after *cupidus.*)

Exercise 265.—1. Rōmānī servōs quī hostēs adjūverant semper occīdēbant. (*Quī,* masc. nom. sing., agreeing with *servōs;* subject of the relative clause.) 2. Montēs Galliae, trāns quōs Caesar cōpiās Rōmānās saepe dūcēbat, altī erant. (*Quōs,* masc. acc. pl., agreeing with *montēs;* acc. after *trāns.*) 3. Caesar ducēs gentium quibuscum pugnāvit saepe occīdēbat. (*Quibuscum,* fem. abl. pl., agreeing with *gentium;* abl. after *cum.*) 4. Caesar cōpiās dūxit trāns multa flūmina quae longa et alta erant. (*Quae,* neut. acc. pl., agreeing with *flūmina;* subject of the relative clause.) 5. Chrīstus, quī Fīlius Deī est, ā Rōmānīs occīsus est. (*Quī*, masc. nom. sing., agreeing with *Chrīstus;* subject of the relative clause.) 6. Legiō quae in silvīs erat fortiter pugnābat. (*Quae*, fem. nom. sing., agreeing with *legiō;* subject of the relative clause.) 7. Legiō cui Gallī frūmentum dedērunt in hīberna ducta est. (*Cui*, fem. dat. sing., agreeing with *legiō;* indirect object of the relative clause.) 8. Legiō cūjus centuriōnēs fortēs erant hostēs vīcit. (*Cūjus*, fem. gen. sing., agreeing with *legiō;* possessive gen. with *centuriōnēs.*) 9. Legiōnēs quās Caesar in prōvinciam dūxit fortēs erant. (*Quās*, fem. acc. pl., agreeing with *legiōnēs;* object of the relative clause.) 10. Legiō quācum Gallī pugnābant fortis erat. (*Quācum*, fem. abl. sing., agreeing with *legiō;* abl. after *cum.*) 11. Mīlitēs quōrum virtūtem Caesar laudāvit in hībernīs sunt. (*Quōrum*, masc. gen. pl., agreeing with *mīlitēs;* possessive gen. with *virtūtem.*) 12. Mīlitēs quibus imperātōr grātiās ēgit multōs impetūs hostium sustinuerant. (*Quibus*, masc. dat. pl., agreeing with *mīlitēs;* indirect object of the relative clause.) 13. Gallī saepe fortiter dēfendēbant oppida quae Rōmānī expugnābant. (*Quae*, neut. acc. pl., agreeing with *oppida;* object of the relative clause.) 14. Fīnēs hostium in quōs Caesar omnēs cōpiās Rōmānās dūxit plēnī perīculōrum erant. (*Quōs*, masc. abl. pl., agreeing with *fīnēs;* acc. after *in.*) 15. Rēs dē quā Caesar cum Gallīs agēbat gravis erat. (*Quā*, fem. abl. sing., agreeing with *rēs;* abl. after *dē.*) 16. Silvae per quās Caesar legiōnēs Rōmānās saepe dūcēbat plēnae perīculōrum erant. (*Quās*, fem. acc. pl., agreeing with *silvae;* acc. after *per.*) 17. Populus Rōmānus prō quō Caesar pugnābat magnus et nōbilis erat. (*Quō*, masc. abl. sing., agreeing with *populus;* abl. after *prō.*) 18. Caesar multās urbēs ā quibus Rōma longē aberat occupāvit. (*Quibus*, fem. abl. pl., agreeing with *urbēs;* abl. after *ā.*) 19. Viae quae ā Rōmānīs mūnītae sunt longae et tūtae erant. (*Quae*, fem. nom. pl., agreeing with *viae;* subject of the relative clause.) 20. Rēs propter quās populī et gentēs bellum gerunt gravēs sunt. (*Quās*, fem. acc. pl., agreeing with *rēs;* acc. after *propter.*) 21. Caesar mīlitibus frūmentum quod servī in castra portāverant statim dedit. (*Quod*, neut. acc. sing., agreeing with *frūmentum;* object of the relative clause.) 22. Caesar mīlitēs quibuscum hostēs pontem complēverant superāvit. (*Quibus*, masc. abl. pl., agreeing with *mīlitēs;* abl. of means.) 23. Ego, quī Chrīstiānus sum, Chrīstum et Marīam semper laudābō. (*Quī*, masc. nom. sing., agreeing with *ego;* subject of the relative clause.) 24. Caesarem, cūjus victōriae multae et magnae erant, omnēs laudāmus. (*Cūjus*, masc. gen. sing., agreeing with *Caesarem;* possessive gen. with *victōriae.*) 25. Gallī castra quae in fīnibus (suīs) posita erant oppugnābant.

(*Quae*, neut. nom. pl., agreeing with *castra;* subject of the relative clause) 26. Caesar imperium cūjus cupidus fuerat obtinuīt. (*Cūjus*, neut. gen. sing., agreeing with *imperium;* case determined by *cupidus.*) 27. Vōbīs quī estis hostēs nōminis Rōmānī neque frūmentum neque arma dabō. (*Quī*, masc. nom. pl., agreeing with *vōbīs;* subject of the relative clause.) 28. Nōs mīlitēs quī prō Rōmā pugnāmus victōriae et glōriae cupidī sumus. (*Quī*, masc. nom. pl., agreeing with *nōs;* subject of the relative clause.) 29. Collis in quō Rōmānī castra posuērunt altus est. (*Quō*, masc. abl. sing., agreeing with *collis;* abl. after *in.*)

Exercise 266.—1. He conquers twice who conquers himself in victory. (The antecedent of *quī* is subject of *vincit* understood. *Sē*, a reflexive, means *himself; eum* would refer to some other person than the subject.) 2. For you are all sons of God through that faith which is in Christ Jesus. (*Filiī* is a predicate nominative. *Omnēs* agrees with the subject of *estis* understood.) 3. Jesus Christ, who conquered death for us once, always conquers death in us. (The direct object of a transitive verb is in the accusative case.) 4. The temple of God is holy, which you are.

Reading No. 15.—We have God's grace through Jesus Christ. Through Jesus Christ and through His death we have salvation and the hope of glory. Through Him we are safe on earth; through Him we shall come to heaven after death. . . . through our Lord Jesus Christ Thy Son, who lives and reigns with Thee in the unity of the Holy Spirit, God, forever and ever (world without end).

Exercise 267.—1. They arrived in the enemy's territory. (*In* with acc. after verbs of motion means *in, into.*) 2. They arrived at the river. (*Ad* with verbs of motion sometimes means *at.*) 3. They fought at the river. (*Ad* with non-motion verbs sometimes means *at.*) 4. They fought until night. (*Ad* is used in expressions of time to mean *to* or *until; usque ad* means *even to, even until.*) 5. Arms are useful for war. (*Ad* with certain adjectives means *for.*) 6. At dawn they arrived at the camp. (*Ad* with verbs of motion sometimes means *at.*) 7. At dawn he arrived at the camp. (*In* with acc. means place to which.) 8. There was a scarcity of all things in our winter quarters. (*In* with abl. expresses place where.) 9. There was bitter fighting at the baggage train. (*Ad* with non-motion verbs sometimes means *at.*) 10. The soldiers were prepared for everything. (*Ad* with certain adjectives means *for.*) 11. He moved the camp into a safe place. (*In* with acc. expresses motion toward.) 12. The grain was being carried into the camp. (*In* with acc. expresses motion toward.) 13. Did he lead the soldiers into (as far as, even into) the city? (*In* with acc. expresses motion toward.) 14. Did he lead the soldiers all the way to the city? (*Ad* with verb of motion means *to;* strengthened by the adverb *usque.*) 15. Roman soldiers, prepared for death, were drawn up before the gates. (*Prō* with abl. expresses *before.*) 16. He was hastening into the forest. (*In* with acc. expresses motion toward.) 17. He was hastening to the forest. (*Ad* with verbs of motion sometimes means *to* or *up to.*) 18. He sent them into the province. (*In* with acc. expresses motion toward.) 19. He sent them to the province. (*Ad* with verbs of motion sometimes means *to.*) 20. He led the soldiers into foreign places. (*In* with acc. expresses motion toward.) 21. He sent a lieutenant into the winter quarters. (*In* with acc. expresses motion toward.) 22. They sent envoys to Caesar. (*Ad* with verbs of motion sometimes means *to.*) 23. The soldier was sent onto the bridge. (*In* with acc. expresses motion toward.) 24. The soldier was sent to the bridge. (*Ad* with verbs of motion sometimes means *to* or *up to.*) 25. Caesar called the chiefs to him from all sides. (*Ad* with certain non-motion verbs sometimes means *to.*) 26. They arrived at the river. (*Ad* with verbs of motion sometimes means *at.*)

Exercise 268.—1. They fought bitterly at the baggage train until night. 2. Envoys swiftly arrived at the camp to ask for help. 3. Will you send a dispatch and envoys to me? 4. Because of Christ (For Christ's sake) Christians are ready for toil and death. 5. Everything which pertains to war is being prepared by our enemies; therefore we too will prepare all those things which are useful for war. 6. The enemy, eager for glory, has come all the way up to our camp. 7. The leaders are treating among themselves in council about all the things which pertain to the safety of the soldiers. 8. Soldiers are easily aroused to effort by means of rewards. 9. At dawn they arrived at the territory of the enemy. 10. The river was wide there, but a bridge stretched to the city which the lieutenant was holding. 11. The commander in chief immediately called to him all the lieutenants and soldiers. 12. He sent the military tribunes away to all the neighboring states to strengthen friendship with them by means of rewards and speeches.

Exercise 269.—1. Ad flūmen quod lātum et altum erat pervēnērunt. 2. Ad flūmen ācriter pugnātum est. 3. Ad Caesarem contendērunt ut eum adjuvārent. 4. Pugnāvēruntne Rōmānī usque ad noctem? 5. Suntne mīlitēs parātī ad proelium? 6. Gladiī et arma ūtilia ad bellum sunt. 7. Omnia quae ad iter pertinuērunt comparāvērunt. 8. In ponte quī ad Rōmam pertinēbat mīlitēs collocāvērunt. 9. Ad flūmen contendērunt ut pontem dēfenderent. 10. Legiōnēs integrae ā lēgātō in Gallōs missae sunt. 11. Ad collem contendērunt atque vallō et fossā eum mūnīvērunt nē hostēs eum occupārent.

Box, page 257.—Ever ready (Always prepared).

Exercise 270.—1. Rōmānīs arma trādidērunt. 2. Ad Rōmānōs contendērunt. 3. Rōmānīs obsidēs dedērunt. 4. Ad exercitum frūmentum portāvērunt. 5. Ad sē lēgātōs vocāvit. 6. Ad omnēs gentēs fīnitimās lēgātōs mīsit.

Exercise 271.—1. *Cum* with the ablative is used to express accompaniment or association. (No. 772) 2. *Ā* or *ab* with the ablative is used to express the living agent. 3. Secondary tenses: imperfect, perfect, and pluperfect. 4. *Sānctī* is an adjective used as a noun, subject of *laudant*.

Box, page 259.—(One) Injustice does not excuse (another) injustice.

Exercise 272.—1. The enemy sent a slave into Caesar's camp to learn his plans. 2. The leader led into the battle line soldiers (who were) ready for everything, in order that they might withstand the forces of the enemy. 3. I will send a messenger to you to treat with you about the wrongs. 4. The leader immediately sent soldiers to the hill to fortify it with a rampart and a ditch. 5. Did the king send a messenger to Caesar to beg help? 6. He sent the cavalry to the river to learn the nature of the place. 7. On account of wrongs (Because of injuries received) he sent a lieutenant to kill the hostages.

Box, page 260.—"But I thank God who has given us victory through our Lord Jesus Christ."—The voice of Saint Paul.

Exercise 273.—1. In castra Caesaris lēgātōs statim mīsērunt quī pācem peterent. 2. Nuntius ad Caesarem missus est quī auxilium peteret. 3. Prō portā mīlitēs collocāvit quī parātī ad omnia erant. 4. In ponte mīlitēs collocātī sunt quī eum dēfenderent. 5. Prīnceps vēnit ut frūmentum peteret. 6. Vallō castra mūnīvit nē hostēs ea expugnārent. 7. In Italiam lēgātum mīsit quī in Galliam legiōnēs novās dēdūceret.

Exercise 274.—1. *Ā* or *ab* with the ablative is used to express the living agent. 2. The ablative without a preposition is used to express the non-living agent, the means, or the instrument. 3. Secondary tenses: imperfect, perfect, pluperfect. 4. See text, 255; GRAMMAR, No. 332.

Reading No. 16.—Porsenna held the royal power (was king) of the Etruscans. He was a brave man, and eager for power and glory. And so he strove with the Romans for the command of Italy and stormed Rome with great forces. The Romans (however) did not have a supply of grain and were violently terrified. Among the Romans, however, there was a brave man, Mucius Scaevola. The courage of the

Romans was strengthened by him. For he said to them: "I will hasten to the camp of the Etruscans and I will kill (their) King Porsenna. Thus shall I serve Rome."

And so he came safely into their camp. The Etruscans therefore led him to the King. Porsenna however (on his part) was violently moved by the danger. And so he said to Mucius: "You have come to me in order to kill me. You have sought my life. You have not done this without help and counsel. If you shall have advised me about your plans (If you reveal your plan to me), I will spare your life and send you away."

Mucius (however) said to the King: "All Romans are ready for death. They will not be moved by the danger of death. Many will be sent into the camp to you in order to kill you. We shall not save our life, (perhaps), but we shall save our state (country). For I am neither terrified by you nor shall I be terrified by the fear of death."

Now there was before the King a fire. Then Mucius, in order that the King should (might) learn what Roman courage was, at once (without hesitation) thrust his right hand into the fire, but was not overcome by the pain. But Porsenna was deeply moved by the courage of Mucius and so he both spared his life and praised his courage. He also sent him away to the camp of the Romans. After this the King sent envoys to the Roman commander to seek peace. Thus the Roman state was saved by the courage of Mucius.

Exercise 275.—1. The lieutenant immediately stationed guards at the river in order that they might more easily defend the bridge. 2. The Roman leaders were ravaging the fields of the Gauls lest they wage war longer. 3. Caesar often called upon the centurions and military tribunes to fight longer. 4. The general sent help into the first battle line in order that the soldiers might longer and more easily repulse the enemy. 5. The cavalry approached the wall; the soldiers, however, approached the gate.

Exercise 276.—1. Custōdēs occīdērunt quō facilius ad castra appropinquārent. 2. Obsidēs occīdērunt nē diūtius hostēs pugnārent. 3. In oppidum hostēs ēgērunt quō facilius agrōs vastārent. 4. Lēgātus mīlitibus praemia dedit quō diūtius pugnārent. 5. In ponte custōdēs collocāvērunt quō facilius eum dēfenderent. 6. Vallō et fossā hīberna mūnīvērunt quō facilius hostēs pellerent.

Exercise 277.—1. Glōriae, gen. sing. of glōria, ae; gen. with cupidī. Cupidī, nom. pl. masc. of cupidus, a, um; predicate adjective agreeing with rēgēs. 2. The ablative without a preposition is used to express the non-living agent, the means, or the instrument.

Box, page 265.—He conquered by means of arms, but he is conquered by (his own) vices.

Reading No. 17.—The enemy approaches. They draw near to our winter quarters. They are approaching swiftly all the way up to the gates. You hear the shouting of both the enemy and of our men. Chiefs and leaders, brave men, are also approaching with them. I see their King too! They are killing our guards at once with swords and they are killing with darts those who are on the wall, in order to storm the winter quarters more easily. Our men are being called to arms at once. (The voices of the centurions are heard through the radio.) The military tribunes are filling the walls with men. The cavalry is being sent swiftly through the gates. They are fighting bitterly with the Gauls! (Suddenly a great shout is heard.) The King . . . The enemy's King has been killed by darts! Now the enemy is being routed! They are yielding! They seek the woods! But our lieutenant, a good and brave man, now sends the cavalry to kill them all. Fortune always aids the Roman legions.

Exercise 278.—1. A loud shout. 2. Hard toil. 3. A loud voice. 4. Great slaughter. 5. Extreme scarcity. 6. A large forest. 7. An extensive number. 8. A bright light.

UNIT SEVEN

Exercise 279.—1. Where were you? 2. To what place are you hastening? 3. From what place have you come? 4. Why did Caesar wage war with the Gauls? 5. Where was the lieutenant sent by the Senate? 6. Why are Christians ready both for efforts (hardships) and for death? 7. Why did the Gauls often exchange hostages? 8. Why shall we always remember our fathers' victories? 9. Why do we Americans strengthen (cultivate) friendship with all nations? 10. Why do we thank God? 11. Why have the Romans fortified the winter quarters with a rampart and a ditch?

Exercise 280.—2. Flūmen Tiberis est in Italiā. 3. Alpēs sunt in Italiā. 4. Prōvincia cūjus imperium Caesar obtinēbat erat trāns Alpēs. 5. Gallī erant in Galliā. 6. Caesar, imperātor Rōmānus, cum Gallīs in agrīs eōrum bellum gessit. 7. Caesar in prōvinciam ā senātū missus est.

Box, page 268.—Through mighty toil we shall come to rich rewards.

Exercise 281.—1. Ubi custōdēs erant? 2. Unde cōpiās novās dūxistī? 3. Unde contendistī? 4. Quō lēgātus legiōnēs dūcet? 5. Quō contendēs?

6. Quō lēgātōs mittis? 7. Cūr hostibus cessistī? 8. Cūr Rōmānī fossā et vallō castra mūnīvērunt!

Exercise 282.—Purpose clauses are introduced by *ut* (negative *nē*); require the subjunctive; require the present subjunctive when the main verb is primary, the imperfect subjunctive when the main verb is secondary.

Exercise 283.—1. Are you well? Valeō. 2. Soldiers do not fight bravely without certain hope, do they? Mīlitēs sine certā spē fortiter nōn pugnant. 3. Did not the Roman legions conquer the barbarians easily? Legiōnēs Rōmānae barbarōs facile superāvērunt. 4. Men who are brave are very strong in the presence of barbarians, are they not? Virī quī fortēs sunt apud barbarōs plūrimum valent. 5. A sure and brave friend is not easily distinguished, is he? Amīcus certus et fortis nōn facile cernitur. 6. Is not a brave man easily distinguished in danger of death? Vir fortis in mortis perīculō facile cernitur. 7. You will praise the victories of the Roman legions, won't you? Victōriās legiōnum Rōmānārum laudābō. 8. Columbus did not reach new lands without a mighty effort, did he? Columbus nōn sine magnō labōre ad terrās novās pervēnit. 9. Have you seen Rome? Will you come to Italy to see it? Rōmam nōn vīdī. Veniam in Italiam ut eam videam. 10. Shall we not fight eagerly to defend our state? Ācriter pugnābimus ut cīvitātem nostram dēfendāmus. 11. Caesar will be very influential among the Romans, won't he? Caesar plūrimum apud Rōmānōs valēbit. 12. Generals are not very influential among Americans, are they? Imperātōrēs apud Americānōs plūrimum nōn valent. 13. Are not friends very influential among friends? Amīcī apud amīcōs plūrimum valent.

Exercise 284.—1. Valēbatne prīnceps apud Rōmānōs propter fidem ējus? 2. Num Rōmānīs arma trādētis? 3. Nōnne nostrum populum līberum dēfendētis? 4. Lēgātus, "Vidētis," inquit, "aciem barbarōrum. Parātī et ad mortem et ad victōriam sunt. Num eōs timētis, mīlitēs? Nōnne fortēs estis? Nōnne Rōmānī estis? Pugnābitisne fortiter prō nōmine Rōmānō? Nōnne cum spē certā victōriae pugnātis? Nōnne equitēs parātī ad proelium sunt? Nōnne magnam cōpiam armōrum et tēlōrum habēmus? Quid timētis? Timētisne mortem? Hominēs autem glōriae cupidī semper parātī sunt aut ad mortem aut ad victōriam. Rōmānī sumus; eī barbarī et Gallī sunt. Num barbarī legiōnem Rōmānam vincent? Nōnne Caesar imperātor noster est? Nōnne barbarī etiam Caesarem laudant, nōnne eum timent? Pugnābunt sine spē certā victōriae. Impetum vestrum nōn sustinēbunt. Cēdent. Pellentur. Victōria vestra erit glōria Senātūs Populīque Rōmānī.

Exercise 285.—1. Purpose clauses are introduced by *ut* (negative *nē*); require the subjunctive; require the present subjunctive when the main verb is primary, the imperfect subjunctive when the main verb is secondary. 2. A pronoun agrees with the word to which it refers in gender and number; its case depends on its use in its own clause.

Box, page 272.—A true friend is (easily) discerned in a dubious affair (when difficulties occur).

Exercise 286.—1. With whom did Caesar fight? 2. To whom did the Gauls give hostages? 3. Who were Caesar's allies? 4. The legion did not show itself to the barbarians in order that it might arrive at the camp secretly. 5. Who now has very much influence among Americans? 6. Who led the army across the river? 7. Who led an army across high mountains and deep rivers in order to wage war with the Romans in Italy? 8. Who has given us a holy law and the light of truth? 9. To whom have you showed our camp?

Picture caption, page 273.—Washington leads the (his) army across the river.

Exercise 287.—1. Cui (quibus) praemia dedistī (dedistis)? 2. Quōcum (quibuscum) erās (erātis)? 3. Quem (quōs) vīdistī (vīdistis)? 4. Cūjus (quōrum) virtūtem laudās (laudātis)? 5. Quid petis (petitis)? 6. Quae audīvistī (audīvistis)? 7. Quid tibi (vōbīs) ostendit? 8. Quis in castra clam vēnit? or Quī . . . vēnērunt? 9. Quī sunt sociī vestrī (tuī)? 10. Ad quid parātus es (parātī estis)? 11. Ad quem (quōs) auxilium mīsistī (mīsistis)?

Exercise 288.—Washingtonius, vir fortis et nōbilis cūjus virtūtem nōs omnēs memoriā tenēmus, imperātor Americānus in prīmō bellō nostrō erat. Cōpiās trāns flūmen Delawarēnse trādūxit ut Germānōs quī in exercitū Britannicō erant vinceret. Nox erat. Mīlitēs ab hostibus neque cernēbantur neque audiēbantur. Ita celeriter et facile hostēs vīcit. Nōnne omnēs cōnsilium Washingtoniī et virtūtem ējus laudābimus?

Answers, page 274.—1. Washingtonius imperātor Americānus erat. 2. Omnēs Americānī eum laudant. 3. Cum exercitū Britannicō bellum gessit. 4. Mīlitēs ējus ab hostibus nōn cernēbantur. 5. Washingtonius Germānōs quī in exercitū Britannicō erant vīcit.

Exercise 289.—1. A pronoun agrees with the word to which it refers in gender and number; its case depends on its use in its own clause. 2. *Quō* is used to introduce a purpose clause when the clause contains a comparative. 3. The ablative without a preposition is used to express the non-living agent, the means, or the instrument.

Exercise 290.—1. Quibuscum sociīs? 2. Cum exercitū cūjus rēgis? 3. Propter quās injūriās? 4. In quibus oppidīs? 5. In quibus castrīs? 6. Apud quās gentēs? 7. Ad quod flūmen? 8. Quō nōmine tē appellāvērunt? 9. Quōs custōdēs collocāvit? 10. Quis vir Caesarem rēgem appellāvit? 11. (In) Quō locō castra posuit? 12. Cui nuntiō litterās dedit? 13. Ad quōs lēgātōs litterās mīsit? 14. Chrīstus nōs frātrēs appellāvit. 15. Ad quid sunt arma ūtilia? 16. Ad quod oppidum (Cui oppidō) appropinquāmus? 17. Quae flūmina sunt lāta et alta? 18. Quae gentēs obsidēs inter sē dant? 19. Ad quod oppidum pōns pertinet? 20. Cui custōdī sē ostendit? 21. Cui rēgī grātiās agunt? 22. In quā rē spem pōnunt?

Exercise 291.—1. On account of what wrongs did we wage war with the Japanese? 2. What messenger whom we all remember hastened through the towns in order that everyone might expect the arrival (be warned of the approach) of the British? 3. What American general led the army across the river which we call the Delaware in order to arrive secretly at the enemy's camp? 4. What nation have we Americans thanked for help which it sent us in our first war? 5. What leader led our forces into Bataan in order to fight longer with the Japanese? 6. In what war did the enemy burn the city of Washington? 7. What leader did the (his) soldiers call "Stonewall"? 8. What Frenchmen first saw the river which we call the Mississippi?

Exercise 292.—1. Augustus was the first Roman emperor. But Augustus did not call himself king, but chief, for the Romans feared the name of king. 2. All Americans called Washington the Father of His Country. For Washington defended and preserved our state as fathers defend and preserve their sons. 3. The king and emperor of the Germans called himself kaiser.

Answers, page 277.—1. Augustus nōmine prīncipis sē vocāvit. 2. Americānī Washingtonium Patrem Patriae appellāvērunt. 3. Rēx Germānōrum sē Caesarem appellāvit.

Reading No. 18.—LIEUTENANT. Who are you? Whence have you come?

GAUL. I do not know.

L. Ha! You do not know! You are a Gaul, aren't you?

G. I do not know.

L. Where are your forces? Who are your allies?

G. I do not know.

L. You shall be led to death! You are not ready for death, are you?

G. Yes, I am ready for death. I will not show you what you are seeking.

L. You will withstand (endure) it for a long time, for you are ready for death.

G. Oh, oh, . . .

L. What? Surely you are not afraid? You are brave, aren't you? Ready for death, aren't you? So now you will be led to death.

G. Oh, no, no!

L. What is this? You do not know now, do you?

G. I know.

L. Who is most influential among your peoples? Whom do you call chief and leader?

G. Ambiorix and Catuvulcus.

L. Who are allies of your tribes?

G. All the tribes of Gaul and the Germans.

L. Germans!

G. Yes! They are leading their forces across the Rhine and will swiftly arrive in our territory.

L. Where are your forces now?

G. They have pitched camp in the forest at the river.

L. They have no supply of grain, have they? We have burned all the crops which were in the fields and a great supply (of grain) has been carried into (our) winter quarters.

G. Yes, they have an abundant supply. The allies have exchanged hostages and have sent us grain. They also have a supply of arms and darts. For we stormed the Roman winter quarters which had been placed in our territory.

L. What? Surely you have not stormed the Roman winter quarters? Which camp? You have not attacked the Roman camp, have you?

G. We have. There was a bloody slaughter.

L. By the immortal gods! For (these) wrongs we will ravage your fields; we will burn the towns; kill mothers and fathers and children!

G. Our soldiers are also ready for war. You will not conquer them.

L. Why have you stormed the winter quarters? Was there not peace and friendship between your tribes and the Roman people?

G. Yes, but we fear the Romans. They are always asking for grain; they seek arms, slaves, hostages. They are always eager for power and for war. We defend our lives and our free states.

L. Because you have not kept faith with the Roman people, you shall all be killed! And you will be the first to be led to death. To death at once!

Exercise 293.—1. Purpose clauses are introduced by *ut* (negative *në*); require the subjunctive; require the present subjunctive when the main verb is primary, the imperfect subjunctive when the main verb is secondary. 2. The ablative without a preposition is used to express the non-living agent, the means, or the instrument. 3. a. Ad prīmam aciem auxilium mīsit. (*Ad* with the accusative after verbs of motion means *to* or *up to.*) b. Hostibus arma trādidērunt. (*Hostibus* is the indirect object.)

Exercise 294.—See Introduction, 3.

Exercise 295.—1. 3rd sing., plu. subj. 2. 3rd sing., perf. subj. or fut. perf. ind. 3. 3rd sing., plu. subj. 4. 1st sing., perf. subj. 5. 3rd sing., plu. subj. 6. 3rd sing., perf. subj. or fut. perf. ind. 7. 3rd pl., perf. subj. or fut. perf. ind. 8. 3rd pl., perf. subj. or fut. perf. ind. 9. 3rd pl., plu. subj. 10. 3rd sing., perf. subj. or fut. perf. ind. 11. 3rd sing., plu. subj. 12. 3rd sing., plu. subj. 13. 3rd sing., plu. subj. 14. 3rd pl., plu. subj. 15. 3rd sing., plu. subj. 16. 3rd pl., perf. subj. or fut. perf. ind. 17. 2nd sing., plu. subj. 18. 2nd sing., perf. subj. 19. 2nd pl., perf. subj. 20. 3rd pl., plu. subj. 21. 3rd sing., perf. subj. or fut. perf. ind. 22. 3rd pl., plu. subj. 23. 1st sing., plu. subj. 24. 1st pl., plu. subj.

Box, page 283.—Water of life.

Exercise 296.—1. He asks whether we have a supply of water. (a) Num . . . habeāmus; (b) num; (c) present subjunctive; action at same time as main verb in primary tense. (The mood in indirect questions is always subjunctive.) 2. He asks whether Caesar conquered the Gauls. (a) Num . . . vīcerit; (b) num; (c) perfect subjunctive; action completed before time of main verb in primary tense. 3. He will ask where the enemy has taken up a position. (a) Ubi . . . cōnstiterint; (b) ubi; (c) perfect subjunctive; action completed before time of main verb in primary tense. 4. He will ask where the supply of water is. (a) Ubi . . . sit; (b) ubi; (c) present subjunctive; action at same time as main verb in primary tense. 5. He asks who the general is. (a) Quis . . . sit; (b) quis; (c) present subjunctive; action at same time as main verb in primary tense. 6. He asks whom Caesar conquered. (a) Quōs . . . vīcerit; (b) quōs; (c) perfect subjunctive; action completed before time of main verb in primary tense. 7. He will ask whether the soldiers are strong. (a) Valeantne mīlitēs; (b) -ne; (c) present subjunctive; action at same time as main verb in primary tense. 8. He will ask whether Caesar conquered the barbarians. (a) Vīceritne Caesar barbarōs; (b) -ne; (c) perfect subjunctive; action completed before time of main verb in primary tense. 9. He asks what races of men dwell in America. (a) Quae . . . incolant; (b) quae; (c) pres-

ent subjunctive; action at same time as main verb in primary tense.
10. He asks what races of men dwelt in Gaul at that time. (a) Quae . . .
incoluerint; (b) quae; (c) perfect subjunctive; action completed before time of main verb in primary tense. 11. He will ask how great the
fortifications (are that) the enemy has prepared. (a) Quantās . . .
parāverint; (b) quantās; (c) perfect subjunctive; action completed
before time of main verb in primary tense. 12. He will ask what kind
of fortifications we are preparing. (a) Quae . . . parēmus; (b) quae;
(c) present subjunctive; action at same time as main verb in primary
tense. 13. He asks what nations dwell in Gaul.[1] (a) Quae . . . incolant;
(b) quae; (c) present subjunctive; action at same time as main verb
in primary tense. 14. He asks what tribes dwelt in the province.
(a) Quae . . . incoluerint; (b) quae; (c) perfect subjunctive; action
completed before time of main verb.

Exercise 297.—A. 1. Rogō quōs obsidēs occīderit. 2. Rogō quem
imperātōrem laudāverit. 3. Rogō quae cōnsilia cognōverit. 4. Rogō quōs
collēs obtinuerit. **B.** 1. Rogō ubi imperātor sit. 2. Rogō ubi hostēs sint.
3. Rogō ubi mūnītiōnēs sint. 4. Rogō ubi hīberna sint.

Exercise 298.—1. a. Ad senātum litterās mīsērunt. (*Ad* with the
accusative after verbs of motion means *to* or *up to*.) b. Servō praemia
dedērunt. (*Servō*, dative of indirect object.) 2. A pronoun agrees with
the word to which it refers, in gender and number; its case depends on
its use in its own clause. (See No. 479.) 3. They fought at the river
for a long time. (*Ad* with the accusative sometimes means *at*. *Pugnātum est* is an idiomatic expression; 3rd sing., perfect indicative passive,
with participle in neuter form; used impersonally. See No. 332.)
4. Purpose clauses are introduced by *ut* (negative *nē*); require the subjunctive; require the present subjunctive when the main verb is primary, the imperfect subjunctive when the main verb is secondary. (See
No. 546.)

Reading No. 19.—Before a battle the general calls the lieutenants
and military tribunes into council. In the council he asks how large a
number of cavalry and soldiers the enemy has, where the enemy's camp
is, how large the fortifications they have prepared; whether they have a
supply of water and of grain; how large a supply of arms they have. He
asks also what harbors, rivers, and mountains there are in the enemy's
territory; what races of men dwell in those parts; whether they have
prepared all the things which pertain to war; whether they are brave

---

[1] In earlier impressions *those places (ea loca).*

and eager for the glory of war; whether they fight eagerly; what leaders they have and whether they are good. Before the battles a general sends horsemen to study the terrain and to find out where the enemy has taken up a position. He finds out whether a battle line had been drawn up; whether they are ready for battle.

Thus Caesar and all great leaders have often conquered the enemy because they had found out everything that pertains to battle (had acquired all the necessary military information).

Exercise 299.—1. The lieutenant asked how great a supply of water the soldiers had. (*Habērent*, imperfect subjunctive; action at same time as main verb.) 2. The lieutenant asked where the enemy had taken up a position. (*Cōnstitissent*, pluperfect subjunctive; action completed before time of main verb.) 3. The barbarians asked how large a force of soldiers the Romans had collected. (*Coēgissent*, pluperfect subjunctive; action completed before time of ma.n verb.) 4. The barbarians asked where the Romans had pitched camp. (*Posuissent*, pluperfect subjunctive; action completed before time of main verb.) 5. He had asked what the nature of the mountain was (asked for a description of the mountain). (*Esset*, imperfect subjunctive; action at same time as main verb.) 6. He had asked how large a number of hostages the lieutenant had collected. (*Coēgisset*, pluperfect subjunctive; action completed before time of main verb.) 7. He was asking what harbors there were in those places. (*Essent*, imperfect subjunctive; action at same time as main verb.) 8. They were asking whether the enemy had seized the hills. (*Occupāvissent*, pluperfect subjunctive; action completed before time of main verb.) 9. "I ask," the Roman said, "whether our god is the true God." (*Sit*, present subjunctive; action at same time as main verb in primary tense.)

Exercise 300.—A. 1. Tribūnus mīlitum quaerēbat num cōpia aquae in hībernīs esset. 2. Lēgātus quaerēbat num pōns in flūmine esset. 3. Barbarī quaerēbant num mīlitēs in silvīs essent. B. 1. Dux quaesīvit ubi hostēs custōdēs collocāvissent. 2. Caesar quaesīvit ubi Gallī mūnītiōnēs comparāvissent. 3. Barbarī quaesīvērunt ubi Caesar cōpiās īnstrūxisset.

Exercise 301.—1. The envoy said, "I ask who your allies are." (*Inquit*, only form given thus far of *inquam*, a defective verb; 3rd sing., present and perfect; used in direct quotations and always put after one or several words of the quotation. See Nos. 452-455. *Quī*, nom. pl. masc. of *quis, quis, quid*, interrogative pronoun; introducing an indirect question; subject of *sint*. *Sint*, 3rd pl., present subjunctive of *sum, esse, fuī, futūrus*, intr.; in indirect questions, action at same time as main verb in primary tense.) 2. The military tribune asked what races of men dwelt in the places. (*Incolerent*, 3rd pl., imperfect subjunctive of *incolō, incolere, incoluī*, 3, tr.; in indirect question, action at same time as main verb in secondary tense.) 3. The Romans prepared immense fortifications in order to repel the enemy more easily. (*Quō*, adverb used to introduce clause containing a comparative; equivalent to *ut eō*.) 4. The barbarians made an attack against the column in order that the soldiers might not preserve fixed rank. (*Servārent*, 3rd pl., imperfect subjunctive of *servō, servāre, servāvī, servātus*, 1, tr.; in negative purpose clause after secondary tense.) 5. I ask whether Caesar was very influential among the Romans. (*Plūrimum*, an adverb (superlative of *multum*); modifies *valuerit*. Although the comparison of adverbs is not taught, *plūrimum* is in the vocabulary on page 269.) 6. He asks whether a true and sure friend is easily distinguished. (*Cernātur*, 3rd sing., present subjunctive passive of *cernō, cernere*, 3, tr.; in indirect question after primary tense, action at same time as main verb.) 7. Do not Christians call Christ (by the name of) king? (*Nōmine*, abl. sing. of *nōmen, nōminis*, n.; idiomatic use with *appellant*.) 8. I ask whether you call Christ king and Lord. (*Dominum*, acc. sing. of *dominus, ī*, m.; predicate accusative with verb of naming.) 9. He asked where the chiefs had assembled. (*Convēnissent*, 3rd pl., pluperfect subjunctive of *conveniō, convenīre, convēnī, conventum*, 4, intr.; in indirect question after secondary tense, action completed before time of main verb.) 10. They fought long and bitterly in a narrow and difficult place in order that the enemy might not lead a column across the river. (*Pugnātum est* is an idiomatic expression; 3rd sing., perfect indicative passive of *pugnō, pugnāre, pugnāvī, pugnātus*, 1, tr.; with participle in neuter form; used impersonally. See No. 332. *Flūmen*, acc. sing. of *flūmen, flūminis*, n.; accusative of the thing over which the direct object is led, with *trādūcerent*.) 11. He sent a lieutenant to lead the hostages away secretly into the camp. (*Dēdūceret*, 3rd sing., imperfect subjunctive of *dēdūcō, dēdūcere, dēdūxī, dēductus*, 3, tr.; in relative purpose clause after a secondary tense.) 12. The leader asked how large a supply of water and grain the slaves had carried into the winter quarters. (*Portāvissent*, 3rd pl., pluperfect subjunctive of *portō, portāre, portāvī, portātus*, 1, tr.; in indirect question after a secondary tense, action completed before time of main verb.) 13. The horseman showed the leader where the enemy's forces had taken up a position. (*Ducī*, dat. sing. of *dux, ducis*, m.; dative of indirect object.) 14. To what place did the chiefs force the troops? (*Quō*, interrogative adverb implying motion or direction and referring to place to which; modifies *coēgērunt.*) 15. They killed the guards and came all the way up to our camp. (*Ad*, preposition governing the accusative *castra*, used with verbs of motion to express *to* or *up to.*) 16. The Romans fortified the hill by means of a rampart and a ditch in order to withstand the enemy's forces longer. (*Vallō*, abl. sing. of *vallum*, *ī*, n.; ablative of means. *Sustinērent*, 3rd pl., imperfect subjunctive of *sustineō, sustinēre, sustinuī, sustentus*, 2, tr.; in purpose clause introduced by *quō* with a comparative; after a secondary tense.) 17. He asks why the barbarian tribes exchanged hostages. (*Dederint*, 3rd pl., perfect subjunctive of *dō, dare, dedī, datus*, 1, tr.; in indirect question after primary tense, action completed before time of main verb.) 18. The leader sent a horseman swiftly to seek help. (*Peteret*, 3rd sing., imperfect subjunctive of *petō, petere, petīvī, petītus*, 3, tr.; in relative purpose clause after a secondary tense.) 19. The general asked whether the military tribunes had prepared everything. 20. He asks from what place the cavalry has hastened. (*Contenderit*, 3rd sing., perfect subjunctive of *contendō, contendere, contendī*, 3, intr.; in indirect question after a primary tense, action completed before time of main verb.)

Exercise 302.—1. Rogāvī ubi hostēs essent. 2. Quaesīvērunt num prīnceps barbarōs trāns flūmen trādūxisset. 3. Rogāvērunt quem rēgem et imperātōrem appellārēmus. 4. Rogāvimus quis imperātor apud eōs valēret. 5. Quaesīvimus ubi barbarī cōnstitissent. 6. Quaerunt quae genera hominum Galliam nunc incolant. 7. Quaerimus quae genera armōrum habeant. 8. Lēgātus quaesīvit quantās mūnītiōnēs comparāvissent. 9. Rogāvimus cūr sine spē certā pugnārent. 10. Quaesīvimus quō sociōs dūxissent. 11. Quaesīvit unde vēnissent. 12. In locum tūtum obsidēs clam coēgerant. 13. Quaesīvit num agmen hostium vīdissent. 14. "Nōnne amīcus," inquit, "fortis et certus es?" 15. Centuriōnēs nōmine appellāvit quō diūtius pugnārent. 16. Quaesīvit ubi cōpia aquae esset.

Exercise 303.—1. Direct questions are introduced by (1) interrogative pronouns, adjectives, and adverbs; (2) *nōnne* if the answer yes is expected; (3) *num* if the answer no is expected or to express surprise; (4) -*ne* to ask for information. The indicative mood is used. (See No. 503.) 2. *Ubi* can be used only when "where" refers to place in which and implies rest; *quō* can be used only when "where" refers to place to which and implies motion or direction. 3. -*Ne* is used to ask for information; *num* when the answer no is expected or to express surprise;

nōnne when the answer yes is expected. For example: Vīdistīne Rōmam? Num Caesar victus est? Nōnne Deus est bonus? Caesar wasn't
conquered, was he? Surely Caesar wasn't conquered? God is good, isn't
He? Is not God good? 4. See No. 140. It is a pronoun because it stands
in place of a noun. 5. See No. 141. 6. *Quis* is used as an adjective for
which or *what* in the nominative masculine singular. (See text, p. 274.)
7. The adjective *quī* is used to express *what sort of, what kind of.* (See
text, p. 274.) It is also used sometimes for *quis* in indirect questions.
(See text, p. 282.) 8. With verbs of transporting the thing over which
the direct object is led is put in the accusative without a preposition or
with *trāns.* (See text, p. 272.) 9. Verbs of calling, naming, making, show-
ing, etc., may take two accusatives, one of the direct object, the other a
predicate accusative. When *nōmen* is used, *nōmen* is in the ablative.
(See text, p. 275.) 10. See Nos. 200-207. The perfect active stem is
used. 11. Indirect questions are those which depend on a verb of asking,
saying, thinking, and the like. 12. The mood in indirect questions is
always subjunctive. They are introduced by the same interrogative pronouns (except that *quī* is sometimes used for *quis*), adjectives, and
adverbs as direct questions; by *-ne* and *num* (meaning *whether, if*);
occasionally by *nōnne.* 13. See answer 12. 14. *Quī* is sometimes used for
quis. (See text, p. 282.) 15. See Nos. 525-541 and text, pp. 282, 286.
16. *Inquit* means *he says* or *he said;* it is used in direct quotations and
is placed after the first word or words of the quotation. 17. Examples
of the four tenses will be found in sentences 1 and 2 of Exercise 296
and sentences 1 and 2 of Exercise 299.

Reading No. 20.—You all knew how great were the forces which
our soldiers withstood for a long time in Bataan. For the Japanese made
a violent and courageous attack against the Philippine Islands. They
had all the kinds of arms and darts which are now useful for war. They
had also led a large number of all types of soldiers into the islands.
They had investigated what harbors there were, what the terrain was
like, and what rivers there were. They had learned everything which
pertained to war. And so our leader, a great and brave man, led our
forces into difficult and narrow places known as Bataan so that he
might hold out longer against the attack of the enemy. He quickly
prepared fortifications, stationed guards, drew up the soldiers; (then)
he awaited the enemy's attacks. On all sides our men were held in by
the enemy and by the nature of the place, and moreover there were not
many American soldiers on Bataan. Nevertheless the battle was fought
there long and bitterly. For our men were valiant and eager for the

glory of the American name. They withstood many attacks bravely; they often drove the enemy back after bloody slaughter.

Meanwhile we knew in what awful peril our battalions were and we were asking why our leaders did not send a large supply of weapons and a large force of soldiers. Nevertheless they had known all the dangers and so they did not send auxiliary troops (reinforcements) lest the enemy kill them.

Finally our men, because of the great number of the enemy, no longer withstood. And so they surrendered to the enemy and handed over (their) arms, But our leader said . . .

Shall we not always praise the courage of our brave soldiers and remember it? For their glory is our glory.

UNIT EIGHT

Exercise 304.—1. Dux, ducēs. 2. Lēgāte, lēgātī. 3. Nuntie, nuntiī. 4. Custōs, custōdēs. 5. Spīritus. 6. Barbare, barbarī. 7. Socie, sociī. 8. Marīa. 9. Jēsū. 10. Centuriō, centuriōnēs. 11. Amīce, amīcī. 12. Eques, equitēs. 13. Chrīste. 14. Frāter, frātrēs. 15. Chrīstiāne, Chrīstiānī. 16. Mīles, mīlitēs. 17. Rōmāne, Rōmānī. 18. Tribūne mīlitum, tribūnī mīlitum. 19. Vir, virī. 20. Homō, hominēs. 21. Domine, dominī. 22. Fīlī, fīliī. 23. Māter, mātrēs. 24. Puer, puerī. 25. Galle, Gallī. 26. Senātus, senātūs. 27. Rēx magne, rēgēs magnī. 28. Amīce bone, amīcī bonī. 29. Frāter mī, frātrēs meī. 30. Domine nōbilis, dominī nōbilēs. 31. Vir līber, virī līberī. 32. Mīles fortis, mīlitēs fortēs. 33. Fīlī mī, fīliī meī.

Exercise 305.—1. Shall we not give thanks, my brothers, to our Lord Jesus Christ, who has taken away the sins of the world and has taught us the truth? 2. Hail, Caesar! I will teach (show) you where the enemy has pitched camp. 3. You, soldiers, will seize the bridge without delay lest the barbarians seize it. 4. We praise Thee, Son of God. 5. The centurion said, "Lieutenant, the enemy has raised a great shout and given themselves up to us without delay." 6. Everyone's hope is in Thee, O good Jesus. 7. O great king, we have conquered the enemy by courage and arms. 8. To Thee, O God, I give thanks; I praise Thee, God; in Thee, O God, is all my hope. 9. Thou, O Lord, wilt save us. 10. Hail, Caesar; you are our emperor and king! 11. Hail, Jesus Christ, who for us endured many labors and a wretched death!

Exercise 306.—1. In Tē, Ō bone Jēsū, omnem spem et fidem nostram pōnimus. 2. Tū, Deus, nōs viās tuās docuistī. 3. Deus, fīlī mī, tē semper dēfendet. 4. Sine morā, mīlitēs, pontēs et collēs occupābimus.

5. Vēnimus, Ō rēx nōbilis, ut pācem peterēmus. 6. Avē, Marīa! 7. Hostēs undique clamōrem sustulērunt ut nōs terrērent. 8. Avē, Caesar! Tibi omnēs grātiās agimus, nam vītās nostrās cōnservāvistī. 9. Undique ab hostibus, mīlitēs, continēmur quī victōriae et glōriae cupidī sunt. 10. Docēbō tē, imperātor, ubi hostēs castra posuerint ut ea oppugnēs.

Exercise 307.—1. In direct questions -*ne* is used to ask information; *num* when the answer no is expected or to express surprise; *nōnne* when the answer yes is expected. (See No. 503.) In indirect questions -*ne* and *num* mean *whether* and *if; nōnne* is seldom used. (See text, p. 282.) 2. *Ubi* can be used only when *where* refers to place in which and implies rest; *quō* can be used only when *where* refers to place to which and implies motion or direction. (See text, p. 268.)

Exercise 308.—1. Laudāte Deum, Chrīstiānī! 2. Adjuvā (adjuvāte) me! 3. Obtinēte collem, mīlitēs! 4. Parāte frūmentum, servī! 5. Trādite arma vestra. 6. Terrēte mīlitēs. 7. Bellum gere, Ō rēx. 8. Tolle peccāta nostra. 9. Oppugnāte oppidum. 10. Timē (timēte) Deum. 11. Pete (petite) auxilium. 12. Portā, serve, gladium. 13. Audī (audīte) ducem. 14. Dīmitte (dīmittite) prīncipēs. 15. Appellā (appellāte) Deum. 16. Exspectā (exspectāte) auxilium.

Moments at Mass No. 2.—Behold the Lamb of God, behold Him who taketh away the sins of the world.

Exercise 309.—1. Rule our minds, Lord, that we may hasten toward heaven. 2. Take away our sins, Lord, take away our sorrows. 3. Draw up the soldiers before the gate, lieutenant, but send the cavalry into the forest. 4. O God, you who rule the whole world, rule my mind and my body too. 5. Jesus, you who have endured heavy sorrows for us, have mercy on us! 6. Help us, Lord, lest the enemy overcome us. 7. Lieutenants, defend our fields. 8. Show us, slave, where the enemy is. 9. Holy Mary, pray for us. 10. Christians, adore your God. 11. Teach me Thy ways, Lord, that I may always have Thy grace. 12. Fear God, ye Christians, the King of heaven and earth. 13. Lieutenant, call the soldiers to arms. 14. Station fresh legions in the first battle line to drive back the cavalry. 15. Slave, carry (the) grain into the camp lest there be a scarcity. 16. Burn the towns, seize the cities, rout the cavalry, kill the soldiers, but spare the lives of the chiefs. 17. Thank God, my brothers. 18. But Christ says to us, "Have peace among you." 19. Fear the Lord, all ye His saints. 20. Christ said, "Give, and it shall be given unto you." 21. Christ said, "Ask, and it shall be given unto you." 22. Abide with us, Lord.

Box, page 293—Do what you do. (Put your heart into your work.)

Exercise 310.—1. Cognōsce, lēgāte, quod cōnsilium hostium sit. 2. Exspectāte, mīlitēs, adventum Caesaris nē hostēs nōs vincant. 3. Memoriā tenēte virtūtem pātrum nostrōrum. 4. Pervenīte, equitēs, ad pontem prīmā lūce. 5. Dēdūce, lēgāte, legiōnem. 6. Appropinquāte celeriter ad hostēs. 7. Vastāte agrōs barbarōrum, mīlitēs. Incendite frūmenta, oppugnāte oppida, occīdite obsidēs, occupāte oppida, collēs, pontēs! 8. Appellā (Appellāte) Caesarem rēgem et imperātōrem. 9. Appellā (Appellāte) nōmine centuriōnēs. 10. Valē (Valēte). 11. Ostende nōbīs, serve, ubi hostēs cusōdēs collocāverint. 12. Trādūc (No. 1020), centuriō, mīlitēs trāns flūmen et in silvās. 13. Rogā (Rogāte) lēgātum cūr vēnerit. 14. Pugnā (Pugnāte) fortiter prō rēge tuō (vestrō). 15. Docē (Docēte) nōs quantus exercitus hostium sit. 16. Tollite clāmōrem et oppugnāte urbem. 17. Rege, Ō Domine, mentem meam et vītam meam. 18. Jēsū Chrīste, miserēre nōbīs. 19. Adōrā (Adōrāte) Jēsūm Chrīstum, Fīlium Deī.

Exercise 311.—1. Caesar called upon the centurions by name. (*Centuriōnēs*, acc. pl., object of *appellāvit. Nōmine*, abl. sing., an idiomatic use with the verb *appellō*. See text, p. 275.) 2. The soldiers had called Caesar the general. (*Caesarem*, acc. sing., object of *appellāverant. Imperātōrem*, acc. sing., a predicate accusative; verbs of calling, naming, etc., may take two accusatives. See text, p. 275.)

Box, page 299.—"Come to Me." (Thus does Christ call all men unto Himself.)

Reading No. 21.—Jesus Christ, as you have learned (know), Christians, is both the Son of God and our brother. For because of us and for our salvation He came into the world. He endured hard labors and heavy sorrows for us. He also suffered for us an ignoble death. He is God, who rules the world, who made earth and heaven; yet nevertheless He was led to death for us. But through His death life and salvation have been given to us. For He came into the world to take away our wretched sins.

Shall we not praise Him, my sons, and adore Him? Shall we not thank Him? Shall we not call Him Lord and King?

O Christians, place your hope in Him lest the enemy confuse you. Keep His holy law in order that you may have God's grace. Keep faith in order that God may rule your minds and show you the way of salvation. Hold bravely and forever the truth of Christ, who is the light of the world. Pray and ask for grace in order that there may be no sin in you. Help all your brothers as our brother Christ has helped us. Withstand, brothers, withstand bravely wrongs and sorrows, that you may be like Him who bravely endured even death for us. For He came to glory through pain and death; we too shall reach glory through pain and death.

And so, Christians, hasten toward heaven that with God's saints, with Joseph and Mary, you may praise the Father, Son, and Holy Spirit forever. Amen.

Exercise 312.—1. May he come. 2. Let us fight. 3. Let us prepare arms. 4. Let us defend our children. 5. May he not conquer. 6. May he storm the city. 7. May they hold the hill. 8. Let us assemble. 9. Let us burn the crops. 10. May they conquer. 11. Let us not yield. 12. May he not kill them. 13. Let us send help. 14. May he not wait.

Exercise 313.—1. Fortiter pugnet! 2. Vincant barbarōs! 3. Deus det nōbīs praemium! 4. Vocēmus mīlitēs. 5. Ōrēmus. 6. Timeant Deum. 7. Nē teneant pontem. 8. Contendāmus ut rēgem videāmus. 9. Cōpiās hostium sustineāmus. 10. Dēfendat nōs Deus! 11. Adveniat (Veniat) rēgnum tuum! 12. In rēgnum Caelī dūcat nōs Deus! 13. Nē cēdāmus. 14. Ad eōs auxilium mittāmus. 15. Caesar vincat! 16. Pellant barbarōs! 17. Audiāmus ōrātiōnem prīncipis. 18. Sit fortis! 19. Maneat nōbīscum Chrīstus! 20. Adjuvet nōs Deus! 21. Cōnfirmet nōs Deus! 22. Cōnservet nōs Deus! 23. Nē exspectēmus adventum ējus. 24. Virtūtem ējus memoriā teneāmus. 25. Perveniat tūtus! 26. Valeant. 27. Valeās!

Exercise 314.—1. Lord, hear my prayer, and let my cry come unto Thee. 2. But may the God of peace be with you all. Amen. 3. Let us pray. 4. May the divine assistance remain always with us. 5. Come, let us adore the Lord, King of martyrs. 6. Saint Paul says, "May the Lord of peace Himself give you eternal peace in every place. May the Lord be with you all."

Exercise 315.—See Introduction, 3.

Exercise 316.—1. May he come swiftly. (*Veniat*, 3rd sing., pres. subj.; a wish.) 2. May Christ the King conquer! (*Vincat*, 3rd sing., pres. subj.; a wish.) 3. Let us be strong. (*Valeāmus*, 1st pl., pres. subj.; hortatory.) 4. May you be well. (*Valeās*, 2nd sing., pres. subj.; a wish.) 5. Let us come. (*Veniāmus*, 1st pl., pres. subj.; hortatory.) 6. Come, let us adore. (*Venīte*, pl. imperative. *Adōrēmus*, 1st pl., pres. subj.; hortatory.) 7. Let us see the child. (*Videāmus*, 1st pl., pres. subj.; hortatory.) 8. Be strong (May you enjoy good health). (*Valēte*, pl. imperative.) 9. Let us not fight. (*Pugnēmus*, 1st pl., pres. subj.; hortatory.) 10. Let us help all men. (*Adjuvēmus*, 1st pl., pres. subj.; hortatory.) 11. Let us beg God's grace. (*Petāmus*, 1st pl., pres. subj.; hortatory.) 12. Call the soldiers to arms. (*Vocāte*, pl. imperative.) 13. May Christ rule our minds. (*Regat*, 3rd sing., pres. subj.; a wish.) 14. May you be good. (*Sis*, 2nd sing., pres. subj.; a wish.)

Reading No. 22.—A Scene from the First Christmas.

CHOIR.   O come, all ye faithful,
    Joyful and triumphant,
    Come ye, O come ye to Bethlehem.
    Come and behold Him born, the king of angels,
    Come, let us adore (Him),
    Come, let us adore (Him),
    Come, let us adore (Christ) the Lord.

FOLK.   What voices de we hear?

SHEPHERDS.   You hear the voices of angels. Listen!

CHOIR.   Glory to God in the highest, and on earth peace to men of good will!

F.   Weren't you afraid?

S.   We were not afraid, for they are angels of God, and they showed us a wonderful sign.

C.   Behold Him born . . .

F.   What did they show you? Tell us! What did you see?

S.   We saw a host of angels in the heavens with a magnificent light. We saw Jesus Christ, the King of kings and Prince of peace—a child—with Mary, His Mother. We saw the glory of God's Son on earth.

F.   The Son of God! On earth! God, a man? Why did God come into the world?

S.   Christ is in the world to take away our sins, to give us life and victory, to lead us wretched men into heaven. Glory be to God! All men will place hope of salvation and peace in the name of Jesus Christ. And so let us praise His name and give thanks to God. And you, our friends and brothers, God's peace and grace be with you!

C.   Christ is born to us;
   Christ is given to us;
  Today Christ came into the world;
  Today has come the world's salvation.

Exercise 317.—1. 2nd sing., perf. ind. of *dō*. 2. 2nd sing., perf. ind. of *dēdō*. 3. 3rd pl., perf. ind. of *dēdō*. 4. 3rd pl., perf. ind. of *dō*.

Exercise 318.—1. They were defending their own fields and cities. (*Suās*, reflexive possessive adjective modifying *agrōs* and *urbēs*, and referring to the subject of its own clause.) 2. They defend themselves bravely. (*Sē*, reflexive pronoun, object of *dēfendunt*, and referring to the subject of its own clause.) 3. After Caesar's victory and the slaughter of their own chiefs, the enemy surrendered themselves and all their possessions to him. (*Suōrum*, reflexive possessive adjective modifying *prīncipum*, and referring to the subject of its own clause. *Sē*, reflexive pronoun, object of *dēdidērunt*, and referring to the subject of its own clause. *Sua*, reflexive possessive adjective used as a noun, object of *dēdidērunt*, and referring to the subject of its own clause. *Eī*, personal pronoun, dative of indirect object, and referring to *Caesaris*.) 4. The barbarians sought safety in flight after the slaughter of their cavalry. (*Suōrum*, reflexive possessive adjective modifying *equitum*, and referring to the subject of its own clause.) 5. Mothers love their sons, don't they? (*Suōs*, reflexive possessive adjective modifying *fīliōs*, and referring to the subject of its own clause.) 6. The barbarians sought the mountains by flight (fled toward the mountains), but a great number of them were killed in flight by the Roman cavalry. (*Eōrum*, personal pronoun modifying *numerus*, and referring to the subject of the preceding clause.) 7. The Gauls sent envoys to Caesar to seek help. Caesar therefore sent them cavalry to defend their territory. (*Eōrum*, personal pronoun modifying *fīnēs*, and referring to the subject of the preceding sentence.) 8. Love God, my brothers. For God will give you His peace. (*Suam*, reflexive possessive adjective modifying *pācem*, and referring to the subject of its own clause.) 9. Did Caesar praise the courage of his men? (*Suōrum*, reflexive possessive adjective modifying *virtūtem*, used as a noun, and referring to the subject of its own clause.) 10. The enemy also often fought bravely. Caesar therefore praised their courage. (*Eōrum*, personal pronoun modifying *virtūtem*, and referring to the subject of the preceding sentence.) 11. The Gauls often sent cavalry to Caesar to fight in company with his forces. (*Ējus*, personal pronoun modifying *cōpiīs*, and referring to the subject of the prepositional phrase in the preceding clause.) 12. The lieutenant sent Caesar a warning of his own danger. And so Caesar immediately led all his forces secretly and swiftly into the territory of the barbarians. (*Suō*, reflexive possessive adjective modifying *perīculō*, and referring to the subject of its own clause. *Suās*, reflexive possessive adjective modifying *cōpiās*, and referring to the subject of its own clause.)

Exercise 319.—1. Pepulēruntne saepe Rōmānī barbarōs et magnum eōrum numerum occīdērunt? 2. Gentēs Galliae obsidēs inter sē dabant ut pācem et amīcitiam inter sē cōnfīrmārent. 3. Caesar ad pontem custōdēs collocāvit quō facilius suōs dēfenderet. 4. Lēgātus servōs rogāvit ubi dominus eōrum esset. 5. Diū et ācriter pugnāvērunt quod vītās suās dēfendēbant. 6. Fossā vallōque castra mūnīvērunt quō facilius sē dēfenderent. 7. Caesar magnus imperātor erat. Rōmānī ējus victōriās atque virtūtem memoriā semper tenēbant. 8. Imperātor centuriōnēs et tribūnōs mīlitum ad sē vocāvit. 9. Urbēs et agrōs nostrōs dēfendēmus.

Box, page 308.—Christ says to us, "As the Father has loved Me, so also I have loved you."

Exercise 320.—1. The lieutenant led the army across the river. (*Exercitum*, acc. sing. of *exercitus, exercitūs*, m.; direct object of *trādūxit*. *Flūmen*, acc. sing. of *flūmen, flūminis*, n.; second accusative with *trādūxit*. See No. 748.) 2. The lieutenant led the army across the river. (*Exercitum*, acc. sing. of *exercitus, exercitūs*, m.; direct object of *trādūxit*. *Flūmen*, acc. sing. of *flūmen, flūminis*, n.; acc. after *trāns*.) 3. Let us come to adore Christ. (*Veniāmus*, 1st pl., pres. subj. of *veniō, venīre, vēnī, ventum*, 4, intr.; hortatory. *Adōrēmus*, 1st pl., pres. subj. of *adōrō, adōrāre, adōrāvī, adōrātus*, 1, tr.; in purpose clause after a primary tense.)

Reading No. 23.—Soldiers, you have learned (know) in what great danger we are. For there is a scarcity of grain and of everything (else) in our camp. We are held in on all sides by the barbarians. I point out to you how overwhelming is the number of the enemy; you yourselves can see how great their courage is. For the enemy of the Roman people is advancing all the way up to the Roman camp. Eager for victory and the glory of war, they fear neither our cavalry nor our legions. We sent a dispatch to Caesar, but the slave to whom we entrusted the dispatch was seen by the enemy and killed. And therefore we do not expect help, and we have no allies.

So what shall we do, Roman soldiers? Shall we sue for peace? Shall we send envoys to the enemy to bargain for our safety? Shall we surrender ourselves and all we have to the enemy of the Roman people?

Soldiers, put your hope in courage! Remember the heroism of our fathers! Fortify the camp! Withstand the enemy's attacks! Rout the forces of the enemy, conquer them, kill them! Fight to the death!

The Roman general (emperor) calls you to arms and to death for the glory of the Roman name!

Exercise 321.—1. The centurion sent to Caesar a slave named Titus to show him in what great danger the garrisons were. Caesar therefore immediately led his own army away and sent horsemen to inform him of his coming. (*Eum*, personal pronoun, object of *docēret*, and referring to the object of the prepositional phrase, *ad Caesarem*. *Suum*, reflexive possessive adjective modifying *exercitum*, and referring to the subject of its own clause. *Eum*, personal pronoun, object of *docērent*, and referring to the subject of the preceding sentence. *Suō,* indirect reflexive possessive adjective modifying *adventū,* in a relative purpose clause, and referring to the subject of the main clause.) 2. The Gauls in truth burned their own towns before Caesar's arrival lest he station garrisons in them. (*Sua,* reflexive possessive adjective modifying *oppida,* and referring to the subject of its own clause. *Eīs,* personal pronoun, abl. after *in,* and referring to *oppida.*) 3. Before the battle the lieutenant told him through messengers what great danger his own legion was in. (*Eum,* personal pronoun, object of *docuit,* and referring to some unnamed person. *Sua,* indirect reflexive possessive adjective modifying *legiō* in an indirect question, and referring to the subject of the main clause.) 4. The Romans built roads in order to lead their troops into the provinces more easily. (*Suās,* indirect reflexive possessive adjective modifying *cōpiās* in a purpose clause, and referring to the subject of the main clause.) 5. Caesar sent fresh legions into Gaul lest the barbarians overcome his men. (*Suōs,* indirect reflexive possessive adjective used in place of a noun (*virī* or *mīlitēs*) as object of *superārent* in a purpose clause, and referring to the subject of the main clause.) 6. The barbarians repulsed the Romans in battle lest they should lead their army through their (the barbarians') territory. (*Eī,* personal pronoun, subject of the negative purpose clause, and referring to *Rōmānōs. Suōs,* indirect reflexive possessive adjective modifying *fīnēs* in a negative purpose clause, and referring to the subject of the main clause.) 7. The Gauls sent Caesar rewards in order to have (find) favor with him. (*Eum,* personal pronoun, acc. after *apud,* and referring to the indirect object of the preceding clause.) 8. But Caesar led his soldiers across the river in order to storm and burn the rest of the towns. (*Suōs,* reflexive possessive adjective modifying *mīlitēs,* and referring to the subject of its own clause.)

Exercise 322.—1. Populus Americānus audīvit quantō in perīculō mīlitēs suī in Bataan essent. (*Their,* reflexive possessive adjective, referring to subject *American people.*) Arma auxiliaque autem nōn mīsērunt quod Bataan ā fīnibus suīs longē aberat. (*Their,* reflexive possessive adjective, referring to subject *they.*) 2. Caesar in prīmam aciem auxilia mīsit quae (quī) legiōnēs suās adjuvārent. (*His,* reflexive possessive adjective, referring to subject *Caesar.*) 3. Barbarōs pepulērunt nē frūmenta sua incenderent. (*Their,* reflexive possessive adjective, referring to subject *they.*) 4. Docuit eōs quae cōnsilia sua essent. (*His,* reflexive possessive adjective, referring to subject *he.*) 5. Deditne Caesar servīs quī in castrīs suīs erant praemia? (*His,* reflexive possessive adjective, referring to subject *Caesar.*)

Exercise 323.—1. He asked whether Christ had come into the world (*Num,* conjunction introducing an indirect question. *Vēnisset,* 3rd sing., plu. subj. of *veniō, venīre, vēnī, ventum,* 4, intr.; in indirect question after secondary tense, action completed before time of main verb.) 2. We do not praise war and slaughter, do we? (*Num,* particle used in questions expecting a negative answer.)

Reading No. 24.—Hail Mary, full of grace, the Lord is with thee: blessed art thou amongst women, and blessed is the fruit of thy womb, Jesus. Holy Mary, Mother of God, pray for us sinners, now and at the hour of our death. Amen.

The angel Gabriel was sent by God into a city of Galilee the name of which was (called) Nazareth. He was sent to Mary. Mary was praying. The angel said to her: "Hail, full of grace, the Lord is with thee! Blessed art thou among women!" . . . "Blessed art thou among women, and blessed is the fruit of thy womb!"

Box, page 314.—Holy Mary, Mother of God, pray for us!

Exercise 324.—1. In silvās vēnērunt nē pellerentur—vidērentur; superārentur; vincerentur; terrērentur; tenērentur; in fugam darentur; audīrentur. (Imperfect tense, in negative purpose clause after a secondary tense.) 2. Manum parvam mīsit quae hīberna mūnīret—occupāret; obtinēret; dēfenderet; incenderet; oppugnāret; expugnāret. (Imperfect tense, in relative purpose clause after a secondary tense.) 3. Mīlitēs monet nē superentur—vincantur; pellantur; in fugam dentur; terreantur; videantur; teneantur; occīdantur. (Present tense, in negative purpose clause after a primary tense.) 4. Equitēs mittit quō facilius oppidum occupētur—incendātur; mūniātur; dēfendātur; oppugnētur; expugnētur; teneātur. (Present tense, in purpose clause after a primary tense.)

Exercise 325.—1. Caesar was calling upon his men by name and was holding in (his) hand the legion's standard, lest they be put to flight by the enemy. (*Suōs,* masc. acc. pl. of *suus, a, um,* reflexive possessive adjective used as a noun, object of *appellābat,* and referring as regards possession to the subject of its own clause. *Manū,* abl. sing. of *manus, manūs,* f.; ablative of means. *Suī,* masc. nom. pl. of *suus, a, um,* reflexive possessive adjective used as a noun, subject of the negative purpose clause and referring as regards possession to the subject of the main clause.) 2. For the sake of water (Because of the available supply of water) Caesar pitched camp at the river in order that the enemy's attack might be more easily and for a longer time withstood by his men. (*Aquae*, gen. sing. of *aqua, aquae*, f.; gen. with *causā* used as a preposition. *Facilius*, comparative form of *facile*, adverb; modifies *sustinērētur*. *Suīs*, masc. abl. pl. of *suus, a, um*, reflexive possessive adjective used as a noun in a prepositional phrase, ablative of agent.) 3. The general led the legions into the enemy's territory secretly in order that they might not be seen by the enemy. They immediately made an attack against the Gauls. But then the chiefs of the Gauls collected a band of men for the sake of war, prepared arms, and according to their own custom strengthened the courage of their men by speeches. (*Vidērentur*, 3rd pl., imp. subj. pass. of *videō, vidēre, vīdī, vīsus*, 2, tr.; in negative purpose clause after a secondary tense. *Bellī*, gen. sing. of *bellum, ī*, n.; gen. with *causā* used as a preposition. *Suōrum*, masc. gen. pl. of *suus, a, um*, reflexive possessive adjective used as a noun, modifying *virtūtem*, and referring to the subject of its own clause. *Suō*, masc. abl. sing. of *suus, a, um*, reflexive possessive adjective modifying *mōre*, and referring to the subject of the main clause.) 4. Caesar hastened across the mountains with a small band of men in order not to be far from his men in their danger. (*Suīs*, masc. abl. pl. of *suus, a, um*, reflexive possessive adjective modifying *mīlitibus* in a negative purpose clause, and referring to the subject of the main clause. *Eōrum*, masc. gen. pl. of *is, ea, id*, non-reflexive personal pronoun serving as a possessive adjective, modifying *perīculō*, and referring to *mīlitibus*.) 5. The Gauls surrendered themselves and all their property to Caesar after the battle in order that the lives of their hostages might be spared by Caesar. (*Sē*, acc. pl. of *suī*, reflexive pronoun, object of *dēdidērunt*. *Sua*, neut. acc. pl. of *suus, a, um*, reflexive possessive adjective used as a noun, and referring as regards possession to the subject of its own clause.) 6. Before a war don't we Americans collect an army and prepare arms and weapons in order not to be conquered by the enemy? 7. The gates were burned, and the cavalry was sent swiftly into the town in order to seize the town immediately. Then the barbarians raised a shout according to their custom and for the sake of safety (to save their lives) surrendered themselves and all their property to the Romans. But Caesar did not spare their lives lest his own envoys be killed by the barbarians. For the injury and slaughter of envoys (injuries done to envoys and their execution) had been the cause of the war. (*Suō*, masc. abl. sing. of *suus, a, um*, reflexive possessive adjective modifying *mōre*, and referring to the subject of its own clause. *Sē*, acc. pl. of *suī*, reflexive personal pronoun, object of *dēdidērunt*. *Sua*, neut. acc. pl. of *suus, a, um*, reflexive possessive adjective used as a noun, object of *dēdidērunt. Eōrum,* masc. gen. pl. of *is, ea, id,* non-reflexive personal pronoun serving as a possessive adjective, modifying *vītās,* and referring to *barbarī* in preceding sentence. *Suī,* masc. nom. pl. of *suus, a, um,* reflexive possessive adjective modifying *lēgātī,* subject of *occīderentur,* and referring to subject of main clause.)

Exercise 326.—1. Deus laudētur! 2. Hostēs vincantur! 3. Oppidum incendātur! 4. Dux moneātur! 5. Nōs cōnservēmur! 6. Custōdēs collocentur. 7. Adjuventur ā Deō! 8. Cīvitās cōnservētur. 9. Vīta mea ā Deō regātur. 10. Deus ab omnibus hominibus dīligātur! 11. In fugam dentur! 12. Peccāta nostra tollantur! 13. Ā Deō doceāmur! 14. Ad nōs auxilium mittātur. 15. Memoriā semper teneātur! 16. Ab omnibus hominibus Marīa laudētur! 17. Omnibus vōbīs grātia Deī dētur! 18. Virīs fortibus praemia dentur!

Box, page 316.—Into Thy hands, O Lord, I commend my spirit.

Exercise 327.—1. Barbarī mōre suō clāmōrem sustulērunt nē ā lēgātō occīderentur. 2. Chrīstus in mundum vēnit ut peccāta nostra tollerentur. 3. Pācis atque salūtis commūnis causā rēs pūblica cōnservētur. 4. Gallī manibus suīs oppida sua incendērunt nē ā Rōmānīs occupārentur. 5. Deus eīs quī pācis causā magnōs dolōrēs sustinent grātiam dabit. 6. Virī fortēs et līberī semper pugnābunt ut cīvitās nostra cōnservētur. 7. Aquae causā ad flūmen castra posuērunt. 8. Auxilia exspectāvit nē ab hostibus premerētur. 9. Parvam manum ibi collocāvit nē ā barbarīs collis occupārētur! 10. Caesar dē mōribus et Gallōrum et suōrum nōs docet.

Exercise 328.—1. For whose salvation did Christ come into the world? (*Quōrum,* masc. gen. pl. of *quī, quae, quod,* interrogative adjective modifying *salūtem.*) 2. Whom did the Roman soldiers call general? (*Quem,* masc. acc. sing. of *quis, quis, quid,* interrogative pronoun, object of *appellāvērunt.*) 3. What tribes did Caesar conquer? (*Quās,* fem. acc. pl. of *quī, quae, quod,* interrogative adjective modifying *gentēs.*)

Exercise 329.—1. Scīvit cūr pulsī essent—laudātī; superātī; vocātī; monitī; occīsī; territī; vīsī; tentī (Pluperfect subjunctive; action before time of main verb in secondary sequence.) 2. Scīvērunt quō ductī essent—missī; coāctī; vocātī. (Pluperfect subjunctive; action before time of main verb in secondary sequence.) 3. Scit quī missus sit—petītus; occīsus; laudātus; monitus; vocātus; superātus; territus. (Perfect subjunctive; action before time of main verb in primary sequence.) 4. Scīvit ubi collocārentur—relinquerentur; occīderentur; īnstruerentur. (Imperfect subjunctive; action at same time as main verb in secondary sequence.) 5. Scit num agrī vastentur—occupentur; dēfendantur. (Pres-

ent subjunctive; action at same time as main verb in primary sequence.)
6. Scit quō dūcantur—cogantur; vocentur; moveantur; mittantur.
(Present subjunctive; action at same time as main verb in primary
sequence.) 7. Scīvit cūr laudārētur—superārētur; vocārētur; monērē-
tur; timērētur; terrērētur; tenērētur; relinquerētur. (Imperfect subjunctive; action at same time as main verb in secondary sequence.)

Exercise 330.—1. When all of Gaul had been pacified, Caesar left
garrisons in winter quarters and hastened into Italy. 2. Before the battle
the centurion asked what plans had been approved by Caesar. 3. You
do not know where the envoys were sent, do you? 4. When the column
was being led through difficult and narrow places, the battle line of the
barbarians was suddenly seen. 5. Do you know whether the legion which
had been in the camp was left behind by the lieutenant? 6. When the
crops were being burned by the cavalry, the soldiers were fortifying the
camp by means of a rampart and a ditch. 7. When Christ was shown by
Pilate to the Jews, the Jews raised a great shout: "We have no king
except (but) Caesar. Take Him away! Let Him be crucified."

Exercise 331.—Cum legiōnēs in hībernīs in Galliā relictae essent
et Caesar in Italiam contendisset, Gallī obsidēs inter sē dedērunt et dē
bellō apud sē ēgērunt. Cum cōnsilia probāta essent in conciliō commūnī, hīberna subitō oppugnāvērunt. Praesidia magnō in perīculō erant.
Itaque nuntius ad Caesarem missus est ut auxilium mitterētur. Caesar
scīvit quantae cōpiae hostium essent et ubi custōdēs collocātī essent.
In Galliam legiōnēs suās integrās statim dūxit nē hīberna expugnārentur. Agmen suum ab hostibus subitō vīsum est. Territī sunt et lēgātōs
statim mīsērunt quī pācem peterent. Tum eī sē dēdidērunt. Ita Gallia
pācāta est.

Box, page 320.—Christ, hear us!

Exercise 332.—1. They were raised (cheered) up by the victories
of (their) allies. 2. They were moved by the arrival of Caesar. 3. They
were terrified by (their) fear of Caesar. 4. They were disturbed by the
envoy's speech. 5. He was moved by the king's dispatch.

Exercise 333.—1. Caede prīncipum vehementer perturbātī sunt.
2. Adventū Caesaris territī sunt. 3. Injūriīs Rōmānōrum commōtī
sunt. 4. Metū lēgātī vehementer mōtī sunt.

Exercise 334.—1. Avē, Jēsū Chrīste, quī salūtis nostrae causā in
mundum vēnistī et per dolōrēs labōrēsque peccāta nostra sustulistī.
Nōs vēritātem docuistī. Nōs viam salūtis docuistī. Rege mentēs ac vītās
nostrās. Ubi pāx vēra sit nōs docuistī. Dīligāmus et adōrēmus eum.
Jēsū Chrīste, Domine noster, miserēre nōbīs! 2. Caesar pācis causā in

cīvitātibus quās pācāverat praesidia relīquit. Tum autem Caesar in Italiam contendit. Cum hoc ā Gallīs cognitum esset, cōnsilia nova ā sē probāta sunt et obsidēs inter sē dedērunt ut pāx amīcitiaque apud sē cōnfirmārentur. Caesar autem, cum cognōvisset quae cōnsilia ā barbarīs probāta essent, Rōmam relīquit et in fīnēs Gallōrum cum manū parvā subitō pervēnit. Interim Gallī lēgātōs quōs Caesar ad sē mīserat retinuerant et hīberna oppugnāverant. Caesar ad hīberna statim contendit nē ā barbarīs expugnārentur. Cum parvā manū pervēnit. Cum agmen Caesaris ab hostibus vīsum esset, impetum in suōs sine morā fēcērunt. Suī pressī sunt; Caesar autem nōmine eōs appellāvit atque signum legiōnis manū tenuit nē pellerentur. Hostēs in fugam datī sunt. Caesar cum omnibus cōpiīs ad castra eōrum contendit; eī autem mōre suō clāmōrem sustulērunt atque sē suaque omnia eī dēdidērunt. Caesar quae causa bellī fuisset cognōvit. Itaque obsidēs Gallōrum occīdit nē lēgātī suī ab eīs posteā tenērentur atque occīderentur. Ita rem pūblicam dēfenderat; Senātus autem Rōmānus propter ējus victōriam sine morā eum laudāvit et eī grātiās ēgit. 3. Lēgātus, nōmine Labiēnus, ā Caesare saepe laudātus est. 4. Deus nōbīs pācem suam det et nōs dēfendat! 5. Jēsū Chrīste, Fīlī Deī, miserēre nōbīs! 6. Adventū Caesaris territī sunt.

Exercise 335.—1. See No. 28. (a) Deus; (b) Jēsū; (c) fīlī; (d) mī; (e) amīce; (f) centuriō. 2. The imperative is formed on the present stem, e.g., laudā, laudāte; monē, monēte; mitte, mittite; audī, audīte. 3. The volitive subjunctive is the present subjunctive in a main clause used to express prayers and wishes, e.g., Deus det nōbīs pācem; Utinam veniat. 4. Latin uses the first person plural of the present subjunctive for exhortations, e.g., Veniāmus; Fortiter pugnēmus. This is called the hortatory subjunctive. 5. See text, p. 305. 6. See text, p. 309. 7. Direct and indirect reflexives of the first and second persons—the pronouns: ego (nōs), tū (vōs); the adjectives: meus, a, um; noster, nostra, nostrum; tuus, a, um; vester, vestra, vestrum. (See Nos. 800-807.) 8. (a) Tē dēde, vōs dēdite; (b) tē dēdis, vōs dēditis; (c) sē dēdit; (d) nōs dēdimus; (e) sē dēdunt. 9. To put to flight. 10. The ablative of *causa* is used as a preposition. It governs the genitive and always stands after the word it governs. (See text, p. 314.) 11. *Cum, when,* in secondary sequence takes the subjunctive; imperfect or pluperfect according to the general rule. (See Nos. 559-563.) 12. The ablative without a preposition may be used to express the cause or reason. Adventū Caesaris territī sunt. (See text, p. 320.)

Reading No. 25.—David, a brave and renowned man, as you know, was king of the Israelites. The Israelites were waging war with the Philistines lest their fields be seized by them. The Philistines were holding (in possession of) Bethlehem, for they had pitched camp there. David was in a garrison with a small band of men and was not far distant from their camp. A garrison had been stationed there in order that David might both defend his own men and learn what was being done by the enemy.

Now there was a great scarcity of water in the Israelites' camp. On that account both David and the soldiers were suffering great hardship. In Bethlehem, however, which was held by the Philistines, there was an abundance of water. And so David said: "If only I had some water from the cistern which is in Bethlehem!"

But when this was heard by the soldiers, three brave men hastened secretly to the enemy's camp in order to bring water to the king. The danger was great, but nevertheless they were not seen by the enemy's guards. And so they carried water safely to the king and gave it to him.

But the king, when he had seen the water, was greatly moved by (their) courage and friendship. For they had gone to the enemy's camp through places full of dangers in order that water might be brought to him. The king knew what great danger they had been in on account of him. He therefore thanked them, but he poured out the water as a sacrifice to the Lord.

UNIT NINE

Exercise 336.—See No. 72.

Box, page 326.—Holy Spirit, God, have mercy on us!

Exercise 337.—(Each may be translated in two ways; e.g., *laudātus, a, um, having been praised* or *praised*.) 1. Cognitus, a, um. 2. Exspectātus, etc. 3. Dēductus. 4. Adductus. 5. Commōtus. 6. Impedītus. 7. Vastātus. 8. Quaesītus. 9. Rogātus. 10. Trāductus. 11. Ostentus. 12. Doctus. 13. Sublātus. 14. Rectus. 15. Obtentus. 16. Retentus. 17. Sustentus. 18. Tentus. 19. Territus. 20. Vīsus. 21. Āctus. 22. Dēditus. 23. Dīlēctus. 24. Pācātus. 25. Adjūtus. 26. Administrātus. 27. Appellātus. 28. Collocātus. 29. Comparātus. 30. Cōnfirmātus. 31. Cōnservātus. 32. Datus. 33. Explorātus. 34. Incitātus. 35. Laudātus. 36. Dēfēnsus. 37. Dīmissus. 38. Ductus. 39. Gestus. 40. Incēnsus. 41. Īnstrūctus. 42. Missus. 43. Occupātus. 44. Oppugnātus. 45. Ōrātus. 46. Parātus. 47. Perturbātus. 48. Portātus. 49. Servātus. 50. Superātus. 51. Vocātus. 52. Complētus. 53. Contentus. 54. Habitus. 55. Monitus. 56. Mōtus. 57. Occīsus. 58. Pulsus. 59. Petītus. 60. Positus. 61. Pressus. 62. Trāditus. 63. Victus. 64. Audītus.

Exercise 338.—1. The barbarians, led on by hope of the common safely, sent the cavalry against the Roman column. (*Spē*, abl. sing. of *spēs, speī*, f.; ablative of cause. *Adductī*, masc. nom. pl. of perf. part. pass. of *addūcō, addūcere, addūxī, adductus*, 3, tr., modifying *barbarī*.) 2. The general encouraged by a speech the soldiers (who had been) alarmed by the slaughter of the cavalry, in order that they might fight longer. (*Commōtōs*, masc. acc. pl. of perf. part. pass. of *commoveō, commovēre, commōvī, commōtus*, 2, tr., modifying *mīlitēs*.) 3. On account of the seized towns and the ravaged fields, the Gauls were not carrying grain into the winter quarters of the Romans. (*Occupāta*, neut. acc. pl. of perf. part. pass. of *occupō, occupāre, occupāvī, occupātus*, 1, tr., modifying *oppida*.) 4. The Senate and the Roman people, aroused by Caesar's authority and dispatch (influenced by the respect Caesar commanded and by his dispatch), sent fresh legions into the province without delay. 5. Then the barbarians and slaves suddenly made an attack from all sides against our column, encumbered by a baggage train. (*Impedītum*, neut. acc. sing. of perf. part. pass. of *impediō, impedīre, impedīvī, impedītus*, 4 tr., modifying *agmen*.) 6. But the Gauls, overcome in many battles and left behind (abandoned) by (their) allies, hastened into difficult and narrow places. (*Impedīta*, neut. acc. pl. of perf. part. pass. of *impediō, impedīre, impedīvī, impedītus*, 4, tr., modifying *loca*.) 7. The messenger said, "Our soldiers, encumbered, did not immediately put the enemy to flight." (*Impedītī*, masc. nom. pl. of perf. part. pass. of *impediō, impedīre, impedīvī, impedītus*, 4, tr., modifying *mīlitēs*.) 8. The centurion led reinforcements to the winter quarters (which had been) stormed by the enemy. (*Hostibus*, abl. pl. of *hostis, hostis*, m.; ablative of agent.) 9. The Gauls, led on by a scarcity of everything and alarmed by Caesar's arrival, sent envoys to the Roman general to sue for peace. (*Adventū*, abl. sing. of *adventus, adventūs*, m.; ablative of cause. *Commōtī*, masc. nom. pl. of perf. part. pass. of *commoveō, commovēre, commōvī, commōtus*, 2, tr., modifying *Gallī*. *Peterent*, 3rd pl. imp. subj. of *petō, petere, petīvī, petītus*, 3, tr.; in a relative purpose clause after a secondary tense.) 10. The English and Americans, aided by their allies, led large forces into France. (*Suīs*, masc. abl. pl. of *suus, a, um*, reflexive possessive adjective, modifying *sociīs*, and referring to the subjects of the sentence. *Adjūtī*, masc. nom. pl. of perf. part. pass. of *adjuvō, adjuvāre, adjūvī, adjūtus*, 1, tr., modifying *Britannī* and *Americānī*.) 11. The Gauls, aroused to war by their chiefs and raised up by hope of victory, stormed our camp (which had been) fortified by a high rampart. (*Incitātī*, masc. nom. pl. of perf. part. pass. of *incitō, incitāre, incitāvī, incitātus*, 1, tr., modifying *Gallī*. *Spē*, abl. sing. of *spēs, speī*, f.; ablative of cause. *Sublātī*, masc. nom. pl. of perf. part. pass. of *tollō, tollere, sustulī, sublātus*, 3, tr., modifying *Gallī*. *Mūnīta*, neut. acc. pl. of perf. part. pass. of *mūniō, mūnīre, mūnīvī, mūnītus*, 4, tr., modifying *castra*.) 12. Meanwhile the soldiers left behind in the camp for the sake of protection were valiantly withstanding the enemy's attack. (*Praesidiī*, gen. sing. of *praesidium, ī,* n., with *causā* used as a preposition.) 13. The enemy, however, drew up their forces (which had been) led to the river. (*Ductās*, fem. acc. pl. of perf. part. pass. of *dūcō, dūcere, dūxī, ductus*, 3, tr., modifying *cōpiās*.) 14. Alarmed by many messages and dispatches, Caesar collected new legions in Italy and sent a lieutenant to lead them into Gaul. (*Commōtus*, masc. nom. sing. of perf. part. pass. of *commoveō, commovēre, commōvī, commōtus*, 2, tr., modifying *Caesar*. *Dēdūceret*, 3rd sing., imp. subj. of *dēdūcō, dēdūcere, dēdūxī, dēductus*, 3, tr.; in relative purpose clause after secondary tense.) 15. The king praised the chiefs on account of the rewards given him by them. (*Data*, neut. acc. pl. of perf. part. pass. of *dō, dare, dedī, datus*, 1, tr., modifying *praemia*.)

Box, page 329.—A learned man always has his wealth in himself.

Exercise 339.—1. The general, greatly aroused, strengthened the soldiers' courage by a speech. (*Commōtus*, masc. nom. sing. of perf. part. pass. of *commoveō, commovēre, commōvī, commōtus*, 2, tr., modifying *imperātor*.) 2. The soldiers, praised by Caesar and called upon by name, withstood the cavalry's attack. (*Laudātī*, masc. nom. pl. of perf. part. pass. of *laudō, laudāre, laudāvī, laudātus*, 1, tr., modifying *mīlitēs*. *Appellātī*, masc. nom. pl. of perf. part. pass. of *appellō, appellāre, appellāvī, appellātus*, 1, tr., modifying *mīlitēs*.) 3. The leaders of the Gauls, violently disturbed by the slaughter of the chiefs, handed over to the Romans the arms prepared by them for war. (*Perturbātī*, masc. nom. pl. of perf. part. pass. of *perturbō, perturbāre, perturbāvī, perturbātus*, 1, tr., modifying *ducēs*.) 4. The leader, a brave man, fortified by means of both a rampart and a ditch the hill seized by the cavalry. (*Occupātum*, masc. acc. sing. of perf. part. pass. of *occupō, occupāre, occupāvī, occupātus*, 1, tr., modifying *collem*. *Vallō*, abl. sing. of *vallum, ī,* n.; ablative of means.) 5. The barbarians made an attack against the soldiers encumbered by a baggage train. (*Impedītōs*, masc. acc. pl. of perf. part. pass. of *impediō, impedīre, impedīvī, impedītus*, 4, tr., modifying *mīlitēs*.) 6. Caesar, disturbed by the danger of the envoys (the danger in which the envoys were), hastened by long marches into the barbarians' territory with all his forces. (*Perturbātus*, masc. nom. sing. of perf. part. pass. of *perturbō, perturbāre, perturbāvī, perturbātus*, 1, tr., modifying *Caesar*. *Cōpiīs*, abl. pl. of *cōpiae, cōpiārum*, f.; ablative of accompaniment.) 7. Alarmed by the envoy's dispatch, Caesar called to himself (summoned) the chiefs of the Gauls and asked how many tribes were in arms. (*Sē*, acc. of *suī*, reflexive pronoun; object of the preposition *ad* and referring to the subject of its own clause. *Vocāvit*, 3rd sing., perf. ind. act. of *vocō, vocāre, vocāvī, vocātus*, 1, tr., verb in main clause.) 8. The cavalry stationed at the river put the enemy to flight and thus killed a great many of them with darts and swords. (*Collocātī*, masc. nom. pl. of perf. part. pass. of *collocō, collocāre, collocāvī, collocātus*, 1, tr., modifying *equitēs*.) 9. The legions stationed in the enemy's territory for the sake of (to maintain) the winter quarters sent a slave to Caesar to ask for reinforcements. (*Collocātae*, fem. nom. pl. of perf. part. pass. of *collocō, collocāre, collocāvī, collocātus*, 1, tr., modifying *legiōnēs*.) 10. The centurions and military tribunes called by name by Caesar withstood the enemy's forces longer. (*Appellātī*, masc. pl. of perf. part. pass. of *appellō, appellāre, appellāvī, appellātus*, 1, tr., modifying *centuriōnēs* and *tribūnī mīlitum*.) 11. The enemy, strengthened by hope of victory, swiftly came all the way up to our first battle line. (*Cōnfirmātī*, masc. nom. pl. of perf. part. pass. of *cōnfirmō, cōnfirmāre, cōnfirmāvī, cōnfirmātus*, 1, tr., modifying *hostēs*. *Usque ad*, adverb and preposition used together to mean *all the way to* or *all the way up to*.) 12. Encouraged by hope of reinforcements, our men fought until night. (*Cōnfirmātī*, masc. nom. pl. of perf. part. pass. of *cōnfirmō, cōnfirmāre, cōnfirmāvī, cōnfirmātus*, 1, tr., modifying *nostrī*.) 13. Greatly alarmed, the general immediately drew up the army before the gates. (*Commōtus*, masc. nom. sing. of perf. part. pass. of *commoveō, commovēre, commōvī, commōtus*, 2, tr., modifying *imperātōr*.)

Exercise 340.—1. Cum hostēs, ā legiōnibus pulsī, fugā montēs peterent, Caesar mīsit equitēs quī eōs occīderent. 2. Barbarī, adventū Caesaris commōtī, collem ā legiōne Rōmānā occupātum nōn oppugnāvērunt. 3. Gallī, spē victōriae ac salūtis adductī, obsidēs inter sē dedērunt atque arma comparāvērunt ut cum Rōmānīs bellum gererent. 4. Gallī, auctōritāte et grātiā Caesaris mōtī, in hīberna frūmentum portāvērunt. 5. In nostrōs impedīmentīs impedītōs et montibus contentōs impetum fēcērunt. 6. Barbarī, multīs proeliīs superātī, sē suaque omnia lēgātō dēdidērunt. 7. Caesar, doctus quantō in perīculō legiōnēs essent, equitēs mīsit quī eās adjuvārent. 8. Imperātor, doctus quae gēns hominum eum locum incoleret, trāns flūmen exercitum clam trā-dūxit. 9. Hominēs ā Deō dīlēctī neque perīculum neque mortem timent. 10. Oppidum expugnātum incēnsum est. 11. In colle ā Rōmānīs occupātō multa corpora relīquērunt. 12. Propter agrōs vastātōs inopia frūmentī erat. 13. Caesar cōnsilia ā barbarīs in conciliō ante adventum suum probāta cognōvit.

Exercise 341.—1. Fem. 2. *Ubi* is used only when *where* refers to place in which and implies rest; *quō* only when *where* refers to place to which and implies motion or direction. 3. Barbarī Caesarī sē dēdidērunt. 4. Ad castra appropinquāvērunt. Castrīs appropinquāvērunt.

Exercise 342.—See Introduction, 3.

Exercise 343.—1. Hōc; with this military tribune. 2. Hās; through this forest. 3. Hoc; to (into) this river. 4. Hanc; on account of this affair. 5. Hōc; before this town. 6. Hōc; on this bridge. 7. Hoc; across this river. 8. Hāc; in this province. 9. Hōc; in this danger. 10. Hoc; after this war. 11. Hīs; in these hills. 12. Haec; on account of these wounds. 13. Hunc; behind this mountain. 14. Hōc; with this boy. 15. Hīs; in these fields. 16. Hōc; without this man. 17. Hanc; after this victory. 18. Hās; on account of these victories. 19. Hōs; into these mountains. 20. Hīs; with these slaves. 21. Hunc; on account of this fear. 22. Hōc; with this general. 23. Hunc; into this world. 24. Hōc; on this march. 25. Hōs; through these fields. 26. Hārum; full of these things. 27. Hoc; at this river. 28. Haec; at this camp. 29. Hōs; against these soldiers. 30. Hāc; without this hope. 31. Hanc; on account of this cause (for this reason). 32. Hōc; in this battle. 33. Hāc; concerning this matter. 34. Hāc; in this state.

Box, page 332.—Saint Joseph, pray for us!

Exercise 344.—See Introduction, 3.

Exercise 345.—1. This free state is ours; these fields and these cities are ours. We will therefore always fight bravely against the enemy for this free state and we will always defend without delay these fields and these cities. (All the italicized words agree with the nouns they modify in gender, number, and case: *haec*, fem. nom. sing. with *cīvitās*, etc.) 2. Many and great were the wars and the victories of our fore-fathers. Will not these wars and these victories always be remembered in this state? 3. The Gauls, forced by Caesar, had sent many hostages to him. When the Gauls waged war, Caesar killed these hostages. Disturbed by this occurrence, the Gauls swiftly collected new soldiers in order to conquer the Romans. 4. The first soldiers had come across the river; the rest were on (in) the river. Suddenly the barbarians made an attack strongly from the rear against these soldiers thus encumbered and killed almost all of them. 5. Friends who help us in difficult affairs are friends true and sure. Let us love these friends. 6. When he had heard this message, Caesar sent a dispatch to the lieutenant. But the lieutenant, violently alarmed by this dispatch and terrified by the attack of the enemy, held the legions in camp, but sent the cavalry to Caesar.

Exercise 346.—1. There were foreign horsemen in Caesar's army. Caesar often praised them on account of their reliability and true courage. (*Hic* as a pronoun, and other pronouns, agree with the noun to which they refer in gender and number; their case depends on their use in their own clauses: *hōs*, masc. acc. pl., agreeing in gender and number with *equitēs* in the preceding sentence, object of the verb *laudāvit*, etc.) 2. The cavalry of the enemy was suddenly seen in the rear. In the first battle line, however, there were fresh legions. And so these withstood almost all the attacks of the enemy. 3. The Romans killed many Christians on account of the law and truth of Christ. Shall we not always praise their memory? 4. Led on by hope of victory and forced by the authority of the king, the Germans had led all (their) forces across the river. They were fighting against the Gauls; they were burning the crops and the towns (that had been) seized; they were killing the chiefs and the kings of the Gauls; they were devastating all the fields. But the Gauls, violently disturbed and terrified, sent envoys to Caesar to ask for help. Caesar, when he had heard all these things (this), immediately hastened into the territory of the Gauls with all (his) forces in order to drive the Germans across the river.

Exercise 347.—1. Hostēs ad bellum gentēs fīnitimās facile commōvērunt, nam hae gentēs fortēs et cupidae glōriae victōriae erant. 2. Caesar cum multīs rēgibus et prīncipibus pugnāvit. Hōs saepe occīdit. 3. Lēgātus in agrīs barbarōrum castra posuit. Haec castra, fossā vallōque mūnīta, fortiter dēfendit. 4. Centuriō ad Caesarem litterās dē hāc rē mīsit. Caesar, hīs litterīs commōtus, in prōvinciam legiōnēs novās mīsit. Hae legiōnēs prōvinciam dēfendērunt et trāns flūmen in fīnēs eōrum hostēs ēgērunt. 5. Barbarī ā tergō in legiōnem impetum subitō fēcērunt. Haec legiō impetum facile sustinuit.

Box, page 335.—"This is Jesus, King of the Jews."

Exercise 348.—1. I call you friends. (*Vōs*, acc. pl. of 2nd person personal pronoun; direct object of *appellō*. *Amīcōs*, acc. pl. of *amīcus, ī,* m.; predicate accusative with *appellō*. See text, p. 275.) 2. He led the legion across the river. (*Legiōnem*, acc. sing. of *legiō, ōnis,* f.; object of *trādūxit. Flūmen*, acc. sing. of *flūmen, flūminis,* n.; acc. of the place with a verb of transporting. See text, p. 272.) 3. Many Romans were with Caesar's army for the sake of friendship. (*Amīcitiae*, gen. sing. of *amīcitia, ae,* f.; genitive with *causā* used as a preposition. *Causā,* abl. sing. of *causa, ae,* f.; used as a preposition governing the genitive.) 4. He put the barbarians to flight. (*Barbarōs,* acc. pl. of *barbarus, ī,* m.; object of *dedit. In fugam,* acc. sing. of *fuga, ae,* f.; acc. after preposition *in;* idiomatic use with *dō,* meaning *put to flight.*) 5. They fought bravely. (*Pugnātum est,* neut. 3rd sing. perf. tense passive; in an impersonal expression. See text, p. 255.)

Exercise 349.—1. Hic mīles dē mūrō cecidit. 2. Caesar ex (or dē) fīnibus hostium contendit. 3. Ā prōvinciā discessit. 4. Ab hōc locō castra mōvit. 5. Exercitus dē (or ex) silvīs vēnit. 6. Hic nauta quī telō occīsus erat dē nāve cecidit. 7. Equitēs ex hīs castrīs missī sunt. 8. Legiō dē hōc colle contendit. 9. Hī barbarī dē (or ex) colle impetum fēcērunt. 10. Ab hōc flūmine discessērunt. 11. Hic exercitus ex hībernīs ductus est. 12. Ex hāc urbe vēnērunt. 13. Centuriō dē hōc ponte in flūmen cecidit. 14. Hic centuriō ex flūmine gestus est. 15. Hic mīles ā flūmine vēnit. 16. Hī ex agrīs barbarōrum ductī sunt. 17. Hōs obsidēs ex oppidō dūcēbant. 18. Caesar ab hāc urbe ad Galliam contendit. 19. Hic ex fīnibus Gallōrum contendit. 20. Hī mīlitēs fortēs ab aciē nōn discessērunt.

Exercise 350.—1. Many sailors, killed by darts, fell from the ships into the water. 2. He had led the army out of the enemy's fields across the river into the province. 3. He led new legions out of Italy into Gaul. 4. When he had heard this, Caesar stormed the town from which the leader of the enemy had led (his) soldiers. 5. There was long and bitter fighting at the river. 6. Almost all the enemy, killed by darts, fell from the wall. 7. Did not many men fall in this battle? 8. At dawn this lieutenant, named Labienus, moved camp from this place to the hill. 9. These barbarians suddenly made an attack from the mountains against the encumbered column. 10. We shall always remember the courage and loyalty of these soldiers of ours who fell in these battles. 11. Caesar sent reinforcements from camp into the first battle line. 12. Alarmed by this dispatch, Caesar, when the fields of the barbarians had been devastated and all the crops burned, for the sake of safety led the army out of the enemy's territory through difficult and encumbered places across the river into the province.

Moments at Mass No. 3.—For this is My Body.

Exercise 351.—1. The soldier sought the forest by flight lest the enemy kill him. (*Sē,* indirect reflexive pronoun, object of *occīderent* in a negative purpose clause, and referring to the subject of the main clause.) 2. The enemy raised a shout according to their custom. (*Suō*, reflexive possessive adjective modifying *mōre* and referring to the subject of its own clause.) 3. The barbarians made an attack against the winter quarters. Caesar therefore killed their hostages. (*Eōrum*, genitive of personal pronoun, serving as possessive adjective, modifying *obsidēs*, and referring to the subject of the preceding sentence.) 4. The Gauls are exchanging hostages. (*Sē*, direct reflexive pronoun, object of preposition *inter*, and referring to the subject of its own clause.)

Box, page 340.—Saint Agnes, pray for us!

Exercise 352.—1. Illīs, eīs; with those sailors. 2. Illā, eā; before that gate. 3. Illā, eā; in that province. 4. Illīs, eīs; out of that forest. 5. Illam, eam; on account of that victory. 6. Illō, eō; with that friend. 7. Illīs, eīs; for those Christians. 8. Illum, eum; against that master. 9. Illīs, eīs; with those sons. 10. Illōs, eōs; through those Gauls. 11. Illīs, eīs; without those swords. 12. Illō, eō; on that wall. 13. Illōs, eōs; among those slaves. 14. Illō, eō; in that town. 15. Illō, eō; down from that hill. 16. Illō, eō; on that bridge. 17. Illō, eō; out of that harbor. 18. Illīus, ējus; for the sake of that matter. 19. Illīs, eīs; to or for those men. 20. Illōrum, eōrum; of those men. 21. Illud, id; across that river. 22. Illa, ea; on account of those wounds. 23. Illōrum, eōrum; on account of the welfare of those Romans. 24. Illārum, eārum; on account of the scarcity of those things. 25. Illīus, ējus; concerning the cause of that war. 26. Illam, eam; on account of that law. 27. Illīs, eīs; down from those mountains. 28. Illī, eī; to or for that man.

Box, page 342.—All ye saints, disciples of the Lord, pray for us!

Exercise 353.—1. All the Gauls were exchanging hostages and were treating of (making plans for) the conduct of the war. Aroused by this occurrence, Caesar immediately led new legions out of Italy into Gaul. But they suddenly sent envoys to him to strengthen friendship with him. (*Sē*, direct reflexive pronoun, acc. after *inter*. *Hāc*, demonstrative adjective modifying *rē*. *Illī*, pronoun, subject of *mīsērunt*. *Eum*, pronoun, acc. after *ad*. *Eō*, pronoun, abl. after *cum*.) 2. Among Americans Lincoln and Washington are very much honored. For the latter founded the republic, but the former preserved it, not without effort. (*Hic*, pronoun, used in contrast with *ille;* referring to the person mentioned last. *Ille* refers to the person mentioned previously. *Eam*, pronoun referring to *rem pūblicam*, object of the verb *cōnservāvit*.) 3. Both Hannibal and Caesar led large forces through the Alps. The latter led soldiers out of Italy to pacify Gaul, but the former led an army into Italy to conquer

the Romans and to seize Rome. (*Hic* and *ille*, used as in No. 2 above.)
4. Those who fight without hope never fight bravely. (*Eī*, personal pronoun, subject of *pugnant*.) 5. We will always remember him (the man) who founded our Republic. (*Eum*, personal pronoun, object of *tenēbimus*). 6. Both Hitler and Caesar led an army into Gaul (France) to conquer the Gauls. The former sent troops from Germany into France to devastate and conquer it; the latter led an army out of Italy through the mountains into Gaul to pacify and seize it. The former was conquered by the French and their allies, but the latter held command of Gaul for a long time. (*Ille* and *hic* used as pronouns in contrast, meaning *the former* and *the latter*. *Eam*, both times, pronoun referring to *Galliam*, as object of verbs in purpose clauses. *Ille* and *hic* again used in contrast. *Eōrum*, genitive of personal pronoun serving as possessive adjective, modifying *sociīs*, and referring to *Gallīs*.) 7. Caesar said: "The Germans and the Gauls were often contending with each other in battle. For either the Gauls were defending their own territory or were leading their forces into the others' territory." (*Sē*, reflexive pronoun, acc. after *inter*, referring to the compound subject of its own clause. *Suōs*, reflexive possessive adjective, modifying *fīnēs*, and referring to the subject of its own clause. *Illōrum*, genitive of pronoun serving as possessive adjective, modifying *fīnēs*, and referring to the more distant group, *Germānī*. *Suās*, reflexive possessive adjective, modifying *cōpiās*, and referring to the subject of its own clause.) 8. The leader of the Gauls said to his men: "I have called you to this place in order to treat of (discuss) the conduct of the war. For they have come into our territory in order to seize and burn these fields and these towns. Furthermore, they are brave and eager for victory. They are prepared for everything. For our lives and the common welfare of Gaul we are contending with them. And so I will kill with my own hand those who shall (do) not fight bravely against them. Fight to the death! Defend from them these fields, these towns, these children of ours. Let us drive the enemy out, conquer (them), and kill (them)!" (The pronouns are explained by the rules given above.)

Exercise 354.—1. Illa ratiō proeliī ā Rōmānīs laudāta est. 2. Praetereā, illae gentēs Rōmānīs obsidēs numquam dedērunt. 3. Propter illās ratiōnēs Caesar ad flūmen castra posuit. 4. Praetereā, illae gentēs contrā legiōnēs Rōmānās semper pugnāvērunt. 5. Illīs ratiōnibus adductī, contrā nōs pugnāvērunt, sed nōs numquam vincent. 6. Hōs pepulērunt; illōs autem occīdērunt. 7. Is quī Deum dīligit, fidem Chrīstiānam numquam relinquet. 8. Hī virī dē montibus vēnērunt; illī vērō in montibus mānsērunt. 9. Castra ab hīs oppugnāta sunt, mīlitēs vērō impedītī in flūmine ab illīs oppugnātī sunt. 10. Equitēs in fugam datī sunt; mīlitēs vērō in illō colle cōnstitērunt et nōn cessērunt. Itaque imperātor hīs grātiās ēgit; illīs vērō praemia nōn data sunt. 11. Illī prīncipēs, auctōritāte Caesaris commōtī, eī obsidēs dedērunt. 12. Rogāvit ubi illae gentēs incolerent. 13. Eī hunc collem numquam occupābunt; nōs vērō illa castra occupābimus. 14. Ille nauta, tēlō occīsus, dē nāve cecidit. 15. Dīligāmus Deum et omnēs hominēs.

Exercise 355.—1. I ask whether Christ is God. (*Sit*, present subjunctive in an indirect question in primary sequence, action at same time as main verb.) 2. I ask whether Caesar conquered the barbarians. (*Vīcerit*, perfect subjunctive in an indirect question in primary sequence, action before time of main verb.) 3. When Caesar was in Gaul, he waged war with the Gauls. (*Esset*, imperfect subjunctive in *cum*-clause in secondary sequence, action at same time as main verb.) 4. When he had seen this, Caesar sent reinforcements to his soldiers. (*Vīdisset*, pluperfect subjunctive in *cum*-clause in secondary sequence, action before time of main verb.)

Box, page 344.—Now or never!

Exercise 356.—1. The life of good (men) is empty of (free from) fear. 2. Kings are never free from fear. 3. But Caesar said, "I will defend you from the enemy." 4. Free me, O Lord, from those who seek my life. 5. The camp, fortified by the nature of the place, was safe from all danger. 6. He asked whether the wall was empty of soldiers. 7. The Gauls often contend in battle with the Germans who dwell across the river Rhine. For they are either warding them off from their own territory or are waging war in their territory. 8. Caesar was sent into Gaul to defend the province from the enemy. 9. After Caesar's arrival the province was safe from the enemy. 10. Lincoln, a great and noble man, freed the slaves in our republic.

Moments at Mass No. 4.—Lamb of God, who takest away the sins of the world, have mercy on us. (Twice.) Lamb of God, who takest away the sins of the world, grant us peace.

Exercise 357.—Sumus līberī metū et imperiō populōrum aliēnōrum. In prīncipiō nōs ā virīs fortibus imperiō populī aliēnī līberātī sumus. Annō mīllēsimō octingentēsimō duodecimō impetūs hostium fīnibus nostrīs ā mīlitibus et nautīs nostrīs prohibitī sunt. Annō mīllēsimō octingentēsimō sexāgēsimō prīmō apud nōs bellum gessimus; in illō bellō autem servī ā dominīs līberātī sunt et rēs pūblica cōnservāta est.

Praetereā, post illud bellum pāx et amīcitia apud nōs cōnfirmātae sunt et semper cōnservātae sunt.

Japōnēs, auctōritāte prīncipum ducumque adductī et cupidī glōriae imperiīque, impetum in portūs et agrōs nostrōs fēcērunt. Contrā eōs autem ā virīs fortibus dēfēnsī sumus. Populī quōs vīcērunt imperiō eōrum līberātī sunt; populī contrā quōs bellum gessērunt ā caede et morte tūtī erunt; agrī eōrum vacuī ab exercitibus aliēnīs erunt. Grātiās agāmus virīs fortibus quī nōs ab hostibus dēfendērunt. Laudēmus et adjuvēmus eōs. Memoriā semper teneāmus eōrum rēs gestās fortēs et, ad mortem et glōriam parātī, rem pūblicam quam metū et bellī perīculīs līberāvērunt semper cōnservēmus. Praetereā grātiās semper agāmus Deō Pātrī nostrō.

Exercise 358.—1. The legion was sent by Caesar out of Italy into Gaul. (*Ex Italiā,* from inside a place. *Ā Caesare,* ablative of agent.) 2. The general hastened into the province with all his troops. (*Cum omnibus cōpiīs,* ablative of accompaniment.) 3. The winter quarters, fortified by the nature of the place and by a rampart, were safe from every attack of the enemy. (*Nātūrā* and *vallō,* ablatives of means. *Impetū,* ablative of separation with *tūta.*) 4. The river is full of water, isn't it? (*Aquae,* genitive with *plēnum.*) 5. The enemy, violently alarmed by this slaughter, were treating of war in a common council of Gaul. (*Caede,* ablative of cause (means). *Bellō,* abl. with *dē.*) 6. For our common welfare I call you to arms. (*Salūte,* abl. with *prō.*) 7. Mary, mother of Jesus Christ, was full of grace. (*Grātiā,* abl. with *plēna.*) 8. The enemy, overcome in many battles, surrendered themselves and all their possessions to the envoy. (*Proeliīs,* abl. without preposition *in.* See Note 3, p. 348). 9. That lieutenant, named Labienus, disturbed by the enemy's attack, filled the wall with men. (*Impetū,* abl. of means or cause. *Hominibus,* abl. of means.) 10. The lieutenant did not pitch camp in an unfavorable place, did he? (When *locō* is modified by an adjective, *in* is often omitted.) 11. Without delay the soldiers were drawn up before the gate. (*Morā,* abl. with *sine. Portā,* abl. with *prō.*) 12. Alarmed by this dispatch, the lieutenant hastened into the territory of the barbarians in order not to be away from the camp. (*Litterīs,* abl. of cause (means). *Ā castrīs,* with *absum.*) 13. The barbarians, raised up (elated) by this victory, made an attack from the mountains against our encumbered column. (*Victōriā,* abl. of cause (means). *Dē montibus,* abl. of place from which.) 14. At dawn he moves the camp from that place. (*Ex eō locō,* abl. of place from which.) 15. From the river he hastened swiftly to the mountains. (*Ā flūmine,* abl. of place away from

100   FIRST YEAR LATIN

which.) 16. Many men, killed by darts, fell from the wall onto (into the midst of) the enemy. (*Tēlīs*, abl. of means. *Dē mūrō*, abl. of place from which, expressing movement downward.)

Box, page 349.—From every evil, O Lord, free us!

Exercise 359.—1. Japōnēs, ex mūnītiōnibus pulsī, fugā silvās petīvērunt. 2. Ab hōc flūmine discessērunt ut impetū tūtī essent. 3. Auctōritāte ductum suōrum adductī, Japōnēs impetum in portūs nostrōs subitō fēcērunt. 4. Hī populī erant sociī nostrī, contrā illōs vērō bellum gessimus. 5. Hostēs ē silvīs clam vēnērunt et ā tergō subitō vīsī sunt. Praetereā equitēs hostium ā fronte impetum fēcērunt. 6. Tēlō occīsus, dē nāve in aquam cecidit. 7. Ā virīs fortibus ab imperiō aliēnō līberātī sumus. 8. Propter magnam virtūtem et fidem ā Caesare laudātus est. 9. Mīlitēs impedītī ab hostium equitibus occīdēbantur. 10. Mīlitēs, nātūrā locī impedītī, discessērunt. 11. Castra erant vacua. Mīlitēs enim, ōrātiōne prīncipis commōtī, in prōvinciam discesserant. 12. Hīs urbibus et agrīs hostēs prohibēbimus. Hōs agrōs ac hās urbēs numquam occupābunt. 13. Equitēs hostium agmen nostrum impediēbant. Itaque ducēs hostium hanc ratiōnem bellī probāvērunt. Nōs autem impetūs eōrum prohibuimus.

Exercise 360.—1. It is the fourth principal part of the verb. 2. (a) Soldiers encumbered by full packs; (b) army encumbered by a baggage train; (c) places in which it is difficult to maneuver. 3. Either as a pronoun or as the demonstrative adjective *this*. 4. As ablatives of place from which they are distinguished as follows: *ex*, the person moving is inside the place; *dē*, the person moving is inside the place, or the motion is downward; *ab*, the person moving is not inside the place. *Dē* and *ab* are also used in other types of ablatives. 5. *Ā* and *ē* may be used for *ab* and *ex* before words beginning with consonants. *Ab* and *ex* before any letter, but rarely before *b, p, f, v, m*. (See Nos. 932, 933, and 958.) 6. See Nos. 792-798. 7. With verbs and adjectives of separating, freeing, depriving, and the like: (1) with things, use the ablative without a preposition; (2) with persons, use the ablative with *dē, ex*, or *ab;* e.g., *Metū līber sum; Ā tyrannīs pātriam līberāvī.* (See No. 766.)

Box, page 350.—The truth shall make you free.

UNIT TEN

Exercise 361.—See Introduction, 3.
Box, page 352.—Glory (be) to Thee, O Lord!
Exercise 362.—1. Possum. 2. Nōn poterat. 3. Poterant. 4. Quis poterat? 5. Poterit. 6. Nōn poterant. 7. Poterantne? 8. Possumus. 9. Nōn

possum. 10. Potuerant. 11. Num possumus? 12. Potuimus. 13. Poterant.
14. Nōnne potes? 15. Cūr nōn possunt? 16. Potuerat. 17. Cūr nōn
poterat? 18. Num potes (potestis)?

Exercise 363.—See Introduction, 3.

Exercise 364.—1. They are preparing to come. 2. It is a sin not to
love one's mother. 3. They can remain. 4. It is useful to prepare arms.
5. They were afraid to wait. 6. They will be able to arrive. 7. Rome
cannot be defended. 8. They are preparing to devastate the fields. 9. To
praise God is holy. 10. They had been prepared to defend the camp.
11. The Gauls can be pacified. 12. They have not been able to fortify
the winter quarters. 13. He cannot be hindered (It cannot be prevented).
14. It is safe to remain in camp. 15. It is not the custom of the Roman
people to give hostages.

Exercise 365.—1. Cēdere parātī sunt. 2. Oppugnāre castra difficile
est. 3. Līberārī nōn possunt. 4. Incitāre Gallōs ad bellum facile est.
5. Discēdere parant. 6. Peccātum est patrem nōn dīligere. 7. Pugnāre
timent. 8. Vincere barbarōs contendit. 9. Vidērī timent. 10. Pugnāre in
montibus difficile est.

Exercise 366.—1. All men are able to pray, aren't they? 2. A sure
friend can easily be distinguished in adversity. 3. It is a mistake to fight
against one's friends. 4. On account of the nature of the place the enemy
could not take up a position facing us. 5. Hannibal, Caesar, and Napoleon were able to lead large forces through mountains difficult (to
cross) and high. 6. It was difficult to pacify Gaul. 7. On account of the
scarcity of all things (material), the American soldiers who were in
Bataan were now unable to withstand the enemy's attack (any) longer.
8. Caesar waged war first with those tribes which were nearest the
province, then he sent envoys and legions into all parts of Gaul to
reconnoiter those parts[1] also, to become acquainted with them, and to
conquer them. 9. It is not easy to fight bravely in adversity. 10. Are we
Americans able to defend our territory against all enemies and to drive
them out of our land? 11. Caesar hastened for a long time toward the
territory of the enemy, then he halted to wait for new forces. 12. The
Americans and the Britains were able to lead a great army into that
part of France which faces Britain. 13. It is holy to praise and love
God. 14. At first the Japanese soldiers were able to press the Americans
hard and repulse them in battle, on account of a scarcity of all the
things that pertain to war. 15. The Germans were neighbors of the

---

[1] In earlier impressions, *regions*.

Gauls, for they dwelt across the Rhine. And they were therefore able to devastate easily the fields of Gaul.

Exercise 367.—Americānī et Britannī prīmum magnum exercitum in Siciliam trādūcere poterant. Germānī adversī eīs cōnstiterant. Ibi ācriter pugnātum est. Germānī autem impetūs Americānōrum et sociōrum eōrum sustinēre nōn poterant. Germānī nōn potuerant cognōscere quae cōnsilia et quae proeliī ratiō ā sociīs probāta essent. Itaque nōn poterant cōpiās collocāre et mūnītiōnēs parāre. Cessērunt; et sociī eōs vīcērunt. Tum sociī in Italiam cōpiās suās celeriter trādūxērunt. In Germānōs et ā fronte et ā tergō impetum fēcērunt. Occupāre magnam partem Italiae poterant. Post multa proelia Rōmam capere poterant. Germānī sustinēre cōpiās sociōrum nunc nōn poterant et fugā salūtem petīvērunt. Ad eās partēs Italiae quae proximae Alpibus sunt contendērunt. Haec loca mūnīvērunt et ibi impetum sociōrum exspectāvērunt.

Selections, page 357.—1. He cannot have God as Father who does not have the Church as mother. 2. Friends are proved by adversity. 3. Without virtue (worth, moral excellence, etc.) friendship cannot exist. 4. Nothing without virtue can be praised. 5. It is a bad plan that cannot be changed. 6. A brave man can fall, but he cannot yield. 7. Saint John said: "For how can he who does not love his brother, whom he sees, love God whom he does not see? And we have this command from God: that he who loves God should love his brother also."

Reading No. 26.—Can kings also be saints? Kings who hold command and royal power are often desirous of the lands of others; aroused by the glory of war they often lead great armies against neighboring tribes and kings. They often fear their own brothers also, and kill them lest they seize their royal power by arms. Nevertheless kings can be saints. Saint Stephen (for instance) was able both to hold royal power and to wage war and yet to love God too. Stephen was king of Hungary and taught his nation the Christian faith.

Once a certain man came to kill Stephen. It was night, and Stephen was sleeping. When he was approaching the king, the sword suddenly fell from his hand. When Stephen learned of the intention of this man, he was neither alarmed nor disturbed, and said, "If God is with me, who will be against me?"

Furthermore, Wenceslaus, king of Bohemia, was able to be both king and saint. Once Ratislaus, leader of a neighboring tribe, was waging war against Wenceslaus, for he was eager for the royal power (to become king) of Bohemia. Wenceslaus sent envoys to him to treat of peace and friendship. Nevertheless he could not strengthen friendship (come to any accord). He therefore hastened against him with all his forces. Now, as he approached the enemy, Wenceslaus was treating of (proposed) a new manner of war, in order that there might be no slaughter. The kings therefore took up a position between the armies to fight each other. But Ratislaus was not able to cast a dart against the holy Wenceslaus. And so, having been conquered by God's grace, he established friendship with him. Thus were preserved both the lives of the soldiers and the royal power of Bohemia.

Box, page 361.—From every sin free us, O Lord.

Exercise 368.—1. I am preparing arms in order to be able to conquer the enemy. You are preparing, etc. 2. I have prepared arms in order to be able to conquer the enemy. 3. I ask whether I can conquer the enemy. 4. I ask whether I could conquer the enemy. 5. I asked whether I could conquer the enemy. 6. I asked whether I could have conquered the enemy.

Exercise 369.—1. Caesar placed soldiers at the river in order to be able to defend the bridge more easily. 2. He asked how great forces (how many troops) he was able to collect from (levy in) those regions. 3. The king determined to show (reveal to) the envoys his opinion. 4. The lieutenant decided to wait for new forces in order that the barbarians might not be able to overcome him. 5. I ask whether Caesar was able to conquer the Gauls. 6. When they had not been able to lead their forces through the province, the Gauls decided to lead them through places (that were) difficult and narrow. 7. When Caesar had not been able to devastate those regions, he decided to lead the legions across the river into the province. 8. I ask who is able to carry on this war strongly. 9. He asked whether the cavalry was able to become acquainted with those regions. 10. The Romans were not accustomed to give hostages. 11. The Roman soldiers were not accustomed to surrender themselves and their standards to the enemy. 12. American soldiers are accustomed to conquering all (their) enemies. 13. The lieutenant will place guards there lest the enemy be able to reconnoiter those regions.

Exercise 370.—1. Rogāvit num Columbus trēs omnīnō nāvēs parāre posset. 2. Lēgātus custōdēs ibi cōnstituit nē barbarī eās regiōnēs explōrāre possent. 3. Sunt omnīnō decem mandāta Deī. 4. Americānī quaerēbant cūr auxilium ad mīlitēs nostrōs tum omnīnō mittere nōn possēmus. 5. Dux Rōmānus, "Nōs," inquit, "obsidēs dare nōn omnīnō cōnsuēvimus." 6. Saepe quaerimus cūr Gallī impetum Rōmānōrum sustinēre omnīnō nōn potuerint. 7. Rogāvit num sententiam senātūs cognōscere possent. "Cōnstituī enim," inquit, "hoc bellum nōn gerere contrā auctōritātem senātūs." 8. Rogāvit num hic vir multīs sententiīs līberātus esset. 9. Sānctī saepe ōrāre cōnsuēverant quō facilius fidem servāre et Deum dīligere possent. 10. Caesar cōnstituerat explōrāre et vincere omnēs regiōnēs Galliae. Itaque prīmum cum eīs gentibus quae prōvinciae Rōmānae proximae sunt bellum gessit, nē impetum in sē ā tergō facere possent. Tum cum reliquīs gentibus bellum gessit et, post multa proelia et magnam caedem, omnem Galliam pācāre et obtinēre poterat.

Exercise 371.—1. It behooves you to defend (your) mother. You ought to defend your mother. 2. It behooves you to pray. It is necessary for you to pray. 3. It behooves you all to love God. You should all love God. 4. It behooves us to keep the law of Christ. We should keep the law of Christ. 5. It behooves all men to love Christ. All men should love Christ.

Box, page 365.—In the hour of my death call me, And bid me come to Thee, That with Thy saints I may praise Thee, For all eternity. Amen.

Exercise 372.—1. Caesar ordered the envoy to remain. 2. The lieutenant ordered the soldiers to assemble. 3. Caesar ordered the hostages to be killed. 4. The Gauls commanded Caesar to depart. 5. The general ordered the soldiers to defend him (themselves). 6. The military tribunes were ordered to remain in the battle line. 7. The enemy was ordered to surrender. 8. We have been commanded by Christ to be holy. 9. Boys have been commanded by God to love (their) mothers. 10. I have been ordered to be brave.

Exercise 373.—1. Oportet nōs amīcōs nostrōs adjuvāre. 2. Chrīstus nōs semper ōrāre jussit. 3. Oportet nōs vītās nostrās cōnservāre. 4. Caesar mīlitēs frūmenta incendere jussit. 5. Oportet nōs Deum appellāre. 6. Eōs silvās explōrāre jussit. 7. Servus esse bonus jussus est. 8. Ā Chrīstō semper ōrāre jussī sumus. 9. Mīlitēs frūmenta incendere jussī sunt. 10. Silvās explōrāre jussī sunt. 11. Oportet nōs mātrēs (mātrem) dīligere. 12. Oportet Americānōs rem pūblicam dēfendere. 13. Lincoln Americānōs servōs līberāre jussit. 14. Prīncipēs discēdere jussī sunt. 15. Barbarī sē dēdere jussī sunt.

Exercise 374.—1. Roman soldiers (when) disturbed by fear did not often seek safety in flight, but nevertheless Caesar always ordered them to remain in battle line. For it was proper for them always to remember Roman courage. 2. Christ has commanded us both to love God and to help all men. And so we should all keep this law. 3. Americans had never been eager for war, but when they had been ordered to fight and to defend the state on account of grave wrongs, without fear or delay they bravely waged war with the Japanese. We should always remember the courage of our soldiers and their (heroic) deeds. 4. When he was leading the soldiers into foreign fields, the leader first ordered the cavalry to reconnoiter all the territory lest he lead the legions into places (that were) difficult and narrow. For it has always been the duty of a leader to defend and preserve the lives of his soldiers.

Exercise 375.—1. Oportet nōs omnēs Deum dīligere. 2. Oportet mīlitēs sine timōre pugnāre. 3. Oportet tē saepe ōrāre. 4. Oportet nōs victōriās patrum nostrōrum memoriā tenēre. 5. Oportet Americānōs rem pūblicam suam dēfendere.

Reading No. 27.—At that time there was in the Roman army a legion called the Theban Legion. In this legion all the soldiers and centurions were Christians. Now at that time there was a war in Gaul. Maximian, therefore, who with Diocletian held power, sent legions into Gaul from all the provinces in order to fight those tribes which were waging war with the Romans. But Maximian was not a good man and he had killed many Christians on account of the name and faith of Christ. And so, when this legion had arrived in Gaul, Maximian ordered it also to kill Christians. But the soldiers of this legion, brave and noble Christians, did not do what the emperor ordered. And so Maximian, violently disturbed (enraged) by this occurrence, ordered every tenth soldier to be killed. But after this slaughter the soldiers (still) did not carry out the orders of the emperor, and yet they would not fight against him. For they were ready to be killed for the Christian faith and for Christ the King, but they were Roman soldiers who did not fight in arms against the Roman Emperor. But Maximian ordered every tenth soldier to be killed. After this second slaughter Saint Maur, who was a centurion in this legion, sent a letter to Maximian, (saying):

"We are your soldiers, Emperor, but we are nevertheless true servants of God. We fight for you, we defend you, for you are our emperor and you give us rations and rewards of our dangers (rewards for the dangers we undergo). But God gives us grace and eternal life. And therefore we cannot leave God—our God and yours, Emperor. In this serious matter we will not obey your commands, for our faith forbids it. If you order us to fight the enemy, if you command us to endure toil and pain or to withstand the barbarians' attack or to seize the enemy's cities and devastate the fields, we will fight, endure, seize, and devastate. But we cannot kill Christians, even (though) commanded by you, O Emperor! You have already killed many of us, good and brave men, on account of Christ; yet we have not fought against you. For behold we have weapons and do not defend ourselves. We are ready for death, and will not abandon Christ out of fear of death. We adore[1] God the Father, King of all men, and His Son, Jesus Christ, God. We cannot kill Christians with (our) swords!"

But when he had heard this, Maximian, violently aroused, immediately determined to kill them all. And he therefore ordered all the soldiers and centurions of this legion to be led to death. The rest of the soldiers, who were not Christians, killed them with swords and thus sent to God in heaven these saints of God. Afterwards all Christians remembered their death and will always remember it. Shall we not also praise them? For they were both brave soldiers and brave Christians.

Box, page 368.—All ye holy martyrs, pray for us.

Moments at Mass No. 5.—P. World without end. S. Amen. P. The Lord be with you. S. And with thy spirit. P. Lift up your hearts. S. We have (lifted them up) to the Lord. P. Let us give thanks unto the Lord our God. S. It is worthy and right. P. Holy, holy, holy, Lord God of Hosts. The heavens and the earth are full of Thy glory. Hosanna in the highest. Blessed is He who comes in the name of the Lord. Hosanna in the highest.

Box, page 370.—Son of God, we beseech Thee, hear us!

Exercise 376.—1. Cum tribus legiōnibus. 2. Post duo proelia. 3. In quīnque urbibus. 4. Sine decem legiōnibus. 5. In duās urbēs. 6. Cum ūnō imperātōre. 7. Post trēs victōriās. 8. Post caedem centum obsidum. 9. Trāns duo flūmina. 10. Post mortem hōrum trium virōrum. 11. Prō ūnō rēge. 12. Ab ūnō virō. 13. Quīnque tēlīs. 14. Propter virtūtem ūnīus virī. 15. Dē salūte trium obsidum. 16. Per duās prōvinciās. 17. Ex tribus urbibus. 18. Propter ūnum peccātum. 19. Ūnī virō. 20. Duōbus prīncipibus.

Box, page 371.—Rome—Head of the World.

Exercise 377.—Answer in Latin 1. How many are five and four? Quīnque et quattuor sunt novem. 2. How many are one and four? Ūnum et quattuor sunt quīnque. 3. How many are six and one? Sex et ūnum sunt septem. 4. How many are five and one? Quīnque et ūnum sunt sex. 5. How many are four and four? Quattuor et quattuor sunt octō. 6. How many are six and four? Sex et quattuor sunt decem. 7. How many are two and one? Duo et ūnum sunt trēs (tria). 8. How many heads has man? Homō habet ūnum caput. 9. How many hands has man? Homō habet duās manūs. 10. How many bodies has man? Homō

---

[1] In editions before 1947, *believe in.*

habet ūnum corpus. 11. How many minds has man? Homō habet ūnam mentem.

Exercise 378.—1. Hear, O Israel, thy God is the one God. 2. To the one God may there be eternal glory. 3. A state is often preserved by the courage of one brave man. 4. The common welfare is often placed in (entrusted to) one man. 5. Through one man, Jesus Christ, we have salvation and eternal life. 6. Two saints, Peter and Paul, taught the Christian faith to those who dwelt in the city of Rome. 7. Christ was led to death with two evil men. 8. The names of two men, Washington, who established our state, and Lincoln, who preserved it, will always be remembered. 9. We adore three Persons in one God, Father, Son, and Holy Spirit. 10. A true Christian can be distinguished by these three virtues, faith, hope, and charity. 11. Man has one head but two hands.

Exercise 379.—1. Per mortem ūnīus virī, Jēsū Chrīstī, ā perīculō mortis aeternae līberātī sumus. 2. In quā urbe magnā et nōbilī erant septem collēs? 3. Nōs Chrīstiānī quīnque vulnera Jēsū Chrīstī, Dominī et Deī nostrī, adōrāmus. 4. Centuriō ita appellātur quod centum virōs dūcit. 5. Quot sunt quattuor et sex? 6. Sunt decem mandāta Deī. 7. Sunt octō beātitūdinēs. 8. Sunt septem dōna Spīritūs Sānctī.

A Saying of St. Paul, page 372.—One Lord, one faith, one baptism, one God and Father of all, who is above all and through all and in us all.

Moments at Mass No. 6.—May the almighty God bless you, the Father, the Son, and the Holy Spirit. Amen.

Box, page 375.—Mother of Good Counsel, pray for us!

Exercise 380.—1. Alterīus rēgis. (See No. 86.) 2. Alterīus centuriōnis. 3. Aliī gentī. 4. Tōtī Italiae. 5. Sōlīus Deī. 6. Nūllīs hominibus. 7. Nūllīus rēgnī. 8. Huic reī pūblicae sōlī. 9. Hūjus virī sōlīus. 10. Nūllī mātrī. 11. Nūllīus mīlitis. 12. Tōtīus Galliae. 13. Tōtī exercituī. 14. Alterīus victōriae. 15. Hūjus puerī sōlīus. 16. Tōtīus populī.

Exercise 381.—1. We have no other way. 2. To the only God, King of heaven and earth, may there be glory. 3. Caesar replied to the Gauls when they were preparing to lead troops through the province: "According to the custom of the Roman people I cannot give to any one a route (permit anyone to go) through the province." 4. No fear nor danger terrifies our soldiers. 5. When the winter quarters had been stormed, Caesar, informed by a dispatch of this occurrence, immediately (and) without any delay led soldiers (out) to help his men. 6. Barbarians praise only those who can fight bravely. 7. All Americans remember Washington and Lincoln. For one established our republic, the other preserved it in the dangers of war. 8. Caesar waged war both with the Gauls and with the Germans. For the one nation was defending itself against him, while the other used to devastate the fields of others. 9. In the battle some are killed by darts, some (others) by swords. 10. Some wage war for the sake of fame, others for the sake of safety. 11. Some praise one general, others another. 12. Some approve one opinion, others another. 13. He ordered the baggage of the whole army sent to one place. 14. He ordered the whole mountain filled with men. 15. Caesar seized command of all Gaul. 16. When the shouting of the enemy was heard, the soldiers in the whole camp were alarmed and asked one another the cause of the shouting.

Exercise 382.—1. Corpora aliōrum in castrīs erant; aliōrum autem in silvīs. 2. Aliī Caesarem laudāvērunt, aliī vērō Hannibalem. 3. Duo virī eōs quī Rōmam incolēbant fidem Chrīstiānam docuērunt. Alter erat Petrus, alter erat Paulus. 4. Caesar et Hannibal summī imperātōrēs erant. Alter tōtam Galliam vīcit, alter ā Rōmānīs victus est. 5. Caesar sōlus tōtam Galliam vīcit. 6. Oppugnāre oppidum sine ūllā morā cōnstituērunt. 7. Aliī cupidī bellī sunt, aliī autem pācis. 8. Nūllī mīlitēs in castrīs relictī sunt. 9. Nōs Americam laudāmus; aliī aliōs populōs laudant. 10. Caesar tōtī exercituī grātiās saepe ēgit. 11. Lee et Grant summī imperātōrēs erant. Alter vīcit, alter victus est. 12. Nōnne Rōma glōria tōtīus Italiae est? 13. Nōs nūllī hostī dēdāmus. 14. Chrīstus sōlus est rēx omnium hominum. 15. Erant duo prīncipēs in hāc gente. Alter amīcus Caesaris et senātūs Rōmānī erat, alter nōn erat. 16. Caesar nūllī prīncipī obsidēs dare cōnsuēvit. 17. Aliī pugnāre timent, aliī pugnāre semper parātī sunt. 18. Agrōs alterīus occupāvit. 19. Prīncipēs tōtīus Galliae ā Caesare victī sunt. 20. Aliī aliud cōnsilium probant. 21. Erant duo Cicerōnēs, quōrum alter in exercitū Caesaris erat, alter in senātū erat. 22. Aliī aliam gentem laudant.

Moments at Mass No. 7.—May the body of our Lord Jesus Christ guard thy soul unto life everlasting.

Reading No. 28.—The Holy Trinity. For there is one person of the Father, another of the Son, another of the Holy Spirit, but the divinity of the Father and of the Son and of the Holy Spirit is one. The Father eternal, the Son eternal, the Holy Spirit eternal; and yet there are not three eternals, but one eternal. So the Father is God, the Son God, and the Holy Spirit God, and yet there are not three Gods, but one God. So the Father is Lord, the Son is Lord, and the Holy Spirit is Lord; and yet there are not three Lords, but one Lord. Therefore there is one

Father, not three Fathers; one Son, not three Sons; one Holy Spirit, not three Holy Spirits.

A Saying of Christ, page 378.—Christ said, "For one is your Father, who is in heaven."

Note on Translation, page 378.—1. For what reason did you kill him? 2. The Gauls were eager for revolution. 3. If the circumstances demand it, a man ought to defend himself even by arms. 4. The envoy informed Caesar of the whole affair. 5. The chiefs were treating of a serious matter.

Reading No. 29.—Peace and War. All men praise peace and seek it, and yet there is no peace.

Hannibal led forces through Gaul across wide rivers and high mountains in order to wage war with the Romans in Italy. His soldiers endured heavy toil and great suffering; many of them fell in the difficult (almost impassable) mountains; many were killed. Yet he neither came to a halt nor sent envoys to the Romans for the sake of peace, for he had determined both to conquer the Romans and to seize Rome. He strove in battle with the Romans for a long time, but finally he was repulsed in battle and conquered.

Afterwards the Romans waged war with the Gauls and nearly all the other neighboring tribes. Led on by (desire of) the glory of war, they surpassed these peoples in courage and arms and conquered them. And so for a long time they held command of all Italy and of many foreign tribes.

Then the barbarians, led on by hope of victory, invaded the Roman cities and provinces in order to devastate and occupy them all. After this many other wars were waged in Europe.

Napoleon, a great and brave man, who had seized power in France (Gaul), led on by hope of power and glory determined to conquer and hold all of Europe. He consequently led (his) armies against all the peoples and states adjoining France in order to seize command of them. For a long time he repulsed them all in battle and overcame them in wars. A great number of men were killed; great sufferings were endured by all. But he too was conquered by courage and arms.

After that another commander, named Hitler, a man eager for glory and royal power, devastated all Europe and overcame it by arms (in war). For a long time he held power over almost all Europe, but now he has been conquered with all his allies.

There is no peace. Nevertheless all good men seek peace and praise it. Yet wars are always being waged, "savage wars." Why are we not able to strengthen (establish) friendship and peace and trust among all peoples? Isn't it good to be at peace? Is it not holy to help others? Isn't it Christian for all men to love one another? For Christ said, "You are all brothers." But it is wrong for brothers to kill brothers. And again Christ said, "Love God with your whole soul and love your neighbor as yourself." But those who love everyone neither fight with others nor kill them. God, the King of heaven and earth, said, "Love peace and truth." It is good and holy to love and keep peace. "Bear one another's burdens," Saint Paul says, for it is Christian to help others. Nevertheless, as you know, there is no peace.

Why do men, violently moved by fear of death and the dangers of war, still wage war, devastate fields, kill the enemy, storm and burn cities? Some are desirous of the broad lands of others. Some are aroused to war by hope of glory. Some fear neighboring tribes. And so they decided to wage war lest they be conquered. Some, aroused by wrongs, call soldiers to arms for the glory of their name.

And so, because the laws of God and of Christ were not kept, there have always been wars, there are wars now on every side, and there always will be wars. But let us Christians encourage peace, seek it, love it, and keep it!

Box, page 380.—He is altogether alone who is without a friend.

UNIT ELEVEN

Box, page 382.—Jesus, King of glory, have mercy on us!

Exercise 383.—1. Quem rēgem fēcērunt? 2. Quantās mūnītiōnēs faciunt? 3. Quō cum omnibus cōpiīs iter fēcit? 4. Fūgitne? 5. Quis fūgit? 6. Quae cōnsilia capient? 7. Quō ex illō locō iter facient? 8. Cūr fugit? 9. Cēpēruntne urbem? 10. Num ante proelium fugiēs? 11. Fēcitne pontem? 12. Num Rōmam cēpērunt? 13. Quis illum collem capiet? 14. Hannibal, Rōmam numquam capiēs. 15. Post proelium in omnēs partēs fūgērunt. 16. Ducēs salūtis causā fūgērunt. 17. Fēcēruntne eum ducem? 18. Nōnne ad montēs fūgērunt? 19. Obsidēs etiam fugiēbant. 20. Mīlitēs Rōmānī nōn fugiunt.

Exercise 384.—1. Soldiers. Soldiers should be brave and eager for victory, for they sustain much toil and heavy suffering. Led out of camp by the leader, soldiers make long marches. They pitch camp. Led into the territory of the enemy, they quickly build large fortifications. Drawn up in battle line by the centurions, the soldiers make an attack against the enemy. Ordered by the leader (At the leader's command) they take hills and bridges. Soldiers who are brave do not flee (when) hard pressed by the enemy, but rather put the enemy to flight and capture (their) supply of grain and arms.

2. **Roman Soldiers.** Roman soldiers were brave. Moved by fear, they did not often flee. They took fortified camps; they captured cities fortified both by walls and by the nature of the place. They also captured a great number of soldiers. They made strong attacks against both battle lines and cavalry. They made long and large fortifications. Roman soldiers, called on by name by the general, fought fiercely and long on account of their good will toward him. They made long marches through the provinces and through the territory of the enemy. Roman soldiers often made their leaders Roman kings.

3. **Caesar, the Leader.** Caesar, a brave leader, managed wars with a strong hand. He made good plans and carried on large-scale maneuvers. He took the cities of the Gauls; he built immense fortifications; he made long marches through forests and through mountains. He never fled, terrified either by darts or by the noise of battle. He had a good will toward the soldiers, and was therefore often greatly saddened by the slaughter of his own men. The soldiers under his command fought bravely because of his good will toward them. Because of their own good will toward Caesar, the soldiers called him commander.

4. **American Soldiers.** American soldiers also are brave, but they are not eager for war, for they love peace. Nevertheless, aroused by wrongs, they will wage war strongly and valiantly. Without hesitation they will make long marches; they will prepare a supply of arms and of weapons. They will take cities and harbors and towns, and will hold (when) taken. They will build large fortifications and seize fortifications already made by the enemy. Without delay or fear they will make attacks against the enemy. They will praise the plan made by the leaders. They will not fear the dangers of death. They will not flee, driven by fear and by missiles. They will show the greatest good will toward the republic, just as our forefathers always showed good will toward our free state. American soldiers will never make their leaders kings, for they will have the greatest good will toward the republic. Shall we not always praise both the Roman soldiers and American soldiers and remember them?

Selections, page 385.—1. Christ said: "I do not seek My own will but the will of Him who sent Me." 2. Lord, Thou art He who made the heavens and the earth, the sea and all the things that are in them. 3. Christ said: "My mother and My brothers are those who hear the word of God and do it."

Exercise 385.—1. Japōnēs cōnsilium bellī cēpērunt. Tum impetum in magnum portum Americānōrum subitō fēcērunt. 2. Mīlitēs longum iter per fīnēs Gallōrum fēcērunt. Tum hī in colle subitō vīsī sunt. Gallī mūnītiōnēs in illō colle fēcerant nē Rōmānī eum caperent. Rōmānī ā fronte impetum in collem fēcērunt. Gallī, tēlīs et gladiīs territī, clamōrem sustulērunt et fūgērunt. 3. Gallī equitēs in silvīs et mīlitēs ad flūmen collocāverant. Hōs Rōmānī cēpērunt, illōs vērō in fugam dedērunt. 4. Prīnceps Gallōrum Caesarī, "Propter voluntātem tuam," inquit, "in gentem meam impetum in hostēs tuōs faciam; agrōs et oppida eōrum capiam; illōs mīlitēs quī nōn fūgerint etiam capiam. 5. Imperātōr, "Quantus," inquit, "numerus hostium est? Quantās mūnītiōnēs fēcērunt? Cēpēruntne cōpiam frūmentī? Fugientne post impetum? 6. Napoleon sē rēgem et imperātōrem Galliae fēcit. 7. Dux sociōrum Caesarī, "Mē et mīlitēs meōs," inquit, "in hōc colle collocāvistī ut eum tenērēmus. Propter voluntātem tuam in mē eum tenēbō et nōn fugiam. Mūnītiōnēs faciam et tēla parābō. Illī hunc collem numquam capient."

Box, page 386.—In the year of the Lord.

Exercise 386.—1. In what year did Columbus arrive at the new lands which we call America? 2. On what day do we thank God for our free land? 3. In what year did Lincoln free the slaves from their masters? 4. On what day was Christ put to death? 5. On what day did men first see the boy Christ? 6. On what day was Christ taken up into heaven?

Exercise 387.—1. Tertiā vigiliā. 2. Secundā hōrā. 3. Tertiā (tertiō) diē. 4. Prīmō annō. 5. Eō tempore. 6. Eō (eā; illō, illā) diē.

Box, page 387.—Time flies.

Exercise 388.—1. Caesar set the day on which all the chiefs of the Gauls should come to him. On that day they all came together. 2. At the first watch the shouting of the guards was heard. 3. At that time war was being waged with the Gauls. 4. On the third day they burned all the crops in the fields. 5. In that year the Romans overcame the Gauls in many battles. 6. On that day many men fell in battle. 7. There were no guards on the wall at that time. 8. The next day grain was given to the soldiers. 9. At the first watch he secretly led the legion out of the camp. 10. On the third day a messenger was sent by the lieutenant to Caesar to ask for assistance. 11. The Romans were brave both in war and in peace. 12. In that year they made (engaged in) many unfavorable battles. 13. At the third watch a slave was sent out of the camp secretly to Caesar.

Exercise 389.—1. Tertiā hōrā fūgērunt. 2. Eō tempore collem cēpērunt. 3. Secundā diē in montēs iter fēcērunt. 4. Tertiā hōrā castra posuērunt. 5. Eō annō mūnītiōnēs in prōvinciā fēcērunt. 6. Tertiā diē rēgem cēpērunt. 7. Proximō annō urbem cēpērunt. 8. Tertiā vigiliā hostēs impetum fēcērunt.

A Saying of Cicero, page 388.—Cicero said: "History is the witness of the times, the light of truth, the life of memory."

Reading No. 30.—Our Father, who art in heaven, hallowed be Thy name: Thy kingdom come: Thy will be done on earth as it is in heaven. Give us this day our daily bread: and forgive us our trespasses as we forgive those who trespass against us. And lead us not into temptation. But deliver us from evil. Amen.

Box, page 390.—Jesus, God of peace, have mercy on us!

Exercise 390.—1. Let us desire the grace of God. 2. May he take the city. 3. May the enemy flee. 4. Let us flee. 5. Let us make a plan. 6. May the king flee. 7. Let us make an attack against them again.

Exercise 391.—1. Cupiāmus vidēre Deum. 2. Iter in montēs faciāmus. 3. Capiant oppidum! 4. Fugiant! 5. Capiāmus cōnsilium. 6. Faciant rūrsus impetum. 7. Capiant rēgem! 8. Fugiāmus.

Exercise 392.—1. They made fortifications in order to hurl darts against the enemy more easily. 2. Cōpiās novās mīsit nē . . . caperent. 3. Caesar in prīmam aciem contendit nē . . . reciperent. 4. Lēgātus auxilia mīserat quō . . . reciperent. 5. In prōvinciam cōpiās dūcere parāvit nē . . . cuperet. 6. Custōdēs cōnstituit nē . . . facerent. 7. Legiōnēs integrās mīsit nē . . . fugerent. 8. Nostrī agmen nē . . . reciperent. 9. Virtus legiōnum cōnfirmābātur ut . . . cuperent.

Exercise 393.—The Roman leader, disturbed by these messages, called the lieutenants and military tribunes to him to make a plan. He had sent a horseman to find out what the enemy was doing. In the council he first asks this horseman on what day the enemy arrived, where they have pitched camp, how large the fortifications they have made, how numerous the troops they have, whether they have a supply of grain and water, which hills they have taken. Then he asked the centurions whether his soldiers desired victory, whether they were ready for battle, whether they had good will toward him, whether they had a supply of darts. After this he made a (his) plan and sent the lieutenants and military tribunes away.

The next day at dawn the leader marched through the forest with all his forces to seize a naturally fortified hill. But the leader of the enemy, when he had seen the Roman column, led troops out of camp and drew them up. Then he advanced toward the Romans in order to make an attack upon them. When the enemy was not far distant, the Romans

hurled darts against them. Immediately many of the enemy, moved by
fear, yielded and fled. The rest nevertheless again made an attack. Then
the Romans waited in order more easily to hurl darts again. And so the
Romans, when they had again hurled their darts against the enemy,
raised a shout and attacked the enemy. They carried on the attack with
swords. There was a bloody slaughter. Some of the enemy swiftly fled,
others raised a shout according to their custom and surrendered themselves and all their possessions to the Romans. Thus the Romans both
took the camp and captured a complete supply of everything. And so
the Romans withdrew to camp.

Exercise 394.—1. Rōmānī virōs in mūrīs collocāvērunt quī in hostēs
tēla conjicerent. 2. Rōmānī mūnītiōnēs fēcērunt nē hostēs in sē tēla
facile conjicerent. 3. Dux rogāvit num mīlitēs signum darī cuperent.
4. Caesar nōbīs ostendit quantum dolōrem Gallī ex obsidum cōrum
caede capiant. 5. Imperātor ā mīlitibus quaesīvit num glōriam et praemia cuperent. Tum, "Pugnāte fortiter," inquit; "hostēs fugient et castra
eōrum capiēmus. Ea sunt plēna omnium hārum rērum quās cupitis."
6. Cum mīlitēs tēla conjēcissent, equitēs in hostēs mīsit nē ē timōre sē
reciperent et impetum rūrsus facerent. Tum barbarī mōre suō clāmōrem
sustulērunt et in omnēs partēs fūgērunt.

Quotation from Martial, page 394.—Diaulus was formerly a doctor and is now an undertaker; what he does as an undertaker, he had
also done as a doctor.

Exercise 395.—1. They marched for five days. (*Diēs*, acc. pl. of
diēs, diēī, m. (f.); acc. of extent of time.) 2. They marched five miles.
(*Mīlia*, acc. of neut. pl. noun *mīlia, mīlium;* acc. of extent of space;
passuum, gen. pl. of *passus, ūs*, m.; gen (partitive) with *mīlia*, the two
words together meaning *miles*. See Nos. 117 and 689.) 3. The camp
was a mile from the mountains. (*Mīlle*, indecl. adj. modifying *passūs;*
passūs, acc. pl. of *passus, ūs*, m.; acc. of extent of space.) 4. The camp
was two miles from the mountains. (*Duō*, acc. neut. of *duo, duae, duo*,
cardinal number, modifying *mīlia; mīlia*, acc. of *mīlia, mīlium*, n.; acc.
of extent of space; *passuum*, gen. pl. of *passus, ūs, m.;* gen. with *mīlia*.)
5. On that day three thousand men fell in battle. (*Diē*, abl. sing. of
diēs, diēī, m. (f.); abl. of time when. *Tria*, nom. neut. of *trēs, tria*,
cardinal number, modifying *mīlia; mīlia*, nom. of *mīlia, mīlium*, n.;
subject of *cecidērunt; hominum*, gen. pl. of *homō, hominis*, m.; gen.
with *mīlia*.) 6. He filled the mountain with three thousand men. (*Tribus*,
abl. neut. of *trēs, tria*, cardinal number, modifying *mīlibus; mīlibus*,
abl. of *mīlia, mīlium*, n.; abl. with *complēvit; hominum*, gen. pl. of

homō, hominis, m.; gen. with *mīlibus.*) 7. The bodies of three thousand men were seen in the fields. (*Trium,* gen. neut. of *trēs, tria,* cardinal number, modifying *mīlium; mīlium,* gen. of *mīlia, mīlium,* n.; possessive genitive; *hominum,* gen. pl. of *homō, hominis,* m., gen. with *mīlium.* See Nos. 680 and 117.) 8. He was in the mountains for a thousand days. (*Mīlle,* indecl. adj. modifying *diēs; diēs,* acc. pl. of *diēs, diēī,* m. (f.); acc. of extent of time.) 9. He was in the mountains for two thousand days. (*Duo,* acc. neut. of *duo, duae, duo,* cardinal number, modifying *mīlia; mīlia,* acc. of *mīlia, mīlium,* n.; acc. of extent of time; *diērum,* gen. pl. of *diēs, diēī,* m. (f.); gen. with *mīlia.* 10. The leader gave rewards to two thousand men. (*Mīlibus,* dat. of *mīlia, mīlium,* n.; dat. of indirect object.) 11. The faith of Christ has been on earth for nearly two thousand years. (*Duo,* acc. neut. of *duo, duae, duo,* cardinal number, modifying *mīlia; mīlia,* acc. of *mīlia, mīlium,* n.; acc. of extent of time.) 12. Caesar waged war with the barbarians in Gaul for seven years. (*Annōs,* acc. pl. of *annus, ī,* m.; acc. of extent of time.) 13. The enemy fled swiftly for four days. (*Diēs,* acc. pl. of *diēs, diēī,* m. (f.); acc. of extent of time.) 14. How wide was that ditch? (*Quam,* interrogative adverb of degree.) 15. How high is this wall? 16. The soldiers made a ditch ten paces wide. (*Passūs,* acc. pl. of *passus, ūs,* m.; acc. of extent of space.) 17. The rampart was ten feet high. (*Pedēs,* acc. pl. of *pēs, pedis,* m.; acc. of extent of space.)

Box, page 395.—Come, let us adore Christ the Son of God, who redeemed us with His own blood.

Exercise 396.—1. Trēs diēs iter fēcērunt. 2. Quīnque mīlia passuum iter fēcērunt. 3. Urbs duo mīlia passuum ā flūmine aberat. 4. Trēs diēs fūgērunt. 5. Quīnque hōrās collem tenuērunt; tum Rōmānī eum cēpērunt. 6. Tribus mīlibus virōrum gladiōs dedērunt. 7. Collis ā duobus mīlibus virōrum captus est. 8. In prōvinciam cum mīlle hominibus iter fēcit. 9. Quam altus est hic mōns? 10. Flūmen mīlle passūs aberat. 11. Duās hōrās pugnāvērunt (pugnātum est). 12. Hoc flūmen multōs pedēs lātum est. 13. Novem diēs exspectāvit. 14. Sānctī ōrāre duās aut trēs hōrās saepe poterant. 15. Americānī multōs diēs Bataan dēfendērunt. 16. Poterimusne multōs annōs pācem cōnservāre? 17. Cīvitās nostra multōs annōs lībera fuit. 18. Trēs annōs bellum gessērunt.

Exercise 397.—1. How many miles long is (the river which is called) the Mississippi? (2,470 miles.) 2. How wide is that river? (300 feet at St. Paul; 1,400 feet at mouth of Illinois River.) 3. How far is the city of Rome from our land? (Rome to New York City, 4,273 miles.) 4. For how many days was Christ on earth after His death? (40 days.) 5. For how many years did Christ teach men on earth the way of salvation?

(Entire life, 33 years; public life, 3 years.) 6. For how many years did Americans wage among themselves that war which is called the Civil War? (3 years, 10 months.) 7. For how many years did Americans fight the Germans? (American participation in World War I, 19 months; World War II, 3 years, 8 months.)

A Saying of Christ, page 396.—Christ said to His apostles, "He who receives you, receives Me; and he who receives Me, receives Him who sent Me."

Exercise 398.—1. Chrīstus trēs diēs post mortem suam nōn vīsus est, sed tum amīcīs suīs sē ostendit. Multōs diēs in terrā mānsit ut amīcōs suōs docēret et eōs cōnfirmāret. Tum in Caelum sublātus est, et ibi in glōriā Patris manēbit in saecula saeculōrum. 2. Cōnfirmēmus et cōnservēmus pācem, ut multōs annōs metibus et dolōribus bellī līberī sīmus. 3. Illī quī ad fīnēs nostrōs prīmī vēnērunt multa mīlia passuum, multōs diēs, per loca angusta, per silvās perīculōrum plēnās, per montēs difficilēs et altōs iter saepe fēcērunt, ut pervenīrent ad agrōs bonōs et habērent cōpiam aquae. 4. Malum est hominēs inter sē pugnāre. In omnibus illīs bellīs quae mīlia annōrum gesta sunt multa mīlia hominum occīsa (occīsī) sunt et capta (captī) sunt. Bonum est in pāce manēre; bonum est pācem dīligere et cōnservāre. 5. Rōmānī castra cotīdiē pōnēbant et mūniēbant. Saepe ea mūniēbant vallō decem pedēs altō et fossā quīnque pedēs lātā. Ita multa mīlia passuum iter cotīdiē faciēbant et multās hōrās mūnitiōnēs parābant.

Reading No. 31.—Saint Peter Claver, Apostle of the Slaves. Saint Peter Claver was a Jesuit. He came to the port of Cartagena, a city in America, to help the slaves there. For in those days evil men were sailing to Africa to seize the wretched men who lived in those regions and to make them slaves. Then they would bring them as slaves to America and there sell them. Those slaves were transported from Africa in small, dirty ships. On these ships there was no supply of water and provisions nor of any of the things useful for life. Saint Peter, therefore, when the ships had come into port, used to hasten to the ships without delay, to help the wretched slaves. He aided both their bodies and their souls. Indeed it is difficult to show with what courage he carried on these things (this work of charity). For he carried out of the ships in his own arms many of them who had fallen (ill) in the ships through suffering and wounds. He aided them by means of (by providing) water and grain (food). Thus he saved the lives of many slaves. Furthermore, he taught them all the Christian faith. He taught them to pray and to love God. He did not hold anyone off, but took everyone to himself. He gave himself wholly to these wretched slaves. The slaves therefore called him father and friend.

Saint Peter, however, endured many sorrows for the sake of the welfare of the slaves. For many of the masters had bad will (were ill disposed) toward him and so they hindered him (in his work). Nevertheless Saint Peter, neither moved nor alarmed by these wrongs, bore everything in order to make Christians (of) the slaves, his beloved brothers. For many years he carried on this work, and at last worn out by his labors, he came to heaven's reward. After many years he was declared a saint and is praised now by all Christians.

Exercise 399.—1. Ab hostibus interficiēbāmur. 2. Capiēbantur. 3. Oppidum captum est. 4. Rōma saepe capta est. 5. Ē manibus hostium ēreptus est. 6. Multa mīlia mīlitum interfecta (interfectī) sunt. 7. Tēla contrā hostēs conjecta sunt. 8. Duo mīlia eōrum interfecta (interfectī) sunt. 9. Mīlle virī captī sunt. 10. Gladiī ēreptī sunt. 11. Nihil captum est. 12. Illud oppidum capiētur. 13. Ab amīcō ē morte ēripiēbar (ēreptus sum).

Box, page 399.—Saint Peter Claver, Apostle of the Slaves, pray for us!

Exercise 400.—1. Our state was saved by Washington from great danger. 2. The Japanese, often forced into places (that were) narrow and difficult to maneuver in, were killed by darts (missiles) and swords (bayonets). 3. The leader said to the soldiers, "What do Roman soldiers fear?" The centurion answered, "We fear nothing." 4. The centurion was saved from the enemy's hands by the cavalry. 5. By whom was the city of Rome taken? 6. The envoys who were sent to the states of the Gauls for the sake of grain were often either captured by the Gauls or killed. This slaughter was often the cause of war, for Caesar determined to kill many thousands of Gauls lest other envoys of his be killed by them. 7. Many men, killed by the darts, fell from the wall. 8. Saints are often saved by God from dangers. 9. I have heard nothing of this matter. Have you heard about it? 10. On account of wrongs on the part of (committed by) the Gauls, (their) hostages were often killed by the Romans. 11. Nothing is desired by him who has an abundance of everything. 12. Many things are desired by men, but salvation most of all.

Exercise 401.—1. Quī ā Caesare interficiēbantur? 2. Nihil ex oppidō ēreptum est. 3. Grātia Deī (ā) nōbīs peccātō ēripitur. 4. Ā Filiō Deī ē morte aeternā ēreptī sumus. 5. Ille vir ā centuriōne fortī ē morte ēreptus est. 6. Multī ā virīs malīs nunc interficiuntur. 7. Virī ab amīcīs suīs ē morte saepe ēripiuntur. 8. Quid ā sānctīs cupitur? 9. Hostēs ā Rōmānīs in fugam saepe conjectī sunt. 10. Haec urbs ab hostibus saepe capta est. 11. Duo mīlia hominum capta (captī) sunt. 12. Capta estne ā Gallīs Rōma? 13. Omnēs aliī aut captī aut interfectī sunt.

Reading No. 32.—A master was punishing a bad slave. The slave shouted, "Why do you beat me, master? I have done nothing." But the master said, "That's why I beat you—because you have done nothing."

Exercise 402.—Ille quī nēminem dīligit, nēminem laudat, nēminem adjuvat, nēminī grātiās agit, sōlus et sine amīcīs est. Brevī tempore dolōribus labōribusque cōnficiētur. Auxilium ā nūllō accipiētur. Nōn poterit magnās rēs gerere, nam nūllōs sociōs et amīcōs habēbit. Erit vir miser, nam vīta sine amīcīs et sine virtūte est misera.

Exercise 403.—1. Tribus diēbus pervenient. 2. Duābus hōrīs agmen hostium vidēbitur. 3. Litterae duōbus diēbus recipientur. 4. Duōbus diēbus bellum cōnficiētur. 5. Duōbus diēbus nāvēs cōnspectae sunt. 6. Tribus hōrīs mīlitēs itinere et labōre cōnficientur. 7. Nēmō vulneribus cōnfectus diū et fortiter pugnāre potest.

Exercise 404.—1. Within six days all the fortifications were finished. 2. The soldiers, worn out with wounds, were not able to stand the effort any longer. 3. The legion marched through the forest secretly and was not seen from the enemy's camp. 4. They came to (arrived at) the river within three days. 5. On the third day they arrived at camp. 6. Barbarians are seen on all sides (in every direction). 7. The Roman leader said to the barbarians: "Romans are accustomed to take hostages, not to give them." 8. The Romans always preserved that glory of war which had been received from (their) forefathers. 9. A dispatch was received by Caesar by (in) which the lieutenant was informed how great the danger was in which the legions were. 10. Among the Romans slaves often received injuries from (were mistreated by) bad masters. 11. Many wounds were received in that battle.

Reading No. 33.—Receive, brother, the viaticum of the body of our Lord Jesus Christ, to (and may He) guard you from the evil enemy and to lead you into eternal life. Amen.

Selected Sayings, page 402.—1. Christ says: "I am the way, the truth, and the life: no one comes to the Father except through Me." 2. "No one," says Saint Paul, "can lay another foundation besides that which has been laid, which is Christ Jesus." 3. Seneca said: "A good man without God is no one (does not exist)."

Exercise 405.—1. Cōnficiantur mūnītiōnēs. 2. Oppidum capiātur. 3. Ex hōc perīculō ēripiāmur. 4. Litterae recipiantur. 5. Capiantur.

6. Pōns cōnficiātur. 7. Fugiant. 8. Satis aquae capiātur. 9. Rēx capiātur.

Exercise 406.—1. Benedict Arnold, who had not kept faith with our republic, left the camp of the Americans and fled into other regions lest he be killed by them. 2. Christ was killed that men be saved from death and sin. 3. Camp was pitched at the river in order that enough water might be taken from the river (to insure an adequate supply of water). 4. He spared the lives of the hostages lest great sorrow be taken (felt) by the Gauls from (because of) their slaughter. 5. It was not safe enough to fight in that place. And so they hastened to the camp lest they be captured and killed by the enemy. 6. He asked the centurions whether the soldiers were worn out with the length of the march and with wounds. 7. Let us prepare arms lest our soldiers be captured and killed by the enemy. 8. All the generals are preparing fortifications lest the cities and towns be taken by the enemy and fortified. 9. He led the legions through the forest to the hill secretly lest they be seen by the barbarians. 10. The leader asked the military tribunes whether the enemy's column had been seen. 11. The lieutenant asked the centurions whether they had enough grain after the taking of the city. 12. He remained there for many days lest the soldiers be worn out with the greatness of their effort and the length of the march.

Exercise 407.—The missing letters are as follows: line 1. a, s; 2. n; 5. u; 6. e; 7. ent; 8. s; 9. e; 10. ant; 11. us; 14. e; 15. em; 16. es; 19. ia; 22. a, c; 24. a, is; 28. en.

Your dispatch was received by me at the first hour. The enemy's column was caught sight of by my cavalry in the second hour. At the third hour their camp was pitched on a hill a hundred feet from the river. They pitched camp there in order to take enough water from the river. I asked whether they had received a sufficient amount of grain also. They have received enough. And so we ought to make an attack against them immediately lest (before) they recover from (their) fear and the toil (the weariness caused by the toil). And therefore I will lead my forces secretly through the forest nearest that hill in order not to be seen by (their) guards. I will station one part of (my) forces in the rear lest the enemy withdraw to the forest; I will send another part against the enemy from the front. I command you to lead the third legion through the mountains secretly lest they be seen from the camp. Station this legion across (on the other side of) the river in order that the enemy may not withdraw across the river into the mountains. The route will be long and difficult enough. And so I will wait a long time and in the third hour I will give the signal. First one division of the troops will remain in the forest, but another will make an attack against the camp from the front. The enemy, confused by fear, will fight against these soldiers. Then those who are in the forest, after the signal has been given, will make an attack from the rear and hurl (their) darts. If I desire help from you I will send a messenger to give you the order to lead the third legion across the river. Farewell.

Selected Sayings, page 406.—1. The Elephant. The trunk was given to the elephant because, on account of the size of its body, it had only difficult access to food. 2. Hope. When asked what was most common to men, Thales said, "Hope, for even those who have nothing else, have hope." 3. A Saying of Epictetus. Epictetus, asked who is wealthy, answered, "He who has enough."

Exercise 408.—When the day decided upon had arrived, the American generals were not able to sail for France on account of the great velocity of the winds. For heavy winds are harmful to ships. And so they remained in Britain longer lest the winds and the sea injure the ships. But afterwards they led large forces across the sea into France in one day in order to do harm to the enemy. The enemy had made immense fortifications. Nevertheless the Americans and their allies, ready for death or for victory, took these defenses and threw the enemy into flight.

A great and valiant leader named Bradley was in command of the American army.

Shall we not always praise both our leader and our soldiers for (their) courage?

Exercise 409.—1. Centuriō centum virīs praeerat; lēgātus duābus aut tribus legiōnibus saepe praeerat; imperātor tōtī exercituī praeerat. 2. MacArthur, dux magnus et fortis, illī exercituī Americānō quī in Austrāliā et proximīs regiōnibus erat praeerat. Nāvibus Japōnum et mīlitibus nocuit. 3. Nautae sunt virī fortēs, nam mare perīculōrum plēnum est, tamen nāvigāre nōn timent. Magnitūdō ventōrum nāvibus nocet et in perīculō mortis saepe sunt. Itaque nautās plūrimum laudō. 4. Multōs annōs populī et cīvitātēs in terrā et in mare inter sē contendērunt. Sed hīs temporibus caelum mīlitibus et armīs complēvērunt. 5. Virī malī cīvitātī plūrimum nocent. Oportet nōs facere virōs bonōs ducēs et prīncipēs. Nam virī sine fide et sine virtūte cīvitātem līberam cōnservāre nōn possunt. Praesuntne nunc virī bonī cīvitātī nostrae?

Reading No. 34.—Columbus. Columbus, a brave and good sailor, determined to sail to India by new routes (a new route). Nevertheless on account of a scarcity of everything he was unable to prepare either ships or all the other useful things. And so he came to the camp (palace) of the king of Spain to ask for help. At first, however, the king did not help him; but then, persuaded by Queen Isabella, he gave him what he desired. And so three ships were made ready and drawn up. The first ship, in which Columbus was, was called the *Santa Maria,* the second ship was called the *Pinta,* and the third the *Nina.* Columbus was in command of these three ships. One hundred and twenty sailors were also collected. And so when everything was now ready these three small ships sailed out of the harbor. The sea was wide. No one before that time had sailed across that sea. Because the ships were small, the sea was full of dangers. It was not often difficult to sail, however, because of the greatness of the winds.

When they had sailed for many days, they saw land. All the sailors were greatly moved. They hastened from the ships and seized that land in the name of the Spanish king. Thus did Columbus come to America.

Box, page 411.—Through Thy coming deliver us, O Jesus!

UNIT TWELVE

Exercise 410.—See Introduction, 3.

Exercise 411.—See Introduction, 3.

Box, page 414.—Show us, O Lord, Thy mercy!

Box, page 415.—Jesus, our God, have mercy on us!

Exercise 412.—**A.** (The present infinitive expresses action as going on at the time of the action of the main verb.) 1. I think that all the saints love God. (*Putō,* main; *sānctōs dīligere,* acc. w. infin.; present infinitive.) 2. I know that Americans fight bravely. (*Sciō,* main; *Americānōs pugnāre,* acc. w. infin.; present infinitive.) 3. I think that all men seek friendship. (*Putō,* main; *hominēs quaerere,* acc. w. infin.; present infinitive.) 4. The lieutenant said that Caesar was conquering the Gauls. (*Lēgātus dīxit,* main; *Caesarem vincere,* acc. w. infin.; present infinitive.) 5. The centurion said that the soldiers were fighting bitterly. (*Centuriō dīxit,* main; *mīlitēs pugnāre,* acc. w. infin.; present infinitive.) 6. The messenger said that the Gauls were storming the city. (*Nuntius dīxit,* main; *Gallōs oppugnāre,* acc. w. infin.; present infinitive.) **B.** (The perfect infinitive expresses action as completed before the action of the main verb.) 1. We know that Caesar conquered the Gauls. (*Scīmus,* main; *Caesarem vīcisse,* acc. w. infin.; perfect infinitive.) 2. We know that Columbus came to America. (*Scīmus,* main; *Columbum pervēnisse,* acc. w. infin.; perfect infinitive.) 3. We know that the Romans killed Christ. (*Scīmus,* main; *Rōmānōs occīdisse,* acc. w. infin.; perfect infinitive.) 4. Caesar heard that the Gauls had killed the envoy. (*Caesar audīvit*, main; *Gallōs occīdisse*, acc. w. infin.; perfect infinitive.) 5. Caesar thought that the cavalry had arrived at camp. (*Caesar putāvit*, main; *equitēs pervēnisse*, acc. w. infin.; perfect infinitive.) 6. The envoy thought that Caesar had conquered the enemy. (*Lēgātus putāvit*, main; *Caesarem vīcisse*, acc. w. infin.; perfect infinitive.) C. (The future infinitive expresses action which will take place after the action of the main verb.) 1. I think that Americans will fight bravely. (*Putō*, main; *Americānōs pugnātūrōs esse*, acc. w. infin.; future infinitive.) 2. I know that good men will see God. (*Sciō*, main; *hominēs vīsūrōs esse*, acc. w. infin.; future infinitive.) 3. I think that Americans will always conquer the enemy. (*Putō*, main; *Americānōs victūrōs esse*, acc. w. infin.; future infinitive.) 4. I know that Mary will always see God. (*Sciō*, main; *Marīam vīsūram esse*, acc. w. infin.; future infinitive.) 5. I think that God will give grace to all men. (*Putō*, main; *Deum datūrum esse*, acc. w. infin.; future infinitive.) 6. Caesar thought that the Gauls would yield. (*Caesar putāvit*, main; *Gallōs cessūrōs esse*, acc. w. infin.; future infinitive.) D. 1. I say that I am a Christian, have been a Christian, and always will be a Christian. (*Mē*, 1st person reflexive, acc., subject of infin.; referring to subject of main verb.) 2. Do you think that you are holy? (*Tē*, 2nd person reflexive, acc., subject of infin.; referring to subject of main verb.) 3. Caesar said that he would conquer the Gauls. (*Sē*, 3rd person reflexive, acc., subject of infin.; referring to subject of main verb.) 4. We say that we are free. (*Nōs*, 1st person pl. reflexive, acc., subject of infin.; referring to subject of main verb.) 5. Do you say that you will give us hostages? (*Vōs*, 2nd person pl. reflexive, acc., subject of infin.; referring to subject of main verb.) 6. The Romans said that they were holding command of all Gaul. (*Sē*, 3rd person reflexive, acc., subject of infin.; referring to subject of main verb.) 7. I say that I will defend my fields. (*Mē*, 1st person reflexive, acc., subject of infin.; referring to subject of main verb. *Meōs*, masc. acc. pl. of *meus, a, um*, reflexive possessive adj., modifying *agrōs* and referring to subject of main verb.) 8. This American points out that no king holds royal power in his state. (*Suā*, fem. abl. sing. of *suus, a, um*, reflexive possessive adj., modifying *cīvitāte* and referring to subject of main verb.) 9. Christ said that we were His brothers. (*Nōs*, 1st person pl. personal pronoun, acc., subject of infin. *Suōs*, masc. acc. pl. of *suus, a, um*, reflexive posses-sive adj., modifying *frātrēs* and referring to the subject of the main verb.) 10. Caesar thought that his men would fight bravely. (*Suōs*, masc. acc. pl. of *suus, a, um*, reflexive possessive adj., used as noun, subject of infin.) 11. Mary knew that she could adore her Son. (*Sē*, 3rd person reflexive, acc., subject of infin.; referring to subject of main verb.) **E.** (All the italicized words are either predicate nouns or predicate adjectives and take the same case as the nouns to which they refer, which in this exercise is always the accusative, in the accusative with infinitive construction.) 1. He says that Christ is the Son of God. 2. I say that almost all men are eager for fame. 3. I know that our state is free. 4. A holy man replied to the Romans that Christ was the Son of God. 5. The Romans knew that Caesar was supreme commander. 6. The Romans knew that Rome was great.

Exercise 413.—A. 1. Americānus dīcit Americānōs fortiter pugnāre. 2. Americānus dīcit Washingtonium fuisse summum imperātōrem. 3. Americānus dīcit mīlitēs suōs fortiter pugnātūrōs esse. **B.** 1. Lēgātus dīxit Caesarem Gallōs vincere. 2. Lēgātus dīxit Caesarem Gallōs vīcisse. 3. Lēgātus dīxit mīlitēs suōs hostēs victūrōs esse. **C.** 1. Sciēmus Deum nōs dīligere. 2. Sciēmus Deum peccāta nostra sustulisse. 3. Sciēmus mīlitēs nostrōs victūrōs esse. **D.** 1. Dīcēbam cīvitātem nostram esse līberam. 2. Dīcēbam cīvitātem Rōmānam fuisse līberam. 3. Dīcēbam cīvitātem nostram semper futūram esse līberam. **E.** 1. Dīxit sē Deum vīsūrum esse. 2. Dīxī mē Rōmam vīsūrum esse. 3. Dīxit sē Galliam vīsūram esse. 4. Dīxērunt sē fortiter pugnātūrōs esse. 5. Dīxistī tē ad nōs obsidēs missūrum esse. 6. Dīxit Caesarem sibi praemium datūrum esse. **F.** 1. Audīverat eōs in armīs esse. 2. Audīverat Gallōs fūgisse. 3. Audīverant Gallōs obsidēs missūrōs esse.

Exercise 414.—A. 1. Dīcō Americānōs fortiter pugnāre. 2. Dīcit Deum hominēs bonōs dēfendere. 3. Dīcunt mīlitēs nostrōs hostēs vincere. 4. Dīxit Caesarem Gallōs vincere. 5. Dīxērunt senātum Caesarem laudāre. 6. Dīxērunt Gallōs obsidēs mittere. **B.** 1. Dīcō Rōmānōs fortiter pugnāvisse. 2. Dīcit Americānōs hostēs vīcisse. 3. Dīcimus Caesarem Galliam vīcisse. 4. Dīxērunt Gallōs hīberna oppugnāvisse. 5. Dīxērunt Caesarem in Galliam contendisse. 6. Dīxit senātum Caesarī grātiās ēgisse. **C.** 1. Dīcō Americānōs fortiter pugnātūrōs esse. 2. Dīcit nōs hostēs victūrōs esse. 3. Scient nōs auxilium missūrōs esse. 4. Dīxit sē barbarōs victūrum esse.

Reading No. 35.—Pyrrhus, King of Epirus. Pyrrhus was king of Epirus. Can you see this kingdom on the map? Pyrrhus was not a Roman. He did not live in Italy nor in Gaul. He was a Greek. He was a king, however, brave and eager for fame. He determined to conquer many other tribes. There was with his army a friend named Cineas. Now this man was good and he did not approve of the plans of Pyrrhus.

Because he was Pyrrhus' friend, he was not afraid to warn (admonish) him strongly. Once Pyrrhus, raised up (elated) by (his) fame, told him he would lead the army into Italy and would conquer the Romans. For he thought he was able to overcome them easily.

But Cineas said: "What have you decided to do after that victory, great king?"

Pyrrhus replied: "Next to Italy is the Island of Sicily, a good and great island. I will lead my soldiers onto it to conquer and occupy it. It will be easy to seize that island by means of arms and courage."

Then Cineas said: "And after that victory, what do you say you will do?"

Pyrrhus replied to him that he would lead his soldiers across the sea into Africa and would conquer those regions also.

Then Cineas said: "What have you decided to do after these battles and these victories?"

Pyrrhus answered: "After these victories I will establish peace."

But Cineas said at once: "Why, O good King, do you not establish peace now? What hinders you?"

Exercise 415.—1. He proves that he is a Christian. 2. We say that good men always seek truth and virtue. 3. I warn you that life is short. 4. The boy replied that he remembered the deeds of Washington. 5. I warn you that God will not give rewards to evil men. 6. I know that Americans can defend themselves. 7. We affirm that our soldiers fight bravely. 8. We Christians affirm that God, our Father, loves all nations. 9. The sailors say that the heavy winds are harmful to (damaging) the ships. 10. We know that all men, alarmed by the danger of death, pray and ask grace of God. 11. We know that memory is the guardian of things known. 12. I advise you, boys, that a good memory is useful for life. 13. Columbus found out that barbarians inhabited America. 14. Cicero, a good and noble man, wrote that he would always praise virtue. 15. Saint Paul wrote that Christ taught him about things that pertain to faith. 16. It is written that Saint Paul suddenly saw Christ on the road. 17. When Washington had heard that Benedict Arnold had fled to the enemy, he found out that it was all true. 18. Christ said that all holy persons would see God with Him in heaven. 19. My friend, haven't you heard that we are all brothers? 20. Christ commanded us to love all men. 21. When He was asked by Pilate, Christ replied that He was a king. 22. Christ denied that He held a kingdom with arms and legions (by force of arms). 23. Thomas More, when he was being led to death, denied that he would depart from the Christian faith. 24. The apostles announced to all men that Christ was the Son of God and that He was killed on our behalf. 25. Pilate thought that Christ was a good man, but he was afraid to dismiss (release) Him. For the Jews said that Christ called Himself a king. And they therefore said: "He who makes himself a king speaks against Caesar." 26. Columbus thought that he had arrived, not at new lands, but at India. 27. The Roman emperors found out that there were Christians in Italy and in all the provinces. And so they ordered many of them to be led to death. Nevertheless they were unable to conquer the faith of Christ.

Exercise 416.—1. Negāvērunt sē eī obsidēs datūrōs esse. 2. Negāvit sē arma deditūrum esse. 3. Negāvērunt sē fugitūrōs esse.

Exercise 417.—1. Repperī illās rēs esse vērās. 2. Repperimus ubi hostēs custōdēs collocāvissent. 3. Vīdimus hostēs mūnītiōnēs parāvisse. 4. Vīdimus ubi hostēs castra posuissent. 5. Dīxērunt magnitūdinem ventōrum nāvī nocuisse. 6. Dīxī Caesarem legiōnī praeesse. 7. Negāvit sē servōs trāditūrum esse. 8. Ostendit sē esse virum fortem. 9. Nuntiāvērunt caedem obsidum. 10. Scīvērunt quanta essent castra Rōmāna. 11. Dīcēbant Gallōs pugnāre timēre. 12. Vīdit barbarōs ē silvīs vēnisse. 13. Vīderat barbarōs mūnītiōnēs parāvisse. 14. Scīvit nōmina centuriōnum. 15. Negāvit cōnsilia ūtilia esse.

Exercise 418.—1. Possum pugnāre. 2. Dīxī mē pugnāre posse. 3. Dīcō mē pugnāre potuisse. 4. Probābō mē pugnāre potuisse. 5. Dīxit sē pugnātūrum esse. 6. Jussus est pugnāre. 7. Eum pugnāre jussērunt. 8. Bonum est fortiter pugnāre. 9. Pugnāre statim cōnstituērunt. 10. Oportuit nōs fortiter pugnāre. 11. Parātī sumus nāvigāre. 12. Dīxērunt sē nāvigāre parātōs esse. 13. Dīxērunt sē nāvigāre quīnque diēs parātōs fuisse (esse). 14. Dīxit sē duōbus diēbus nāvigāre parātum futūrum esse. 15. Tertiō diē nāvigāre poterat. 16. Oportet nōs statim nāvigāre. 17. Cōnsuēvērunt ex hōc portū nāvigāre. 18. Dīxērunt sē ex illō portū nāvigāre cōnsuēvisse. 19. Negāvērunt aquae satis esse. 20. Ōrāre difficile nōn est. 21. Dīxit hostēs quīnque mīlia passuum fūgisse. 22. Propter magnitūdinem ventōrum negāvit sē nāvigātūrum esse. 23. Jussit eōs collem usque ad noctem dēfendere. 24. Dīxērunt sē trēs diēs collem dēfensūrōs esse. 25. Nōn scīvit num agmen oppugnāvissent. 26. Chrīstus dīxit sē omnēs hominēs adjūtūrum et dēfēnsūrum esse.

Reading No. 36.—A Brave King. Leonidas, who was king of the Spartans, and to whom Xerxes, king of the Persians, had written, "Send arms," replied to him, "Come and take them."

Box, page 425.—Let us adore Christ the King.

Reading No. 37.—They placed on the cross of Jesus a sign on which was written: "This is Jesus, King of the Jews." And so the leaders of the Jews, when they had seen this sign, violently moved, came to Pilate. "Do not write: King of the Jews," they said, "but: He said that He was King of the Jews."

Pilate answered: "What I have written, I have written!"

A Latin Riddle, page 426.—Who is he who is not and yet has a name and answers to one asking?

Box, page 427.—O good Jesus, have mercy on us!

Reading No. 38.—The War Waged with Pyrrhus. We have already shown that the Romans had conquered many tribes of Italy and were holding command of a great part of Italy. When they had conquered the tribes nearest them, they waged war with other tribes. And so the Tarentini, who feared the Romans, were fighting them lest they be conquered by them. The Tarentini, because alone (by themselves) they were not able to repulse the Romans, sent envoys to Pyrrhus, king of Epirus, to seek help from him. Pyrrhus, eager for fame, said he would lead (his) army into Italy for the sake of help (in order to help them).

Meanwhile the Romans were preparing everything which pertained to war. Pyrrhus therefore, when he had led (his) army into Italy, found out that the Romans were prepared for war. He therefore hastened against them with all (his) forces. The Romans drew up a battle line and were awaiting the attack of Pyrrhus. But Pyrrhus had many elephants with him. These he sent in first against the Roman cavalry; then, when the cavalry had been put to flight, he sent them against the battle line of soldiers. Now the Romans had never before (that) seen elephants in battle. And so their ranks were confused by the elephants and many soldiers were killed. Nevertheless the Romans were fighting bravely. But terrified by the greatness of the body (size) of the elephants, they were unable to conquer the enemy. After a bloody slaughter the Romans withdrew to camp lest they all be killed.

Seven thousand Roman soldiers fell in this battle. The fields were full of (strewn with) bodies, but Pyrrhus, when he had seen that the bodies of the dead Romans had (their) wounds in front, said that with these Roman soldiers he could conquer all lands. Of the soldiers of Pyrrhus, four thousand were killed. The Romans could easily collect other soldiers, but it was difficult to get new forces from Epirus. And so Pyrrhus, on account of the great number of the slain, saw that this victory was not useful enough. He said, "If I conquer . . ."

Exercise 419.—1. I say that all men are loved by God. 2. I say that the Gauls were conquered by Caesar. 3. He said that Caesar was praised by the Senate. 4. He said the Gauls were routed by Caesar. 5. Caesar said that he was not praised by the Gauls. 6. I say that I am defended by God. 7. You said that you were praised by the Senate. 8. He says he is being helped by the barbarians. 9. We say that we are seen by the enemy. 10. You say that you are being helped by God. 11. They say that they are being called by the leader. 12. I said I had been captured by the barbarians. 13. He said that you had not been captured by the barbarians. 14. He said that he had been praised by Caesar. 15. We say that we have been freed by brave men. 16. They said that they had been called into camp by Caesar. 17. The envoy had said that Caesar had not been conquered by the Gauls. 18. The envoy had denied that Caesar was being conquered by the Gauls. 19. I deny that I was stationed there.

Box, page 429.—May the Lord bless us and defend us from every evil and lead us into eternal life.

Exercise 420.—1. Exīstimō Lincoln ā virō malō interfectum esse. 2. Sentiō collem occupātum esse. 3. Exīstimāvit Rōmam oppugnārī. 4. Negāvit Rōmam occupātam esse. 5. Exīstimō Lincoln ab omnibus (virīs) bonīs laudārī. 6. Dīximus nōs ā virō fortī līberātōs esse. 7. Scīs servōs nostrōs ā Lincoln līberātōs esse. 8. Audīvistī Americam ā Columbō repertam esse. 9. Scīmus grātiam omnibus hominibus darī. 10. Scīvimus mūnītiōnēs ab hostibus parārī. 11. Scīvimus hostēs ad bellum ā ducibus eōrum commovērī. 12. Scīvimus arma ā ducibus nostrīs nōn parārī. 13. Scīs omnēs hominēs ā Deō dīligī. 14. Putāsne Deum semper adōrātum esse? 15. Putāmus Deum ā Chrīstiānīs bonīs adōrārī et laudārī.

Exercise 421.—1. We know that Washington has been called by all a brave man. (*Virum,* acc. sing. of *vir, ī,* m.; verbs of calling, naming, etc., in the passive take a predicate nominative, but in the acc. w. infin. construction the predicate nominative becomes accusative to agree with the subject to which it refers.) 2. We said that hostages were often killed by Caesar on account of the wrongs of (committed by) the Gauls. (*Occisōs,* acc. pl. of the perf. part. pass. of *occīdō, occīdere, occīdī, occīsus,* 3, tr.; in the perf. infin. pass. agreeing with *obsidēs;* in acc. w. infin.; tense by relation.) 3. We have already shown that Christ was killed by the Romans. (*Rōmānīs,* abl. pl. of *Rōmānus, ī,* m.; ablative of agent.) 4. We say that mothers are often killed in war. (*Interficī,* pres. infin. pass. of *interficiō, interficere, interfēcī, interfectus,* 3, tr.; in acc. w. infin.; tense by relation.) 5. When they had heard that their men had been captured in Bataan, the Americans were violently moved. (*Suōs*, masc. acc. pl. of *suus, a, um*, reflexive possessive adj. used as a noun, subject in acc. w. infin.) 6. The Gauls heard that their hostages had been killed by Caesar. Furthermore they knew that all the crops had been burned by him; that the cities and towns either had been or were being stormed; that arms and slaves had been taken, their armies conquered, all Gaul devastated; and that they themselves could not be defended from him. And so the wretched men were forced to send envoys to him to seek peace from him. (*Eō*, masc. abl. sing. of *is, ea, id;* abl. of agent. *Sē*, acc. pl. of *suī*, reflexive pronoun; subject in acc. w. infin.; referring to the subject of *scīvērunt* (*Gallī*).) 7. The Germans were violently moved and disturbed when it had been announced that great forces had been led by the Americans and their allies into France. (*Nuntiātum esset*, 3rd sing., plup. pass. subj. of *nuntiō, nuntiāre, nuntiāvī, nuntiātus*, 1, tr.; in a *cum*-clause in secondary sequence; action completed before time of main verb. *Esse trāductās*, perf. infin. pass. of *trādūcō, trādūcere, trādūxī, trāductus*, 3, tr.; in acc. w. infin.; participle in acc. pl. agreeing with *cōpiās. Mōtī*, masc. nom. pl. of perf. ind. pass. of *moveō, movēre, mōvī, mōtus*, 2, tr.; agreeing with *Germānī*.)

Reading No. 39.—Pyrrhus and Fabricius. After that battle about which we have already shown (which we have already described) the Romans did not treat of (sue for) peace. They collected new forces; they were getting ready arms and darts. For they had now determined to conquer Pyrrhus and his elephants and to drive them out of Italy.

Fabricius was made general and sent against Pyrrhus. When he had approached the camp of Pyrrhus and pitched camp, a doctor came out of Pyrrhus' camp to Fabricius. This man said that he would kill Pyrrhus the king and that thus he would free the Romans from him. He asked for rewards, however. But Fabricius took him and ordered him to be led bound to Pyrrhus. Furthermore he wrote to Pyrrhus that the Romans fought not with treachery but with swords. Pyrrhus, thus warned by the enemy of his own danger, was greatly moved, "It is easier," he said . . .

The Romans on their part sent Fabricius, a brave man, to Pyrrhus to treat (with him) concerning an exchange of prisoners. When he had treated of this matter with Fabricius, Pyrrhus saw that he was a brave and noble man. And so he gave (offered) rewards (gifts) to him in order that he might fight with him. But Fabricius did not accept these gifts. Thus he showed himself to be a true Roman. Then Pyrrhus said, "Why will you not come to Epirus with me? I shall give you a large part of my kingdom." Again Fabricius said that he would not accept the kingdom and that he would always remain in a free state.

After this Pyrrhus sent envoys to the Roman Senate to sue for peace. And they were therefore led into the Senate, and they pointed out (stated) what the terms of peace were. In the Senate some desired to establish peace, but others said that they would not accept the terms of peace. Furthermore these men pointed out that the Roman army had been conquered, that the fields of the allies had been devastated, that the glory of the Roman name had not been preserved. They argued the matter for a long time. But one of them, a very great man named Appius Claudius, greatly moved, said, "The Roman people . . ." And so the Senate did not approve the terms and decided to wage war again.

Box, page 431.—A brave man can be conquered neither by arms nor by rewards (bribes).

Reading No. 40.—On a bull's back there was a little fly. The fly said: "If I am pressing (bothering) you, I will leave immediately." But the bull replied: "Where are you? For I feel nothing."

Exercise 422.—1. (a) The present infinitive active is the second principal part of the verb. (b) The perfect infinitive active is formed by adding *-isse* to the perfect stem. (c) The future participle active is formed by dropping the *-us* of the perfect participle passive and adding *-ūrus*. (d) The future infinitive active is a compound tense made up of the future participle active and *esse*. (e) The present infinitive passive is formed on the present stem. (f) The perfect infinitive passive is a compound tense formed by using the perfect participle passive with *esse*. 2. Noun clauses after verbs of saying, etc., are put in the accusative with the infinitive. In this construction (1) the verb is always an infinitive, (2) the subject is always in the accusative case, and (3) the tense of the infinitive is determined by the rule: tense by relation. 3. See Nos. 885-887. 4. A predicate noun or adjective agrees with the subject; that is, in the accusative with the infinitive construction it is in the accusative case. 5. An impersonal verb in the accusative with the infinitive construction is in the infinitive without a subject expressed, and in a compound infinitive the participle is always neuter. 6. An important difference between the use of the accusative with the infinitive construction after verbs of saying, etc., and after other verbs is in tense. The former construction follows the rule, tense by relation; when the infinitive is used after other verbs and expressions such as *jubeō* and *oportet*, the tense is generally present. 7. Verbs which may take an accusative with the infinitive do not always do so. When the sense requires, they also take indirect questions, accusative objects, etc.; e.g., Haec nuntiāvit, *He reported these things;* Nuntiāvit quot essent hostēs, *He reported how many (numerous) the enemy were.*

Exercise 423.—1. I say that God is good. (*Deum esse bonum* is the acc. w. infin. after a verb of saying; action at same time as main verb.) 2. He replied that he would not deny the Christian faith. (*Sē negātūrum esse,* acc. w. infin.; action which will take place after the time of main verb.) 3. Caesar thought that all Gaul had been pacified. (*Esse pācātam,* acc. w. infin.; action completed before time of main verb.) 4. The saints have written that God loved all men. (*Dīligere,* infinitive after a verb of saying; action at same time as main verb.) 5. Columbus found that many tribes dwelt in America. (*Incolere,* infinitive after a verb of saying; action at same time as main verb.) 6. He said that he would not come. (*Sē,* acc. sing. of reflexive pronoun, subject of infinitive after a verb of saying.) 7. It was announced that there had been bitter fighting. (*Pugnātum esse,* an impersonal verb in the acc. w. infin. construction; no subject expressed; participle neuter; action completed before time of main verb.) 8. He pointed out that they ought to surrender. (*Oportēre,* impersonal verb used in the acc. w. infin. construction; no subject expressed; action at same time as main verb. *Sē,* acc. pl. of reflexive pronoun, object of *dēdere.*) 9. I think that we Americans will always be free. (*Futūrōs esse,* future infinitive after a verb of saying; action that will take place after time of main verb.) 10. He felt that he was in great danger. (*Sē,* acc. sing. of reflexive pronoun, subject of infinitive after a verb of saying.) 11. He said that he had been in Gaul that year. (*Fuisse,* perfect infinitive after a verb of saying; action completed before time of main verb.)

UNIT THIRTEEN

Exercise 424.—See Nos. 89-93.
Exercise 425.—See Nos. 94-96.
Exercise 426.—See Introduction, 3.
Exercise 427.—1. Propter vītam miseriōrem. 2. In altiōre mūrō. 3. Propter amīcitiam vēriōrem. 4. Trāns fossam lātiōrem. 5. Cum tribūnīs mīlitum fortiōribus. 6. Cum virō sānctissimō. 7. Sine cōnsiliō difficillimō. 8. Cum lēgātō fortiōre. 9. Propter labōrem gravissimum. 10. In longiōre ordine. 11. Prō obsidibus miserrimīs. 12. In locum tūtiōrem. 13. In altiōribus montibus. 14. In longiōre itinere. 15. Per lōca difficillima. 16. Trāns lātissimum flūmen. 17. Cum amīcīs vērissimīs. 18. Propter rēs gravissimās. 19. Ducī nōbiliōrī. 20. In cīvitāte līberiōre.

Exercise 428.—1. The mind is the noblest part of man. 2. Mary is the holiest of all the saints. 3. This route is shorter than that. 4. What can be truer than our faith? 5. Caesar was very eager for glory. 6. Do you judge Lincoln to have been braver and nobler than Washington? 7. Do you think that Americans are more free than others? 8. Are not arms and darts very useful for war? 9. He who without delay helps us in adversity is the surest and truest of friends. 10. Don't you judge saints to be more like Christ than other Christians are? 11. Mary is most full of grace. 12. It is safer to remain in camp than to fight in the battle line. Nevertheless all the bravest soldiers ought to fight in the battle line (when) commanded by the officer. 13. It is very difficult to march through mountains.

Exercise 429.—1. Was Lincoln braver than Washington? 2. Is the Mississippi the longest river of all? 3. Is the Mississippi longer than the Missouri? 4. What river is the longest of all? 5. What are the highest mountains in our country? 6. Is Pike's Peak higher than Mount Wilson?

Exercise 430.—1. What things are most useful for war? Aren't arms and darts very useful for war? Are not a supply of grain and a large army also very useful? Are we prepared for war? Are we more ready for war than other peoples and nations? Do you judge it necessary for us always to be of all peoples the best prepared for war? You do not fear an enemy, do you? Surely you don't think there will be war again! 2. What man can be the truest and surest friend? The truest friend has the greatest faith in us and the greatest good will toward us. A brave and holy man can be the truest friend, for even Cicero, who was not a Christian, says that there can be no friendship without virtue and faith. Do we not judge (think) that a very true and sure friend ought to help and love us always? Don't we ask for and expect help from him in adversity? A true friend also remains in faith and friendship even after a very long time. And so who can be a truer friend than Christ? For He endured heavy sorrows on our behalf and was led to death (for us). Who can be a surer friend than Christ? For He loves us and helps us always. No one can be more friendly (a better friend) to us than Christ. Shall we not love Him? Let us always remain in faith and friendship with Him. 3. In our land there are many high and large mountains. Do you know what mountain is the highest of all the mountains in our land? Is Pike's Peak higher than Mount Wilson? Is it the highest of all our mountains? 4. There are many rivers in our land (that are) long and wide. Do you know which rivers are (the) longest? Is the Mississippi longer than the Missouri? Is the Mississippi the longest of all the rivers (which are) in our land? What is the widest river? Is the Missouri or the Ohio wider than the Mississippi? Is the Mississippi the widest of all our rivers?

Box, page 439.—Come, Holy Spirit!

Exercise 431.—1. Fuitne Caesar fortissimus omnium Rōmānōrum? 2. Putāsne Caesarem fortiōrem fuisse quam omnēs aliōs imperātōrēs? 3. Haec via est facilior quam illa. 4. Jūdicāsne hanc viam faciliōrem esse quam illam? 5. Quis tē certiōrem fēcit hanc viam esse tūtissimam? 6. Hic mōns altior est. 7. Tūtius est discēdere ā prīmā aciē, fortius autem est sustinēre impetum hostium. 8. Spēs commūnissima est omnium rērum. 9. Imperātōrēs cōpiās trāns flūmina lātissima et per altissimōs montēs saepe dūcunt. 10. Servī Rōmānī saepe miserrimī erant. 11. Quae cīvitās est līberrima omnium cīvitātum? 12. Ducēs Caesarem certiōrem fēcērunt hanc gentem esse fortissimam omnium Gallōrum. 13. Fuitne Caesar victōriae cupidior quam Napoleon? 14. Nōnne putās Chrīstum esse vērissimum omnium amīcōrum?

Exercise 432.—1. Nothing is truer than our faith. 2. Caesar was braver than other leaders. 3. What is more noble in man than the mind? 4. Who was braver than Caesar? 5. Whom do you judge to have been more noble than our Washington? 6. No one can be holier than Christ. 7. That mountain is not higher than this one, is it? 8. It is often safer to fight than to flee.

Exercise 433.—1. Quod flūmen hōc flūmine longius est? 2. Quid commūnius spē est? 3. Quis mōns est illō monte altior? 4. Altera via est angustior, altera autem tūtior. 5. Haec fossa lātior illā est. 6. Nēmō sānctior Chrīstō est. 7. Via per montēs brevior alterā viā est. 8. Quid certius amīcitiā Chrīstī est? 9. Quis Caesare fortior erat? 10. Quis servō Rōmānō miserior erat?

Box, page 440.—A quotation from Cicero: Nothing is sweeter than the light of truth.

Exercise 434.—1. Cum mājōribus cōpiīs. 2. Ad maximam urbem. 3. Cum virīs optimīs. 4. In castrīs minōribus. 5. In maximō perīculō. 6. Propter plūra praemia. 7. Mājōris glōriae causā. 8. Cum virīs pessimīs. 9. Post maximam caedem. 10. Post minimās rēs. 11. Propter maximum perīculum. 12. Maximōrum praemiōrum causā.

Exercise 435.—1. What is better than virtue? 2. Do you judge that friendship is better than virtue? 3. I think that nothing is better than virtue. 4. Most men think that fame or power is better than virtue, don't they? 5. Nevertheless they are the very (of) worst men who, for the sake of glory, fill every place with the greatest slaughter and the deepest sorrow. 6. And so we say that virtue is the best and greatest thing. 7. What is worse than sin? 8. Do you judge that death is worse than sin? 9. Isn't it the worst sin to leave Christ and deny the faith? 10. We therefore think that nothing is worse than sin, for God teaches us that sin is the very worst of all things. 11. But it is difficult to reach the highest virtue, for we reach the highest virtue (only) through the greatest toil and very great suffering. 12. Let us give thanks to God, the best and greatest (being). 13. Let the welfare of the people be the highest law. 14. Cicero said: "The greatest sorrow cannot last many days." 15. Nothing is worse than to flee from the battle line. 16. Let us leave behind both the greatest and the smallest sins. 17. It is better to be free of kings and masters. 18. There are very many and very great cities in our land. 19. A very short life is better and easier than a very long one. 20. A very bad envoy sought more grain, but the Gauls were unable to give more grain. 21. We know that Rome is smaller than many other states. 22. There are more men in our territory than in France. 23. Whom do you judge to be the worst of all men? 24. The Romans always pitched camp in the higher places. 25. Rome is nearer to France than our cities are. 26. He who makes an attack against the enemy with the greater forces often conquers. 27. In Bataan our forces were less than those of the Japanese. 28. Caesar called the legions to him from the other winter quarters in order to have greater forces with him.

Selected Thoughts, page 442.—1. He who conquers anger overcomes the greatest enemy. 2. Virtue is the best reward. 3. Nothing is better than virtue. 4. To the greater glory of God.

Box, page 442.—One from (out of) more (many).

Exercise 436.—1. Caesar in locō superiōre cōnstitit et mājōrēs cōpiās exspectāvit. 2. Plūrimī (hominēs) virtūtem laudant, sed hōrum multī pessimī virī sunt. 3. Oportet hominēs optimōs cīvitātī praeesse. 4. Nōnne erat Jūdas pējor Benedictō Arnold? Hic hostēs cīvitātis suae adjūvit; ille autem Jēsum Chrīstum pessimīs virīs trādidit. 5. Jūdicāsne Lincoln meliōrem virum esse quam Washingtonium? 6. Virī fortēs cum minōre cōpiā armōrum mājōrem manum hostium saepe vincunt. 7. Nōnne aestimās nautās mīlitēsque saepe esse in maximō perīculō? Prō eīs ōrēmus. 8. MacArthur cum minimā manū maximōs impetūs hostium diū sustinuit. 9. Nōn potuimus mittere ad MacArthur plūra arma et plūs frūmentī quod multa mīlia passuum aberat et nāvēs hostium undique erant. 10. Plūrēs (virī) in hōc bellō occīsī sunt quam in aliō ūllō bellō. 11. Suprēma lēx est lēx Chrīstī.

Reading No. 41.—The Romans always remembered the courage of (their) best men. We Americans also praise and remember many very good men who performed the greatest deeds for (this) our republic.

Once our men were waging a very important war with the British in order to free our state from their power. The American general was Washington, a very good and brave man, who performed great deeds for his state over a long period of time and endured the greatest pains (sufferings).

When the leader of the British had led his forces into Manhattan, Washington took up a position facing him with all his troops. He was not able to make a plan, for he did not know where the general of the enemy had stationed his soldiers. There was, however, in the American army a very brave officer named Nathan Hale. He was ready to hasten into the enemy's camp and to reconnoiter the whole place in order to learn in what places the enemy had stationed guards and how great their fortifications were. Washington sent him into the enemy's camp.

Without delay Hale hastened to the camp of the enemy. He arrived secretly. He reconnoitered the whole territory. He saw the guards, the supply of arms, and the fortifications, but the enemy at last perceived what he was doing. They therefore led him captive to the leader. The leader, informed of the affair, ordered him led to death. But when that very brave Nathan Hale was led to death, he said, "I regret . . ."

Aroused and encouraged by the supreme courage of this man, are we not more ready to love and defend our republic?

Reading No. 42.—The Spartans had great fame for war and courage. Once they were waging war. A messenger came to the king of the Spartans and said: "The number of the enemy is great." The king, a very brave man, replied to him: "So much the greater will our glory be."

Exercise 437.—See Introduction, 3.

Exercise 438.—See Introduction, 3.

Exercise 439.—1. Cōnābāmur. 2. Centuriōnem sequēbantur. 3. Tribūnum mīlitum verētur. 4. Nāvēs sequēbantur. 5. Fugere cōnātur. 6. Sociōs veritus erat. 7. Vulnera gravia verentur. 8. Nūllum ducem sequētur. 9. Id nōn patientur. 10. Clāmor ortus est. 11. Deum sōlum verentur. 12. Capere rēgem cōnātus erat. 13. Manus eōs secūta est. 14. Patiēturne nōs trādūcere cōpiās nostrās trāns flūmen? 15. Capere mūnītiōnēs et oppidum incendere cōnābuntur.

Exercise 440.—1. I do not fear the enemy. 2. Christians follow Christ. 3. Christ suffered many things (much). 4. A new war has arisen. 5. He was not afraid (did not fear) to kill them. 6. Christians were suffering very many things (very much). 7. You did not try to pray. 8. He who follows Christ follows the best leader. 9. The Romans did not fear the true God. 10. He did not allow them to hasten through the province. 11. I will follow Thee, Christ. 12. They were trying to flee. 13. Why were they following him? 14. Mary suffered very great sorrows. 15. The cavalry followed (pursued) the enemy. 16. A very great shout arose from all sides. 17. Fear suddenly arose among the soldiers. 18. The Jews feared God strongly (greatly). 19. He was trying to take that city. 20. We tried to kill them.

Exercise 441.—1. I will not allow very large forces to be led through the province. 2. When Caesar had thought that all Gaul had been pacified, a new and very difficult war suddenly rose. 3. Pilate feared Christ and tried to help (Him). Nevertheless he feared the Jews and the Romans too. And so he allowed them to lead (put) Christ to death. 4. Very many tribes tried to conquer the Romans, but no tribe conquered them. 5. All the saints, aroused by the grace of God, followed Christ. 6. Christ suffered the most serious pains for our salvation. 7. Very many soldiers followed Napoleon on account of his greatness of soul. 8. Very many tribes feared not-true (false) gods. 9. I will not follow you, leader, for, desirous of glory, you will fill every place with sorrow and slaughter. 10. When the legions had approached the walls of the town a very great shout arose, for the Gauls, according to their custom, shouted that they would surrender everything to the Romans.

Box, page 447.—A Thought from Ovid. I see and approve the better (things), (but) I follow the worse.

Exercise 442.—1. Caesarem sequor. 2. Deum vereris. 3. Dolorem patitur. 4. Eum venīre nōn patimur. 5. Pugnāre cōnāminī. 6. Propter injūriās factās bella oriuntur. 7. Fugere cōnābantur. 8. Caesarem verēbāminī. 9. Eōs fugere patiēbāmur. 10. Bellum oriēbātur. 11. Imperātōrem sequēbāris. 12. Mortem verēbar. 13. Bella semper orientur. 14. Nōs pugnāre nōn patiētur. 15. Capere Rōmam cōnātus est. 16. Rōmānī hostēs celeriter secūtī sunt. 17. Passī erant obsidēs discēdere. 18. Novum bellum ortum erat. 19. Chrīstum diū secūtus es. 20. Nōn veritī sumus pugnāre.

Exercise 443.—1. May he not let them flee. 2. May a new war not arise. 3. May he follow the leader. 4. May they fear God. 5. May they allow us to come into the camp.

Box, page 448.—Come, let us adore the King who made us!

Exercise 444.—1. Let us follow Christ even unto death. 2. Let us suffer for Christ. 3. Let us try to be saints. 4. Let us allow all (men) to be in peace. 5. Let us not fear death. 6. Let us fear God. 7. Let us try to preserve peace. 8. Let us not follow bad leaders.

Exercise 445.—1. He asked whether a new war had arisen. 2. He asked the soldiers whether they violently feared death. 3. He asked whether the saints followed Christ. 4. He informed them who had followed them. 5. I ask which tribes tried to conquer the Romans. 6. The Senate asked Caesar whether he had allowed the Gauls to lead very large forces through the province. 7. The leader asked the military tribune how great were the forces which followed him. 8. I ask why all men do not fear the one (and) true God.

Exercise 446.—1. The enemy, when they tried to lead very large forces across a very wide river, were thrown into flight by Caesar. 2. When the enemy had followed by a very difficult route, Caesar put them to flight. 3. When Christ was suffering the gravest pains, He gave us His mother. 4. When a war had arisen (broken out) in our country, Lincoln freed all the slaves from their masters. 5. When Caesar had not allowed the Gauls to march through the province at all, he defended the territory of the province by arms.

Exercise 447.—1. Jēsūs Chrīstus, Fīlius Deī, dūcī ad mortem sē passus est prō salūte nostrā. Itaque etiam sequāmur eum sine morā et sine timōre. Nē vereāmur maximum perīculum. Nē vereāmur pessimam mortem. Spem nostram in Deō pōnāmus nē nōs ab hostibus in rēbus adversīs superārī patiātur. 2. Mīlitēs nostrī, cum ducēs fortissimōs et imperātōrēs optimōs sequerentur, neque impetūs hostium neque perīcula maris silvārumque veritī sunt. Cum hostēs eōs ē mūnītiōnibus suīs pellere cōnārentur, cum hostēs impetūs suōs sustinēre cōnārentur, eī neque ab aciē discessērunt neque fūgērunt. Dux noster, Chrīstiānī, omnium ducum fortissimus et optimus est. Cōnēmur semper facere rēs quās jubet, ut eum ad victōriam certam et glōriam maximam sequāmur. 3. Rogās quantās rēs Chrīstus passus sit. Passus est maxima et pessima. Rogās cūr maximōs dolōrēs passus sit. Passus est maximōs dolōrēs ut nōs, dolōre ējus mōtī, eum sequerēmur, ut semper manēre in ējus amīcitiā cōnārēmur. 4. Quaesivērunt semper cūr bella orīrentur. Nunc hīs temporibus quaerunt rūrsus cūr bella oriantur. Bella oriuntur quod rēgēs et illī quī gentibus praesunt Chrīstum nōn sequuntur.

Exercise 448.—1. Caesar, having set out for Gaul, came to the Roman camp in three days. 2. Christ, having spoken of many things with His friends, was taken up into heaven. 3. The Romans halted, having found a suitable place for a camp. 4. The cavalry, having followed the enemy swiftly, killed very many of them. 5. Christ, having suffered the greatest pains and the worst death for us, came to His glory. 6. The barbarians, having feared Caesar, sought the mountains in flight. 7. Caesar drove into the forest the Gauls (who had) tried to storm the camp. 8. Caesar, having set out for the city, arrived on the third day. 9. The barbarians, very brave men, made an attack against the Romans who had set out from camp. 10. On account of the new war which had arisen, Caesar had set out for Gaul.

Box, page 451.—(It of said) Of Christ: "No man has spoken as this man."

Exercise 449.—1. Chrīstus, multōs diēs cum amicīs suīs locūtus et sē Spīritum Sānctum ad eōs missūrum esse pollicitus, in Caelum sublātus est. 2. Sānctus Polycarpus, rogātus num Chrīstiānus esset, respondit sē, secūtum Chrīstum plūrimōs annōs et veritum Deum semper, eum nōn negātūrum esse. 3. Columbus, pollicitus sē datūrum esse nautīs suīs maxima et optima praemia, parvam manum virōrum fortium coēgit et trēs nāvēs parāvit. Nactus ventum bonum profectus est. 4. Ducēs Jūdaeōrum, saepe cōnātī Chrīstō nocēre, tandem eum cēpērunt et interfēcērunt. Tum amīcī ējus, duo aut trēs annōs eum secūtī, fūgērunt et, veritī Jūdaeōs, in locum tūtum discessērunt. Cum autem Spīritus Sānctus ad eōs missus esset, ex urbe profectī sunt et omnibus hominibus nuntiāvērunt Chrīstum esse Fīlium Deī.

Reading No. 43.—Tarpeia's Reward. The Sabines, who were neighbors to the Romans, were waging war with them. Having set out from their own territory with very great forces, they came to the fields of the Romans. The Romans, having feared their forces, withdrew into the city of Rome. And so the Sabines, having swiftly followed, devastated and seized all the fields. In a short time they led troops even into the city of Rome, for the Romans were unable to withstand their attack. The Sabines, however, were not able to take the Capitoline, fortified by defenses (fortifications) and by the terrain.

The Sabines, when they were not far from the Capitoline, saw Tarpeia, the daughter of the Roman leader, who was carrying water to the Capitoline. They therefore led her captive to their leader. Now the leader thought that she could lead his army into the Capitoline, and so he promised to give her very great rewards. He asked Tarpeia what reward she desired. She said that she wanted those things which the Sabines wore on their left hands. The leader therefore promised that he would hand these things over to Tarpeia. The Sabines, having followed her, in a short time seized the Capitoline.

Tarpeia, having feared neither God nor her own father, had handed over into the hands of the enemy her own people and city, for the sake of a reward. Behold her reward! When they had taken up a position on the Capitoline, the Sabines suddenly all hurled (their) shields at Tarpeia. Thus nevertheless they kept faith and gave what they promised, for the Sabines wore their shields also on the left hand. Thus that most wretched maiden was killed.

Box, page 453.—Help of Christians, pray for us!

Exercise 450.—See Introduction, 3.

Box, page 454.—May the divine help always remain with us. Amen.

Exercise 451.—1. After a very difficult battle Caesar ordered his men to advance. 2. They were not able to advance from the very difficult places. 3. Caesar often ordered the military tribunes to urge and encourage their men. 4. We ought to set out at dawn, ought we not? 5. The worst men ought to fear God strongly (to have a great fear of God). 6. Christians ought always to try to be saints. 7. Caesar ordered the envoy to talk with the leaders of the enemy. 8. It is best to follow Christ, but it is also very difficult. 9. We ought to suffer many and very severe things. 10. We cannot go out, but, ordered by you, we will try. 11. We ought all to follow Christ, to suffer a great many pains, and so to attain our glory.

Exercise 452.—1. The messenger said that the enemy had gone out at dawn. 2. They said that they had not gone out from the most difficult place. 3. He thought that the military tribunes had encouraged their men. 4. He said that we ought to set out at dawn. 5. He informed us that the enemy had set out. 6. He affirmed that the legion had gone out. 7. We heard that the Gauls had tried to lead very large forces across the river. 8. Christians think that it is best to follow Christ.

Exercise 453.—1. Caesar said that he would set out within three days. 2. He promised that he would do all these things in two days. 3. The Roman envoy said that he would never speak with the enemy. 4. We thought that they would go out within five days. 5. He said that he would not allow them to lead very large forces by this route. 6. We know that the leader, a very brave and good man, would encourage his men. 7. The apostles promised that they would always follow Christ. 8. The king said that he would advance to the safest (possible) place.

Box, page 455.—A Thought from Livy. To act and to suffer bravely is Roman.

Exercise 454.—1. Putō hostēs duo mīlia passuum prōgressōs esse. 2. Nuntiāvit equitēs ē castrīs subitō ēgressōs esse. 3. Vīdimus tribūnōs mīlitum et centuriōnēs mīlitēs hortārī. 4. Obsidēs pollicitī sunt sē ē castrīs nōn ēgressūrōs esse. 5. Putāvērunt sē prīmā lūce ēgredī nōn oportēre. 6. Veritī sunt loquī vēritātem (vēra). 7. Profectī, hostēs tria mīlia passuum secūtī sunt. 8. Dīxit eōs profectōs quattuor mīlia passuum hostēs secūtōs esse. 9. Dīxit nāvēs, ventum bonum nactās, tertiā diē profectās esse. 10. Dīxit sē tribus diēbus profectūrum esse. 11. Mīlitēs negāvērunt sē illum ducem secūtūrōs esse. 12. Dīxit sē eōs per prōvinciam iter facere nōn passūrum esse. 13. Cōnfirmāvērunt sē dolōrēs pessimōs passūrōs esse. 14. Cōnātus est proficīscī sed ab equitibus captus est. 15. Eques nuntiāvit hostēs, progressōs tria mīlia passuum in prōvinciam, trāns flūmen venīre cōnārī. 16. Caesarem certiōrem fēcērunt hostēs collem occupāre cōnārī.

UNIT FOURTEEN

Exercise 455.—See Introduction, 3.

Exercise 456.—1. They went (traveled) all night. (*Noctem*, acc. of extent of time.) 2. He went out at the second watch. (*Vigiliā*, abl. of time when.) 3. He went two miles. (*Mīlia*, acc. of extent of space.) 4. He will go out within three days. (*Diēbus*, abl. of time within which.) 5. He had gone a hundred feet. (*Pedēs*, acc. of extent of space.) 6. At what hour will you go out, my friend? (*Hōrā*, abl. of time when.) 7. They entered upon a new plan. (*Cōnsilium*, direct obj. of a tr. verb.) 8. For how many days did they go (travel, march)? (*Diēs*, acc. of extent of time.) 9. One legion went out from the camp; the other remained in the camp. (*Altera, altera*, pronouns expressing one and the other of two only. *Castrīs*, abl. after *ē*.) 10. They went into the towns for the sake of safety. (*Salūtis*, gen. after *causā*. *Oppida*, acc. after *in*.) 11. Almost everyone is going out. 12. They were going out from their own territory. (*Fīnibus suīs*, abl. after *dē*.) 13. He is going to the river (*Flūmen*, acc. after *ad*.) 14. He was going out on the third day. (*Diē*, abl. of time when.) 15. The centurion will go out with a hundred men. (*Hominibus*, abl. of accompaniment with *cum*.) 16. The legion went out without any delay. 17. How long had he gone (traveled)? (*Quam*, interrog. adv. of degree.) 18. Where will you go, my son? (*Quō*, interrog. adv. expressing place to which.) 19. He had gone through places full of obstacles and very difficult. (*Loca*, acc. after *per*.) 20. Christ said, "I will go to the Father."

Exercise 457.—1. Quīnque mīlia passuum iērunt. 2. Secundā diē ad castra exiit. 3. Aliī ē castrīs exībant. 4. Tribus diēbus in urbem inībit. 5. Ībimusne omnēs ad Caelum? 6. Per maximās silvās it. 7. Quō istī? 8. Caesar in prōvinciam iit. 9. In hīberna vēnērunt. 10. Novum

140 FIRST YEAR LATIN

cōnsilium bellī iniērunt. 11. Quīnque diēbus ībunt. 12. Ē castrīs exiē-runt. 13. Tertiā diē prōvinciam iniērunt. 14. Illā diē profectī, quattuor mīlia passuum iērunt. 15. Flūmen altissimum iniērunt. 16. Nactī ventum bonum, ē portū exiērunt. 17. In Galliam brevissimā viā iērunt. 18. Duōs diēs per montēs altissimōs ībant. 19. Prīmā vigiliā ex oppidō clam exiit. 20. Profectī, trēs mīlia passuum iērunt et castra posuērunt.

Exercise 458.—A. American soldiers went out of our territory across a very wide sea into France in order to fight against the enemy. 1. From what place did they go? Ex nostrīs fīnibus iērunt. 2. Did they go across a very wide sea? Trāns mare lātissimum iērunt. 3. Why did they go to France? In Galliam iērunt ut contrā hostēs pugnārent. **B.** Having spoken with His friends for many days, Christ went to heaven to His Father. 1. With whom did Christ speak? Chrīstus cum amīcīs suīs locūtus est. 2. For how long did He speak with them? Multōs diēs cum eīs Chrīstus locūtus est. 3. Where did He go? In Caelum īvit. 4. To whom did He go? Ad Patrem īvit. **C.** All the saints, having followed Christ bravely, will go to heaven. 1. Who have followed Christ? Omnēs sānctī Chrīstum secūtī sunt. 2. Where will they go? In Caelum ībunt. **D.** Marquette, a very good and brave man, had gone for many days through forests full of dangers and through places full of obstacles and very difficult. Then he heard that a very wide and very long river was not far away. This river was called by those who lived in those regions the Father of Waters. Having again set out therefore in a small boat, he traveled for very many days and at last went first (was the first to go) into that river which is now called by us the Mississippi. 1. How many days had Marquette gone? Marquette multōs diēs ierat. 2. Through what places had he gone? Per loca impedīta et difficillima ierat. 3. He did not go through a forest, did he? Per silvās perīculōrum plēnās ierat. 4. What did he hear then? Tum audīvit nōn longē abesse flūmen lātissimum et longissimum. 5. What was this river called? Hoc flūmen Pater Aquārum vocābātur. 6. Who called it the Father of Waters? Illī quī eās regiōnēs incolēbant id Patrem Aquārum vocābant. 7. Did Marquette set out again? Marquette rūrsus profectus est. 8. To what river did he come? Tandem ad flūmen quod nunc ā nōbīs Missis-sippi vocātur pervēnit. 9. Do you know at what place Marquette first saw this river? Marquette hoc flūmen prīmum cōnspexit ad Prairie du Chien. 10. Do you know who was Father Marquette's companion? Joliet socius Patris Marquette fuit. 11. Was Marquette a Jesuit? Marquette fuit Jesuīta. **E.** We have already shown that our soldiers in Bataan were not able to withstand any longer the attack of the enemy. For, as you know, the Japanese were making attacks against our men with larger forces and more arms. MacArthur, who was in command of our garrison, was ordered to leave the troops and to go out from the place which is called Corregidor. And so without delay he went out in a small boat with a few companions. They went for very many nights through seas full of dangers. They often went into harbors naturally fortified and remained there through the day lest they be seen by the enemy. Having set out again by night, they went swiftly. Thus they saved themselves from the hands of the enemy and at last entered a port held by our men. 1. Why were our men unable to withstand the attacks of the Japanese? Nostrī nōn potuērunt· impetūs hostium sustinēre quod Japōnēs mājōribus cōpiīs et pluribus armīs impetūs faciēbant. 2. Of what garrison was MacArthur in command? MacArthur praesidiō nostrō praeerat. 3. What was he ordered to do? Jussus est mīlitēs relinquere et ex Corregidor exīre. 4. Did he go out immediately? Statim exiit. 5. With whom did he go? Cum paucīs sociīs exiit. 6. Where did they often remain? Per diem saepe in portibus nātūrā locī mūnītīs mānsērunt. 7. Why did they remain there? Ibi mānsērunt nē ab hostibus cōnspicerentur. 8. Did the enemy see them? Hostēs eōs nōn cōnspexērunt. 9. Where did they finally arrive? Tandem ad portum ā nostrīs occupātum pervēnērunt.

Box, page 460.—From an evil death, O Lord, deliver him!

Exercise 459.—1. When Columbus was crossing the very wide sea, he was often in the greatest danger. (*Trānsīret*, imp. subj. in a *cum*-clause in secondary sequence; action at same time as main verb. *Note.* All the other italicized verbs in this exercise are pluperfect subjunctives in *cum*-clauses in secondary sequence, action completed before time of main verb.) 2. When Columbus, having gone out of the harbor, had crossed the sea, he came to America. 3. When Caesar had visited all the tribes of Gaul, he returned to Italy. 4. The legions, when they had been gone a whole night, halted and pitched camp. 5. The leader, when he had entered upon a very good plan of war, conquered the enemy more easily. 6. When the cavalry, commanded by the leader, had gone out of the camp, they swiftly followed (pursued) the enemy.

Exercise 460.—1. Let us go. (*Eāmus*, hortatory subjunctive.) 2. Let us not go out of the first battle line. (*Nē exeāmus*, negative hortatory subjunctive.) 3. Let us return to the winter quarters. (*Redeāmus*, hortatory subjunctive.) 4. Let us visit all the states of Italy. (*Adeāmus*, hortatory subjunctive.) 5. May he not go. (*Nē eat*, subjunctive, a negative wish.) 6. May they return swiftly. (*Redeant*, subjunctive, a wish.)

Exercise 461.—1. He asks how great are the forces crossing the river. (*Quantae*, interrog. adj. introducing an indirect question. *Trānseant*, pres. subj. in indirect question, action at same time as main verb in primary sequence.) 2. The leader asked at what hour the enemy had gone out of the camp. (*Quā*, interrog. adj. introducing an indirect question. *Exiissent*, pluperf. subj. in an indirect question, action completed before time of main verb in secondary sequence.) 3. I ask whether you have gone into the camp. (*Num*, interrog. particle introducing an indirect question. *Ierīs*, perf. subj. in indirect question, action completed before time of main verb in primary sequence.) 4. He informed Caesar how many (of the) enemy had crossed the river. (*Quot*, interrog. indecl. adj. introducing an indirect question. *Trānsiissent*, pluperf. subj. in indirect question, action completed before time of main verb in secondary sequence.) 5. I ask by what route they went through the mountains. (*Quā*, interrog. adj. introducing an indirect question.)

Exercise 462.—1. Caesar built (made) a bridge across (on) a very wide river in order that the cavalry might more easily return. (*Quō*, conj. before comparative in purpose clause. *Redīrent*, imp. subj. in purpose clause after secondary tense.) 2. He is stationing guards on all sides in order that the barbarians may not go out of the forest. (*Nē*, conj. in negative purpose clause. *Exeant*, pres. subj. in negative purpose clause after primary tense.) 3. American soldiers seized many harbors lest the enemy's ships return to them. (*Nē*, conj. in negative purpose clause. *Redīrent*, imp. subj. in negative purpose clause after secondary tense.) 4. He sent cavalry swiftly to cross the river. (*Quī*, relative pronoun referring to *equitēs*, in relative purpose clause. *Trānsīrent*, imp. subj. in relative purpose clause after secondary tense.) 5. The general called the centurions to him in order to adopt a new plan. (*Ut*, conj. in purpose clause. *Inīret*, imp. subj. in purpose clause after secondary tense.) 6. They built fortifications in the harbor in order that ships might not enter into it. (*Nē*, conj. in negative purpose clause. *Inīrent*, imp. subj. in negative purpose clause after secondary tense.)

Box, page 462.—Defend us, we beseech Thee, O Lord, from all dangers of mind and body.

Exercise 463.—When a new war had arisen in Europe and all the nations of that region were contending in arms among themselves on land and sea, we first came to the aid of the French and the British with a supply of arms and rations, then we waged war against the enemy along with them. And so we prepared a great many ships in order that our soldiers might cross the sea; we prepared an immense

supply of darts and arms in order that our men, when they had crossed over into Europe, would be able to fight bravely and long against the enemy. In this war American soldiers visited many places. For some crossed over into Africa; others crossed first to England and then to France; still others crossed to other regions. We know that our men are fighting bravely and will fight bravely in all these places. They will return to us after the victory, having suffered many pains and very many wounds. Let us always remember them and their (valiant) deeds.
1. Where had a new war arisen? Novum bellum ortum est in Eurōpā.
2. What nations were contending in arms among themselves? Omnēs illīus regiōnis gentēs inter sē contendēbant. 3. With what things did we first help our allies? Prīmum cōpiā armōrum et frūmentī sociōs nostrōs adjūvimus. 4. Did we wage the war with them? Bellum cum eīs gessimus. 5. Where did our soldiers go? Mīlitēs nostrī in multa loca iērunt. 6. Didn't some cross over into England and some into Africa? Aliī in Britanniam, aliī in Africam trānsiērunt. 7. Do you think that our soldiers fight bravely? Arbitror mīlitēs nostrōs fortiter pugnāre et semper pugnātūrōs esse. 8. When will they return to us? Post victōriam ad nōs redībunt.

Exercise 464.—1. Japōnēs, cum ē mūnītiōnibus exiisent, fugā silvās petīvērunt. 2. Ab hōc flūmine rediērunt ut ab impetū tūtī essent. 3. Nāvēs Japōnum mare clam trānsiērunt ut in portūs nostrōs impetum facerent. 4. Hī mīlitēs ē castrīs redeunt, illī autem in castra eunt. 5. Hostēs ē silvīs clam exiērunt et ā tergō subitō vīsī sunt. 6. Cum ad nāvem rediisset, tēlō occīsus est et in aquam cecidit. 7. Hī mīlitēs fortēs in Galliam iērunt ut Gallōs ab imperiō aliēnō līberārent. 8. Equitēs hostēs pepulērunt ut mīlitēs impedītī flūmen trānsīrent 9. Mīlitēs, locī nātūrā impedītī, in castra rediērunt. 10. Castra vacua erant, nam cum mīlitēs in prōvinciam exiissent, nūllī rediērunt. 11. Prohibēbimus hostēs hīs agrīs et hīs urbibus ut eī quī eās (ea) incolēbant redeant. 12. Ducēs hostium ratiōnem bellī novam iniērunt. Equitēs suī ex oppidīs exiērunt ut agmina nostra impedīrent. 13. Impetum equitum pepulimus ut legiō in hīberna redīret. 14. Lēgātus, "Rogō," inquit, "quō sociī vestrī īerint." 15. Dux lēgātōs rogāvit quās gentēs (hominum) adiissent. 16. Rōmānī viās mūnīvērunt quō facilius prōvinciās adīrent. 17. Equitēs impetum ā tergō fēcērunt nē hostēs ad castra redīrent. 18. Ad ducēs īvit ut rogāret quis apud eōs plūrimum valēret. 19. Ducēs Jūdaeōrum, cum ad Pilātum iissent, dīxērunt Chrīstum sē rēgem appellāvisse. 20. Chrīstus apostolōs rogāvit quō nōmine appellārētur. 21. Prīncipēs convēnērunt ut nova cōnsilia inīrent. 22. Ibi ācriter pugnātum est et plūrimī nōn rediērunt. 23. Lēgātōs mīsit quī prīncipēs illārum gentium adīrent. 24. Dux rogāvit quantīs cum cōpiīs hostēs in prōvinciam iissent. 25. Cum dē colle iissent, ibi cōnstitērunt. 26. Cum Caesar ē castrīs exiisset, hostēs vallum adiērunt. 27. Rōmānī, cum in fīnēs hostium iissent, castra posuērunt eaque fossā vallōque mūnīvērunt. 28. Rogāvit num obsidēs ē castrīs clam exiissent. 29. Caesar, cum ex Italiā rediisset, rogāvit num omnia ad bellum ūtilia parāta essent. 30. Rogāvērunt unde rediisset. 31. Barbarī, adventū Caesaris territī, in fīnēs suōs iērunt. 32. Caesar, cum ad hīberna rediisset, repperit novum bellum in Galliā ortum esse.

Exercise 465.—1. Christ said that He would go to heaven within a few days. (*Sē itūrum esse*, acc. w. infin. after a verb of saying; future infinitive expressing action which will take place after time of main verb.) 2. We must return. (*Nōs redīre*, acc. w. infin. after *oportet*.) 3. To return to evil companions already left is very bad. (*Redīre*, infin. used as subject.) 4. He replied that the cavalry had not yet returned. (*Equitēs rediisse*, acc. w. infin. after a verb of saying; perfect infinitive expressing action completed before time of main verb.) 5. Christ promised to return. (*Sē reditūrum esse*, acc. w. infin., future infinitive with *pollicitus est*.) 6. The cavalry found out that the barbarians had already crossed the river. (*Barbarōs trānsiisse*, acc. w. infin. after a verb of saying, etc.; perfect infinitive expressing action completed before time of main verb.) 7. Caesar did not allow the hostages to go out of the camp to their own people. (*Obsidēs exīre*, acc. w. infin. after *passus est;* present infinitive expressing action at same time as main verb.) 8. The leader wrote that he would return in two days. (*Sē reditūrum esse*, acc. w. infin. after a verb of saying; future infinitive expressing action which will take place after time of main verb.) 9. The messenger showed how many men had gone into the camp. 10. Pilate said that the Jews had not proved that Christ was the worst of men (a very evil man). (*Jūdaeōs probāvisse*, acc. w. infin. after a verb of saying; perfect infinitive expressing action completed before time of main verb. *Chrīstum esse*, acc. w. infin. after *probāvisse;* present infinitive expressing action at same time as main verb. *Pessimum*, superlative of *malus;* modifies *hominem*.) 11. I think that most men will go to heaven. (*Hominēs itūrōs esse*, acc. w. infin. after a verb of thinking; future infinitive expressing an action which will take place after the time of main verb.) 12. The leader thought it best to cross the river immediately. (*Optimum*, pred. adj. with *esse*, modifying *trānsīre flūmen; esse*, acc. w. infin. after *arbitrātus est*.) 13. He informed Caesar that the barbarians had gone three miles. (*Barbarōs iisse*, acc. w. infin. after a verb of saying; perfect infinitive expressing action completed before time of main verb.) 14. He ordered the cavalry to cross the river without delay. (*Trānsīre*, present infinitive with *jussit*.) 15. The lieutenant decided he ought to go to Caesar immediately with all his forces in order to help him against the barbarians. (*Oportēre*, impersonal verb in the infinitive with *cōnstituit. Sē īre*, acc. w. infin. with *oportēre*.) 16. The cavalry found out that the enemy had already returned to camp. 17. The military tribune wrote that he would cross over into the enemy's fields. (*Trānsitūrum esse*, future infinitive in acc. w. infin., expressing action which will take place after time of main verb.) 18. The Jews determined to approach Pilate in order that Christ might be put to death. (*Adīre*, present infinitive with *cōnstituērunt*.) 19. Christ, worn out with sorrows and with wounds, was led through the streets. (*Cōnfectus*, perf. part. pass. of *cōnficiō*, used as adj. modifying *Chrīstus*.) 20. Christ could have saved Himself from their hands, for He was God. (*Ēripere*, present infinitive with *potuit*.) 21. The Jews, when they saw that Pilate was trying to help Christ, said to him that Christ had made Himself king. (*Cōnārī*, present infinitive in acc. w. infin.; action at same time as main verb. *Adjuvāre*, present infinitive with *cōnārī. Fēcisse*, infinitive in acc. w. infin. after a verb of saying; perfect tense expressing action completed before time of main verb.)

Exercise 466.—1. Nōn potuērunt īre. 2. Caesar Helvētiōs īre nōn patiētur. 3. Dīxit sē tribus diēbus itūrum esse. 4. Centuriō nūntiāvit hostēs rediisse. 5. Oportuit Caesarem Galliam adīre. 6. Jussī sunt ē castrīs exīre. 7. Dīxērunt sē cum mājōribus cōpiīs reditūrōs esse. 8. Nōn passus est eōs flūmen trānsīre. 9. Bonum est hoc cōnsilium inīre. 10. Caesarem certiōrem fēcērunt Gallōs tria mīlia passuum iisse. 11. Propter mīlitēs Rōmānōs flūmen trānsīre nōn potuērunt. 12. Cōnstituit tertiā diē redīre.

Exercise 467.—When Caesar had arrived in Gaul, he heard that the Helvetians had determined to go through the province in order to arrive at new fields. The Helvetians were a tribe of Gauls which was next (lived nearest) to the province. They had prepared all the things which pertained to the march, in order more easily to go out of their own territory. But Caesar thought that he ought to prevent (stop) them. He therefore said that he would not allow them to go through the province. He stationed guards lest they cross the river which was between the province and their fields. They tried for many days, however, to cross with all their forces. Caesar prevented them by means of arms. And so, when they could not cross the river and enter the province, they decided to go by another way, more difficult and narrow. When it was announced to him that they had gone out of their own territory to go into new fields by way of this route, Caesar immediately went out of camp with all his forces and followed them. He followed them for many days; at last he overcame them in battles. The Gauls, overcome altogether by Caesar, surrendered themselves and all their property (possessions) to him. He ordered them to return to their own territory. They therefore returned. For Caesar never allowed the tribes of Gaul to cross over from their own territory into other territory. 1. What did Caesar hear after his arrival? 2. Where did the Helvetians dwell? 3. Why did they decide to go through the province? 4. Did they not prepare all the things which are useful for a march? 5. Did Caesar allow them to go out of their own territory? 6. What river did they try to cross? 7. Were they able to cross that river? 8. Why were they unable to cross the river? 9. What did they do then? 10. Did Caesar hear that they had gone out of their own territory? 11. Did Caesar follow them? 12. Do you think that Caesar had crossed the river about which we have already spoken? 13. With what (whom) did Caesar set out? 14. For how many days did he follow them? 15. Did Caesar conquer them? 16. Did the Helvetians return to their own fields when they had been ordered by Caesar to return? 17. Caesar did not allow other tribes to go out of their own territory, did he?

Reading No. 44.—For two or three years Christ had taught the Jews the way of salvation. He had spoken to them of the kingdom of heaven and of the will of His Father. He had showed that He was the Son of God and King of all men. He had always showed good will toward all men. He had called all men to Him, for He said, "Come to Me." He had received them all and helped them all. Nevertheless a great many leading men of the Jews, the very worst men, feared Him. For they thought that He would seize the kingdom of the Jews and would raise up His own power (establish Himself as ruler). They therefore were making plans in order to take Christ and to kill Him. When they were making a plan, one of the disciples of Christ named Judas came to them. This man promised that he would deliver Christ into their hands. "What will you give me," he said, "and I will deliver Him to you?" But they set the price at thirty pieces of silver. From this time Judas was ready to betray Christ.

Now Christ, after that supper in which He left us the Most Holy Sacrament, went out of the city. Having gone out, He crossed the river which was called the Cedron and went to the place which was called Gethsemani. For He was accustomed to withdraw to this place with His friends to pray. And so on this night, having gone ahead a few feet from His friends, He fell upon the earth and prayed fervently. For He knew that He was about to suffer the greatest pains for our sake. He prayed a long time. "Not My will," He said, "but Thine be done." After this He came to the disciples and said to them: "Behold, the hour has approached (come) and the Son of man will be delivered into the hands of sinners. Let us go; behold, he who will betray Me has drawn near." Now when He was speaking, Judas, one of the Twelve, came up. With him there was a band of soldiers sent by the leading men of the Jews. Judas came up to Christ and kissed Him. Now this sign had been given to them in order that they might know who Christ was. But Jesus said to him: "Friend, for what have you come? Judas, do you betray the Son of man with a kiss?" Then Jesus, having advanced (gone) to those who were sent, said, "Whom do you seek?" They answered, "Jesus of Nazareth." Jesus said to them, "I am He." When He had said to them, "I am He," they fell to the earth. He asked them again, "Whom do you seek?" And they answered, "Jesus of Nazareth." Jesus replied: "I have said that I am He. Therefore if you seek Me, permit these to go away."

They took Christ and led Him to the council. The high priest questioned Him about His disciples and about His teaching. Jesus answered him: "I have spoken openly to the world. I have always taught in the synagogue and in the temple, where all the Jews assemble; and in secret I have spoken nothing. Why do you question Me? Question those who heard what I spoke. Behold, these men know what I have said."

The chief priest asked Him, "Art Thou Christ the Son of the blessed God?" And Jesus answered, "I am." And they all shouted that He was guilty of death.

And so in the morning they led Christ to Pilate. Pilate went out to them and asked why they had led (brought) Christ to him. They replied that Christ was the very worst of men. But Pilate said to them: "You take Him, and judge Him according to your law." But the Jews said that they could not put Him to death. Pilate therefore went in and called Jesus and said to Him, "Art Thou the king of the Jews?" Jesus replied, "Do you say this of yourself, or have others told you this about Me?" Pilate answered: "Am I a Jew? Your people and priests have delivered You up to me. What have You done?" "My kingdom is not of this world," Jesus replied. "If My kingdom were of this world, My servants would certainly strive that I be not delivered up to the Jews;

but now My kingdom is not from here (of this world)." Pilate therefore said to Him, "Are You a king, then?" Jesus answered: "You have said that I am a king. Unto this I was born and for this I have come into the world, that I might give testimony to the truth; everyone who is of the truth hears My voice." Pilate said to Him, "What is truth?" And when he had said this, he went out again to the Jews and told them that he found no cause in Him. It was a custom, however, to release a prisoner at the time of the festival of the Pasch. And so Pilate said to the Jews, "Shall I release to you the king of the Jews?" They all shouted: "Not this man, but Barabbas. Take Him! And release to us Barabbas." Now Barabbas was a robber.

"What shall I do about Jesus who is called the Christ?" Pilate asked them. "Let Him be crucified," they all shouted. "What evil has He done?" Pilate said to them. But they shouted again, "Let Him be crucified."

Then Pilate ordered Christ scourged. But the soldiers, platting a crown of thorns, placed it on His head and put on Him a purple garment. And they went up to Him and said, "Hail, King of the Jews." And they slapped Him.

Pilate went out again and said to the Jews: "Behold, I lead Him to you in order that you may know that I find no cause in Him." Jesus went out. He was wearing the crown of thorns and the purple garment. And Pilate said to them, "Behold the man!"

But the leaders of the Jews shouted when they had seen Him, "Crucify Him, crucify Him." Pilate said to them: "You take Him and crucify Him. For I find no cause in Him." The Jews answered: "We have a law, and according to the law He ought to be put to death, because He made Himself the Son of God." When Pilate had heard this, he feared greatly. Again he went in and said to Jesus, "Whence are you?" But Jesus answered nothing. Pilate says to Him: "You do not speak to me? Do you not know that I have the power to crucify You and the power to let You go?" Jesus replied: "You would not have any power against Me, unless it were given to you from above. Therefore those who have delivered Me up to you have the greater sin."

From this time Pilate tried to release Him. But the Jews were shouting: "If you release this man, you are no friend of Caesar; for everyone who makes himself a king speaks against Caesar." But Pilate, when he had heard this, said to the Jews, "Behold your king." And they kept shouting: "Take Him away, take Him away! Crucify Him!" Pilate said to them, "Shall I crucify your king?" The leaders of the Jews replied,

"We have no king except Caesar." And Pilate therefore, fearing both Caesar and the Jews, delivered Jesus up to them. And they led Him to a place which was called Golgotha and there they crucified Jesus Christ, the Son of God.